FAMINE EARLY WARNING AND RESPONSE

Famine Early Warning and Response

The Missing Link

MARGARET BUCHANAN-SMITH and SUSANNA DAVIES

INTERMEDIATE TECHNOLOGY PUBLICATIONS 1995

Intermediate Technology Publications
103–105 Southampton Row, London WC1B 4HH, UK

© IT Publications 1995

A CIP catalogue record for this book
is available from the British Library

ISBN 1 85339 291 X ✓

Typeset by Dorwyn Ltd, Rowlands Castle, Hants
Printed by BPC Wheatons, Exeter, UK

Contents

LIST OF TABLES viii
LIST OF FIGURES ix
ACKNOWLEDGEMENTS x
ACRONYMS xi

1: The Missing Link 1
Introduction 1
Understanding famine 3
Early warning 4
Famine prevention: the relief response 5
The Sahel and Horn of Africa: conditions ripe for famine 6
The actors 8
Conclusions 10

2: What are Famine Early-warning Systems? 12
Introduction 12
EWS as information systems 12
Information generated by EWS 15
Use of EW information 18
Constraints to the use of EW information 19
Conclusions 24

3: The International Relief System 26
Introduction 26
Preventing famine: whose responsibility? 27
What is the international relief system? 28
Profile of four donor agencies 30
The political context of emergency aid to Africa in 1990–91 33
Sources of EW information used by donor agencies 36
Influence of the media 41
Influence of formal political channels 43
Making decisions about the relief response 44
Executing decisions: the relief response 48
Donor co-ordination 50
Conclusions 51

4: Ethiopia   55
  Introduction   55
  Food security   57
  The EW/response system   61
  The story of EW/response in 1990–91   66
  Evaluating the EW information   71
  Use of EW information   74
  Implications for the final response   77
  Insecurity and the EW/response process   78
  Conclusions   80

5: Sudan   84
  Introduction   84
  Food security in north Sudan, focusing on Darfur 86
  The EW/response system   88
  The story of EW/response in 1990–91   91
  Evaluating the EW information   97
  Use of EW information   100
  Implications for the final response   105
  Insecurity and the EW/response process   106
  Conclusions   107

6: Chad   111
  Introduction   111
  Food security   113
  The EW/response system   116
  The story of EW/response in 1990–91   119
  Evaluating the EW information   124
  Use of EW information   128
  Implications for the final response   134
  Insecurity and the EW/response process   135
  Conclusions   135

7: Mali   139
  Introduction   139
  Food security   141
  The EW/response system   144
  The story of EW in 1990–91   148
  Evaluating the EW information   151
  The story of response in 1990–91   151
  Use of EW information   155
  Implications for the final response   156
  Insecurity and the EW/response process   159
  Conclusions   160

8: Turkana District, Kenya   165
    Introduction   165
    Food security   167
    The EW response system   175
    The Emergency Livestock Purchase Scheme: 1990   178
    Food crisis and food-for-work in Kakuma Division: 1991   181
    District-wide drought in 1992   183
    Evaluating the EW information   185
    Use of EW information   189
    Implications for the final response in 1990 and 1991   193
    Insecurity and the EW/response process   196
    Conclusions   197

9: Forging the Link   202
    Introduction   202
    EWS are necessary   204
    Common patterns in how EW information is used   205
    Forging the link   208

GENERAL REFERENCES   212

CASE-STUDY REFERENCES   214
    Ethiopia   214
    Sudan   216
    Chad   217
    Mali   218
    Turkana District, Kenya   219

INDEX   221

List of Tables

Table 2.1	Typology of early-warning systems	17
Table 2.2	Constraints to the timely use of early-warning information	20
Table 3.1	Profile of donors' food aid programmes	31
Table 3.2	Food aid to case-study countries, by category, 1991 (cereals only)	35
Table 3.3	Response to early warning: ODA, EU, USAID, WFP	37
Table 3.4	Relief decision-making within donor agencies	45
Table 4.1	Ethiopia: annual food aid donations (imports and local purchases)	59
Table 4.2	Ethiopia: outputs of the national EWS in 1990–91	62
Table 4.3	Ethiopia: timetable of food aid pledges and deliveries, 1991	70
Table 4.4	Ethiopia: comparison of the final results of the FAO, WFP and RRC (October) assessments, 1990–91	72
Table 4.5	Ethiopia: relief ration rate, or annual consumption rate, on which different agencies' assessments are based	72
Table 5.1	Sudan: malnutrition rates reported by Oxfam in North Darfur during 1991	97
Table 6.1	Chad: domestic cereals production, food aid distributions and commercial imports	114
Table 6.2	Chad: SAP's food-needs assessment for 1991	120
Table 6.3	Chad: results of anthropometric surveys carried out during 1990–91	122
Table 7.1	Mali: stages of SAP early warning and response	145
Table 7.2	Mali: comparison of national food deficit/surplus in 1990–91 according to different harvest and consumption estimates	150
Table 7.3	Mali: authorized free food aid distributions from SNS stocks in 1991	152
Table 8.1	Turkana District: EW/response interventions between 1990 and 1992	166
Table 8.2	Turkana District: major periods of drought and food crisis	171
Table 8.3	Turkana District: indicators used by EWS	176
Table 9.1	Summary of time-lags between EW and response	203

List of Figures

Figure 1.1   The timing of response in the downward spiral of famine   6

Figure 2.1   An EWS as information system (as process)   14

Figure 3.1   The international relief system *circa* 1990   29

Figure 3.2   UK newspaper coverage of African famine, December 1990 to August 1991   42

Figure 4.1   Map of Ethiopia   58

Figure 4.2   Ethiopia: main components of the national and international EWS in 1990–91   64

Figure 4.3   Ethiopia: number of people at risk, 1990–91 – comparison FAO, WFP/NGO and RRC   67

Figure 4.4   Ethiopia: assessments of relief needs, 1990–91 – comparison FAO, WFP/NGO and RRC   67

Figure 4.5   Ethiopia: emergency food aid, 1990–91 – record of availability and deliveries   69

Figure 5.1   Map of Sudan, 1991   85

Figure 5.2   Sudan: emergency food aid, 1990–91 – record of availability and deliveries   94

Figure 5.3   Sudan: emergency food aid to Darfur, 1990–91 – record of availability and deliveries   96

Figure 6.1   Map of Chad showing vulnerable groups at the beginning of the 1990 agricultural season   112

Figure 6.2   Chad: diagram of components of EWS and links with decision-makers   118

Figure 6.3   Chad: distribution timetable for relief food aid – recommended compared with actual   123

Figure 6.4   Chad: relief food aid distribution by *préfecture* – recommended, planned and actual   129

Figure 6.5   Chad: decision-making and response time for the relief operation, by donor agency   130

Figure 7.1   Map of Mali, showing the harvest assessment for 1990–91   140

Figure 7.2   Mali: cereals production, 1971–2 to 1990–91   142

Figure 7.3   Mali: crude national food balance, 1971–2 to 1990–91   143

Figure 7.4   Mali: SAP recommendations vs decisions to distribute food aid by region, 1989–90   152

Figure 7.5   Mali: SAP recommendations vs decisions vs actual distributions of food aid by region, 1990–91   153

Figure 8.1   Map of Turkana District, Kenya   168

Figure 8.2   Turkana District: TLU/person ratio   173

Figure 8.3   Turkana District: household food consumption pattern, 1988–91   174

ix

Acknowledgements

IDS research for this book was generously funded by a grant from the Food Aid Division of DG VIII of the European Commission and by a grant from Band Aid. Research for this project was jointly conceived with SCF (UK). The fieldwork and writing of three of the original case-study documents (Sudan, Ethiopia and food-aid donors) was undertaken in collaboration with SCF, who were jointly responsible with IDS for the international conference held in 1992 to discuss the results of the work, entitled 'Predicting and Preventing Famine: an Agenda for the 1990s'. We are grateful to ODA and to the Training and Cultural Co-operation Unit of the European Commission for funding the conference. Above all, we would like to thank Celia Petty of SCF, for working with us on this project.

We should like to thank all those who participated in the conference in 1992 for their useful comments on earlier drafts. We are also indebted to those who helped us while carrying out fieldwork for unselfishly sharing their understanding of the issues and cheerfully responding to our incessant questions. We received support, information and advice from many people, too numerous to mention, but in particular we should like to thank: Berhane Gizaw in Ethiopia; Dr Abu Aouf, Leyla Omer Bashir and Ibrahim Diraige in Sudan; Thierry Godbille and Ali Adoum in Chad; Mamadou Bangaly, Mary Diallo and Karim Sacko in Mali; and Frederick Wekesa Lukhanyo and Rudolf Van Den Boogaard in Turkana District, Kenya. We are very grateful to all those who helped us with our research within ODA, USAID and especially the FEWS project, the EU and WFP.

Comments from our colleagues in the IDS Food Security Unit, particularly Simon Maxwell, Jeremy Swift and Hans Singer, were very much appreciated, as were comments on the Turkana chapter from Karen Twining, Jennifer Bush and Stephen Anderson. Karim Hussein provided excellent research assistance. Caroline Neville and Annie Jamieson tirelessly typed earlier drafts of this book.

Finally, we should like to thank both Jane Kennan and Margaret Cornell for their sterling help in editing the manuscript. The views expressed and any mistakes are entirely the responsibility of the authors.

Acronyms

ACC/SCN	Administrative Committee on Co-ordination /Sub-committee on Nutrition
AEDES	Association Européenne pour le Développement et la Santé
AGRHYMET	Agrometeorology and Remote Sensing Unit (CILSS)
APU	Agricultural Planning Unit, Darfur Regional Government (Sudan)
ASAL	Arid and Semi-arid Lands (Kenya)
BET	Borkou-Ennedi-Tibesti (Chad)
BSA	Bureau de la Statistique Agricole (Chad)
CASAAU	Comité d'Action pour la Sécurité Alimentaire et l'Aide d'Urgence (Chad)
CCE	Commission des Communautés Européennes
CFA	Committee on Food Aid Policies and Programmes (WFP)
CFAfr	Communauté Financière Africaine franc
CIDA	Canadian International Development Agency
CILSS	Comité Permanent Inter-Etats de Lutte Contre la Sécheresse dans le Sahel
CNAUR	Comité National d'Actions d'Urgence et de Réhabilitation (Mali)
CNNTA	Centre National de Nutrition et de Téchnologie Alimentaire (Chad)
COC	Comité d'Orientation et de Coordination (Mali)
CRA	Comité Regional d'Action (Chad)
CRDA	Christian Relief and Development Association (Ethiopia)
CSA	Central Statistical Authority (Ethiopia)
DHA	Department of Humanitarian Affairs (UN)
DIAPER	Projet Diagnostique Permanent (CILSS)
DMC	(District) Drought Management Committee (Kenya)
DMP	Drought Monitoring Programme of SRC, North Darfur (Sudan)
DNA	Direction Nationale de l'Agriculture (Mali)
DNSI	Direction Nationale de la Statistique et de l'Informatique (Mali)
DPASA	Direction de la Promotion des Productions Agricoles et de la Sécurité Alimentaire (Chad)
ELP	Emergency Livestock Purchase Scheme (Kenya)

xi

EPLF	Eritrean People's Liberation Front
EPPG	Emergency Prevention and Preparedness Group (UN Ethiopia)
ERA	Eritrean Relief Association
EU	European Union
EW	early-warning
EWPS	Early Warning and Planning Services (within RRC of Ethiopia)
EWS	early-warning system(s)
EWSU	Early Warning System Unit (within RRC of Sudan)
FAO	Food and Agriculture Organisation (UN)
FEWS	Famine Early Warning System (USAID)
FFW	food-for-work
FIAA	Front Islamique Arab de l'Azawad (Mali)
GIEWS	Global Information and Early Warning System (FAO)
GTZ	Deutsche Gesellschaft für Technische Zusammenarbeit
IDS	Institute of Development Studies, Sussex
IEFR	International Emergency Food Reserve (WFP)
IER	Institut d'Economie Rurale, Bamako (Mali)
IFPRI	International Food Policy Research Institute, Washington, DC
IFRC	International Federation for Red Cross and Red Crescent Societies
ILO	International Labour Organization (UN)
IMF	International Monetary Fund
INRA-ESR	Institut National de la Recherche Agronomique, Montpellier
IRA	Immediate Response Account (WFP)
IUCN	International Union for the Conservation of Nature and Natural Resources
KANU	Kenya African National Union
MATDB	Ministère de l'Administration Territoriale et du Développement à la Base (Mali)
MEP	Member of the European Parliament
MPA	Mouvement Populaire pour l'Azawad (Mali)
MSAPS	Ministère de la Sécurité Alimentaire et des Populations Sinistrées (Chad)
MSF	Médécins sans Frontières, Belgium
MUAC	middle upper-arm circumference
NCPB	National Cereals and Produce Board (Kenya)
NDPPS	National Disaster Prevention and Preparedness Strategy (Ethiopia)
NDVI	Normalised Difference Vegetation Index
NMSA	National Meteorological Services Agency (Ethiopia)
NORAD	Norwegian Agency for Development

NSP	Nutritional Surveillance Programme (SCF (UK), in Ethiopia)
ODA	Overseas Development Administration of the UK Government
ODI	Overseas Development Institute, London
ODNRI	Overseas Development Natural Resources Institute, Chatham (now Natural Resources Institute)
OFDA	Office of US Foreign Disaster Assistance, State Department of the US Government
OLS	Operation Lifeline Sudan
ONC	Office National des Céréales (Chad)
ONDR	Organisation Nationale de Développement Rural (Chad)
OPAM	Office des Produits Agricoles du Mali
PADEM	Projet de la Mise en Place de Dispositifs Permanents d'Enquêtes auprès des Ménages (UNDP) (Mali)
PNSA	Programme National de Sécurité Alimentaire (Chad)
PRMC	Programme de Restructuration du Marché Céréalier (Mali)
RDI	Relief and Development Institute (formerly International Disaster Institute, now amalgamated with Overseas Development Institute), London
REST	Relief Society of Tigray
RRC	Relief and Rehabilitation Commission (Ethiopia and Sudan)
SADS	Suivi Alimentaire Delta Seno (SCF (UK) project in Mali)
SAP	Système d'Alerte Précoce (Chad and Mali)
SCF (UK)	Save the Children Fund of the United Kingdom
SEPHA	Special Emergency Programme for the Horn of Africa (UN)
SIM	Système d'Information sur le Marché des Céréales (Mali)
SNS	Stock National de Sécurité (Mali)
SRC	Sudanese Red Crescent Society
TCC	Technical Co-ordination Committee (Sudan)
TDCPU	Turkana Drought Contingency Planning Unit (Kenya)
TLU	Tropical Livestock Unit
TPLF	Tigray People's Liberation Front
TRDP	Turkana Rural Development Programme (Kenya)
TRP	Turkana Rehabilitation Project (Kenya)
UDPM	Union Démocratique du Peuple Malien (Mali)
UNDP	United Nations Development Programme
UNDRO	United Nations Disaster Relief Organization
UNICEF	United Nations Children's Fund
USAID	United States Agency for International Development
WFP/PAM	World Food Programme/Programme Alimentaire Mondiale (UN)
WHO	World Health Organisation (UN)

CHAPTER 1

The Missing Link

Introduction

By the early 1990s, most drought-triggered famines and food crises in Africa were not hard to predict. This is testimony to the success of famine early-warning systems (EWS), many of which were set up during the 1980s. In 1984–5, failure to prevent famine in the Sahel and Horn of Africa was widely attributed to a lack of early warning (EW). Since then, better prediction has been a major policy concern, for both donor agencies and national governments. Greatest attention has been paid to the establishment of purpose-built EWS. In the Sahel and Horn of Africa alone, more than eight new EWS were set up between 1985 and 1990. Considerable progress has been made, in improving data-collection methods, developing indicators, and making use of sophisticated information technology. By 1990 more information on the likelihood of famine was available to donors and governments than ever before.

Famine prevention, however, has remained an elusive goal. Better prediction has not led to corresponding improvements on the response side. There is clearly a missing link between the provision of EW information and the use of that information to trigger a timely preventive response. Anecdotal evidence abounds as to why EW information has not been influential. The EWS was not sufficiently vociferous; the information was inappropriate, late or untrustworthy; donors were ill-disposed to help a particular government; adequate resources were not available; institutional and logistical obstacles overwhelmed good intentions; the domestic political will to react was lacking, and so on. Intuitively such explanations make sense, but they do not amount to a systematic analysis of what happens to EW information once it enters the decision-making process and how it is used by policy-makers. How and when do they receive the information, and what kind of data are most influential and why? Most important, what are the missing links between prediction and prevention?

That is the subject of this book. It is based on an analysis of early warning and relief responses in 1990 and 1991 in five African countries: Ethiopia, Sudan, Chad, Mali and Kenya focusing on Turkana District in the north; and in a number of donor agencies. Our approach is to begin with the decision-making processes which determine the response to a threatened crisis. From there, it is possible to ascertain the relative importance of information and of other factors in triggering or inhibiting the response.

The agricultural year 1990–91 was a year of drought across much of the Sahel and Horn of Africa, with early indications that food crises would be

1

widespread. In some regions, it was the combination of drought and conflict that threatened to cause the most severe cases of famine and suffering. Elsewhere, the drought was not necessarily as bad as in the mid-1980s. Nevertheless, conditions deteriorated to the point where relief aid was necessary, to protect livelihoods and often lives as well. A number of EWS in the region were being put to the test for the first time. Could they fulfil their ultimate objective of triggering an adequate and timely response to prevent acute food insecurity and/or famine developing? The results have been mixed. In some countries the EWS were remarkably ineffective. In others, they had much greater influence.

The reasons why EW information is, or is not, used fall into four broad categories: first, reasons to do with the EWS itself, and the information provided; second, reasons to do with the institutional context within which the EWS sits, and the institutional links to decision-makers; third, reasons to do with the broader political environment; and fourth, logistical obstacles to launching a timely and adequate response. Much has been written about the technical aspects of EW and numerous evaluations of different systems have been carried out.[1] Most have focused on the internal workings of the EWS: the scope of indicators, accuracy of the data and timeliness of the warnings. These relate to the first category of reasons, concerned with the performance of the EWS itself. But few have looked at how EWS fit into the wider context.[2] From the analysis presented in this book, the second and third categories of reasons emerge as the most important explanations of whether EW information is used, and of variations in performance between the different case-studies.

Most countries in the Sahel and Horn of Africa rely on the international relief system to provide resources to run relief operations in times of food crisis. National governments rarely have adequate resources or capacity to respond. Donor agencies and non-governmental organizations (NGOs), the key actors within the international relief system, have been particularly influential in developing famine prediction for the Sahel and Horn of Africa, both in funding and operational roles. But much less attention has been paid to developing the response side of the equation. There are two key reasons for the persistent failure to translate EW into timely response, illustrated in the case-studies in this book. First, the international relief system responds to famine once it is under way but is ill-equipped to respond to genuinely *early* warning, to intervene in time to prevent it. Second, it is not the severity of the crisis, but relations between international donors and national governments which tends to be the single most important determinant of the timing and scale of the international response. Thus, in the case of the southern African drought in 1992–3, as well

---

[1] See Lambert *et al.*, 1991, for an annotated bibliography of the literature on famine EWS.
[2] Although after each episode of severe drought and famine in Africa there has been a prolific literature which looks at what went wrong, and what needs to be done to ensure that the same mistakes are not repeated (for example, Gill, 1986; Glantz, 1987; Curtis *et al.*, 1988; Downing *et al.*, 1989), rarely has this investigated in any detail how the decision-making processes work, which trigger or inhibit the launching of a timely relief response.

as national capacity to respond, the desire of the donors to keep structural adjustment programmes on track and a determination to avoid further political unrest in the region combined to initiate a timely response by the international relief system (SADC, 1993). The same factors did not conspire to trigger a timely response to food crisis in the Sahel and Horn in 1991.

Understanding famine

A common theme running through this book is that a gap exists between theory and practice in famine prevention. Our understanding of famine as 'outsiders' has improved in leaps and bounds during the last 10 to 20 years. This should improve our ability to prevent it with appropriate policies and interventions. Instead, conventional and often inappropriate relief responses persist. Explanations of the causality of famine have shifted from a preoccupation with supply-side factors in the 1970s, towards a recognition of the pre-eminence of access or entitlement to food in the 1980s. Famine is no longer solely — or indeed even primarily — attributed to food availability decline (FAD), but increasingly to food entitlement decline (FED). Thus 'starvation is the characteristic of some people not *having* enough food to eat. It is not the characteristic of there not *being* enough food to eat' (Sen, 1981:1). This key distinction has fuelled much of the subsequent development of famine theory. The notion of entitlements has been refined in the light of recent famines in Africa. The health-crisis model of famine, for example, challenges Sen's assumption and the popular Western notion that famine mortality is caused primarily by starvation. Instead, the major killer is epidemic disease, either during or after periods of food shortage (de Waal, 1990; Dyson, 1993). The outbreak of mass communicable disease is often caused by economic and social collapse leading to large-scale migration and social disorder, itself a function of declining entitlements. A further refinement has been to move away from a narrow focus on exchange relations towards a wider bundle of entitlements incorporating different types of assets, including investments, stores and claims (Swift, 1989). In addition to buffering vulnerable people when famine threatens, however, this broader range of entitlements can also undermine food security, for example, via demands from kin for food, or various claims exacted by the state or by more powerful neighbours (Davies, 1995 (forthcoming)).

Linked to this is improved understanding of the strategies famine-prone people pursue to cope with famine. Interest in coping strategies arose in the mid-1980s as a means of trying to understand why it was that some people survived periods of dearth while others did not. Studies have revealed different stages of coping, from insurance, through to disposal of productive assets, to destitution as the crisis deepens and coping capacity runs out (Corbett, 1988). At the centre is a constant trade-off between short-term consumption and the preservation of longer-term capacity to produce: it is now widely recognized that households threatened by famine often choose to go without food rather than sell productive assets (de Waal, 1989; Devereux, 1993). Emphasizing indigenous strategies marks a

3

shift towards a more people-focused understanding of famine, paying attention to the perceptions and priorities of famine victims.

Famines caused by conflict are increasingly common on the African continent, but are as yet poorly understood. There are at least three major ways in which war causes famine: first, the direct destruction of battle, and consumption of resources by armies; second, when famine is used as a weapon of war, for instance through restrictions on population movement, especially during sieges and for counter-insurgency purposes; and third, when state structures and warlords sustain themselves as predators of the poor, thereby creating famine (de Waal, 1993). Conflict, especially when it is prolonged, also serves to divert attention away from the pursuit of preventive policies. Furthermore, it tends to weaken those institutional structures not directly geared to sustaining and/or winning the war; and also creates a climate of suspicion and mistrust between governments and donors.

Early warning

There are many systems for predicting famine, from informal indigenous information systems through to formal EWS. This book is principally concerned with the functioning of formal EWS. An EWS can be defined as a system of data collection to monitor people's access to food, in order to provide timely notice when a food crisis threatens and thus to elicit appropriate response (Davies *et al.*, 1991).

To some extent improved understanding of famine processes has fed into and informed the design of, and approach to, EWS. Inevitably there is a time-lag before theory is applied in practice, although the lag for EW has not been that long. The first major impetus to establish EWS in Africa came after the famines of the early 1970s in the Sahel, which the international community failed to recognize in time. EWS were set up to service donor and UN food aid institutions, and this remains their *raison d'être*. The earliest modern (and still one of the most influential) EWS, the FAO's Global Information and Early Warning System (GIEWS) is unequivocally supply-side oriented.

With the influence of entitlement theory of famine in the 1980s, most EWS began to incorporate indicators of effective demand for food, including price data and other socio-economic indicators, and a number responded to the work on coping strategies by trying to incorporate behavioural indicators of famine vulnerability. Measurement difficulties and scaling-up of local experiences make this one of the more challenging episodes in EWS development. Much of the most successful work has happened within small-scale, local-level information systems. Although most formal EWS operate at national and international level, after the mid-1980s a number of pioneering local-level systems were set up, often by NGOs.

Food-production and food-supply forecasts are in many ways still the best-developed EW capability. A number of EWS continue to be food-supply driven. However, many have now developed multi-indicator models, incorporating a wider range of socio-economic indicators, which

4

enable them to be sensitive to less-dramatic changes in food situations than famine. The complexity of famine processes implies that multi-indicator local-level EWS are most likely to be able to: detect deterioration in food security sufficiently early to launch a timely response; monitor and be sensitive to complex famine processes within different groups in a population; and identify appropriate public action in line with local people's priorities. Nevertheless, the original rationale for setting up EWS, to service food-aid donor agencies, has changed very little during the last 20 years. Their reference point, particularly for the recommendations they make, continues to be large-scale famine catastrophes.

Least progress has occurred in conflict situations, despite growing demands for EWS to enter this arena. The problems here are overwhelming, not least because of political sensitivities which can undermine the 'technical neutrality' most EWS strive to preserve.

Famine prevention: the relief response

Response can be defined as additional resources channelled to famine-prone people in order to assist them in withstanding the effects of declining access to food. For the international relief system, this means resources over and above normal development aid. In practice, response usually means saving lives or providing food to prevent starvation. Much less often, it means saving livelihoods, or providing food and other resources to protect future capacity to subsist, as well as to ensure current consumption.

The conceptual advances in our understanding of famine processes have major implications for preventive public action. First, they imply that famine policy cannot be limited to preventing large-scale excess mortality due to starvation, but instead must be viewed as halting the progress of a downward spiral of increasing vulnerability, leading to economic and social disintegration, destitution and eventually death from one of a number of causes, of which the outbreak and transmission of communicable disease is particularly serious. This spiral is illustrated in Figure 1.1. For famines to be prevented, intervention on the spiral must occur well before the point of death has been reached, as indicated.

Second, intervention must be early enough to protect livelihoods before lives are threatened, in accordance with people's own priorities (cutting back on consumption to preserve productive assets). This requires a more developmental approach to relief early enough in the spiral to prevent destitution and to reinforce existing capacity to cope.

Third, the preventive process is institutionally and politically more complex than a narrowly defined humanitarian relief operation which aims to prevent death by starvation. It implies that a range of interventions is required, including improved health care and the protection of water sources. This suggests a heavy institutional load, both for donor agencies and national governments, and a restructuring of bureaucratic procedures which tend to separate famine and related emergencies from more general development activities.

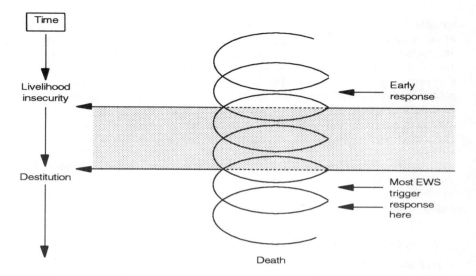

Figure 1.1 *The timing of response in the downward spiral of famine*

The current international relief system falls far short of this ideal. Its approach is founded on a simplistic and reductionist model of famine — of death by starvation, to which the most logical response is to provide food aid. Of course there are other factors feeding these assumptions: at least until recently, readily available food surpluses in the North, whereas money and other relief resources have been more difficult to obtain. The principal characteristics of the international relief system are that it is geared to saving lives, not livelihoods; that it mainly provides food aid, on the premise that starvation is the main cause of famine mortality; and that it delivers inadequate quantities of relief too late — after the start of the hungry season.

Figure 1.1 shows how far down the famine spiral people must sink before they usually receive international relief assistance. This is supported by evidence from the case-studies in this book. What is conspicuously clear is that our improved knowledge has not percolated through to famine-prevention practice. And this cannot be blamed on lack of information; famine EW is where greatest progress has been made. Instead, the problems are to do with inherent institutional and political weaknesses in how the international relief system functions. These themes are explored in Chapter 3.

The Sahel and Horn of Africa: conditions ripe for famine

Coupled with this poorly functioning international relief system is a constellation of forces in Africa which conspire to create conditions ripe for famine. What makes the Horn of Africa, in particular, and to a lesser but significant extent the Sahel, so vulnerable to famine when other countries, such as India, are succeeding in preventing it?[3] First is the fact that the underlying scale and intensity of food insecurity on the African continent are increasing. More people are vulnerable to famine now than 20 years ago, due both to deteriorating trends and rising incidence and severity of short-term shocks. Nearly half the population of sub-Saharan Africa — an estimated 235 million people — face conditions of chronic food insecurity. A third of all children under five are chronically undernourished. Population growth has resulted in the absolute number of hungry children rising from 18 million in 1975 to 30 million in 1990 (ACC/SCN, 1992).

Second, economic performance in sub-Saharan Africa contrasts sharply with the rest of the world. While global per capita food production has increased by approximately 10 per cent during the last 20 years, in Africa it has declined by 15 per cent. From being more or less self-sufficient, Africa now produces less than 90 per cent of its food needs. GNP per capita has decreased since 1981 to about US$300 a year, approximately equivalent to the level in the 1970s. The International Food Policy Research Institute has highlighted economic policy failure as one of the most important root causes of famine in Africa today (von Braun et al., 1993). Recent structural adjustment programmes have had mixed effects on economic performance, often making the poor in sub-Saharan Africa potentially more vulnerable to internal and external shocks (Elbadawi et al., 1992).

Third, the shock of drought exacerbates this underlying impoverishment. The Sahelian belt has experienced an unusually dry period over the last 30 years, during which time the frequency of drought has increased. Despite the estimated effects of global warming and reduced rain-forest cover, the reasons for this desiccation are not known with any certainty. Historically, such episodes are not abnormal: the region has experienced similar dry periods in the past. What has changed is people's vulnerability. A vicious circle is set in motion. Macro-economic decline, frequently accompanied by a marginalization of the traditional farming and pastoral sectors, has increased inequalities, cut the real incomes of many rural people, and reduced their assets. The increased frequency of drought makes it even less likely that in the interim wetter years they will be able to reconstitute assets, whether of livestock or some other store of wealth, to build the buffer needed for survival in the dry years.

Fourth, the shock of armed conflict has intensified in Africa. In addition to the long-running civil war in south Sudan, war has broken out in Somalia and Rwanda, and many other countries have intermittent internal conflicts (e.g. Chad). Initially attributable to war by proxy under Cold War conditions, in the post-Cold War era internal conflict is increasingly prevalent, fuelled by the availability of sophisticated weaponry and the struggle for resources and economic survival (Duffield, 1991). In some cases, rapid political transition has further increased the likelihood of conflict, for example, in Kenya. Internal wars are easier for the international community to ignore than the proxy wars of the Cold War era; and it is harder for it to

---

[3] For example, India successfully averted famine in 1987, despite the worst drought in a hundred years.

7

assist in peace brokering, as the case of Rwanda illustrates. Against this unstable background the international community's attention is increasingly diverted away from Africa, where the geopolitical stakes are low, towards the Gulf, eastern Europe and the former Soviet Union.

The effect of both these short-term shocks — drought and conflict — has been a growing number of people displaced from rural areas, swelling the ranks of the urban poor who are dependent on unreliable food and labour markets, or in the case of war, precipitating large movements of people and influxes of refugees across borders.

Fifth, the last ten years or so have witnessed the withdrawal of individual African states from many spheres of economic activity, due to macroeconomic decline, mounting debt, deteriorating terms of trade and enforced reduction of the public sector via structural adjustment programmes. This has prompted a drive towards liberalization of the economy, market-driven efficiency, reduced public-sector deficits and a smaller civil service. Liberalization of cereal markets may theoretically offer some opportunities for private sector contribution to famine mitigation, but in most instances the contribution is small. Thus, despite recent donor emphasis on good government, the capacity of the state to provide basic safety nets to protect people from famine has been eroded from an already low starting-point. The climate of political liberalization has not always facilitated the state's role in this respect. Democratically elected governments are usually more sensitive to the threat of famine. For example, a free press can publicize famine, as it did in Kenya in 1992 (see Chapter 8), and it has been argued that in India this has been a principal reason for ensuring famine prevention (Drèze and Sen, 1989). But this presupposes that the government has adequate resources to respond. Instead, in most African countries, the government is dependent on the goodwill of the international donor community, and as new zones of crisis emerge outside Africa, in more geopolitically strategic places, African countries may no longer be accorded priority.

This is the context within which more information about the threat of famine in the Sahel and Horn of Africa has been generated than ever before. The inability to use this information to prevent famine is rooted in the constraints which national governments face in responding and the consequential dependence on the international relief system, which cannot be guaranteed to mobilize an adequate or timely response.

The actors

People who live in famine-prone areas have little — if any — direct input into the decision-making process about public action to prevent famine. There are isolated examples of EWS which rely on local people's own perceptions and responses as a source of information. But these are rarely influential at the decision-making stage, despite the fact that, of all the actors concerned, it is famine-prone people who can least afford to make mistakes and who have shown themselves best able to anticipate and plan for shocks in their livelihood strategies, especially in their ability to plan for drought in those agro-ecological zones where it is endemic.

Recognition of this capacity is reflected in policy-makers' interest in indigenous coping strategies. But there is a danger of overestimating the capacity of people to cope, as vulnerability intensifies. Coping strategies can be thwarted by conflict (migration routes disrupted); exhausted by over-use (wood-fuel reserves depleted); rendered useless by market forces (the terms of trade between goats and cereals may collapse if too many people sell livestock), and so on. Macro-economic decline in many African countries during the last decade has adversely affected local people's ability to cope, leaving them more vulnerable as a result. In Sudan, for example, finding employment in urban areas to supplement rural incomes is no longer as feasible nor as lucrative an option as it was in the early 1980s. Community safety nets, reciprocal ties between households in different agro-ecological zones and between richer and poorer neighbours are all under stress. Increasingly, studies show that people's coping strategies run out earlier than they used to; and that they offer piecemeal, poorly remunerated and uncertain means of filling food gaps (Davies, 1995 (forthcoming); Holt and Lawrence, 1993). Reinforcing indigenous coping capacity is currently a much-advocated but rarely implemented policy option. Before this can happen, far more needs to be known about the potential for reinforcing these strategies — the starting-point for developing more flexible response options than are currently offered by the international relief system.

International donor agencies, recipient governments and NGOs are the principal players in the implementation of exogenous famine-prevention exercises. It is they who determine whether, when and how resources are allocated once an EWS has signalled the threat of famine. Relations between them are of central importance in understanding how decisions are made. For example, donors and recipient governments can be sceptical of each other's motives. Foreign NGOs, which often have a high profile in implementing relief programmes, may play an ambivalent role in this climate of mistrust: at times independent, at other times beholden to one or other side.

International donor agencies

These include Western bilateral donors and multilateral institutions such as the UN agencies. Donors have assumed a responsibility to respond to food shocks in Africa, whether caused by drought, war or a combination of both. This role has become especially prominent since the perceived failure to respond in time to prevent the Ethiopian famine of 1984. Demands from Western electorates for their governments to intervene on humanitarian grounds, irrespective of wider political interests, have given famine relief a high political profile in recent years.

The amount of money now being spent by the main donors on famine relief has increased substantially, from less than two per cent of overseas development assistance in 1988 to more than six per cent in 1991 (Borton, 1993). Relief expenditure in Africa accounts for a large part of the increase. This is against a backdrop of stagnating or declining aid budgets. But it is politically more sensitive to cut emergency aid which enjoys greater media coverage than development expenditure, and this to some extent protects the emergency portion of aid.

Recipient governments
In stark contrast to Asian examples of famine mitigation, where domestic public action has been the corner-stone of success, government capacity to respond to the threat of famine in the Sahel and Horn of Africa has never been strong. Where it did exist, it has been eroded by a decade or more of public expenditure cuts and economic stagnation. As well as being crippled by a lack of economic and institutional resources, governments do not necessarily have the political will to prevent famine, especially if they are under threat from rival interest groups. Elsewhere, political upheaval and change have diverted government attention away from food crises.

Local government capacity to respond has tended to be even weaker. In exceptional cases where local capacity is strong, this is invariably due to localized investment by a foreign donor or NGO. Democratization, and the accompanying trend towards decentralization of government service provision, offers real opportunities for more appropriate and flexible famine-prevention policies; but, again, these will inevitably be contingent on the availability of external resources. Building up local government capacity is a lengthy and costly process.

Non-governmental organizations
Over the last 10 to 15 years, the role played by Northern but also by some Southern NGOs in providing relief assistance has increased dramatically (Borton, 1993). In sub-Saharan Africa, 40 per cent of emergency food aid is now channelled through NGOs. Western donors have actively encouraged Northern NGOs to play a bigger role, tending to become the favoured distributors of relief. There are a number of reasons for this sub-contractual relationship. First is mounting frustration with inadequate government capacity to run relief operations. Second, NGOs are seen to be more flexible, able to deliver relief more rapidly and be more accountable to donors for the resources they handle. Third, as a growing proportion of relief is destined for conflict areas, NGOs are chosen by donors as the most trustworthy and neutral distributors, less constrained by issues of sovereignty where cross-border operations are to be launched (Borton, 1993; see also Chapter 3). But there are also drawbacks to the use of NGOs. Their geographical coverage is usually limited. Relying on NGOs is often at the expense of government structures which become marginalized and weakened even further.[4] And national governments do not necessarily agree with donors' perceptions of the suitability of foreign NGOs.

Conclusions

There is growing concern about the poor record of famine prevention in the Sahel and Horn of Africa, despite the quantity of resources allocated to it. The time has come to shift the debate forward from a preoccupation with information and EW towards tackling constraints on the response

---

[4] See Buchanan-Smith, 1990, for the case of Sudan in the mid-1980s.

side. There is little point in further improving the ability of EWS to provide decision-makers with the certainty they crave, until there are changes in the institutional framework within which they operate, to reflect better what actually happens during a famine. Prediction will always be more akin to art than science; decision-makers must learn to live with this, but adapt their response systems accordingly rather than waiting for the definitive forecast. If the policy failure of famine prevention is to be reversed, the institutional and political constraints to realizing the benefits of early, albeit imprecise, warning must be tackled.

The starting-point is that EWS must not only be capable of warning of large-scale famine (quite a rare event), but also be sensitive to changes in food-security status long before famine threatens and be able to detect localized pockets of acute food stress. As many EWS evolve into multi-indicator systems, this wider remit is now within their reach. On the response side, interventions should be geared to protecting livelihoods, not only to saving lives. This means *early* response, and is consistent with local people's priorities. It is also a more rational response than waiting for destitution as the trigger, especially if post-famine rehabilitation is part of the overall policy objective. The analysis presented in this book about how the international relief system works, and the five country case-studies of EW and response in 1990–91, are judged against these benchmarks of what an EWS and a relief response *ought* to be able to do.

In Chapter 2, the complexity of EWS for famine prevention is situated in the wider context of the debate about the use of information in decision-making. Empirical evidence on the generation and exploitation of famine early-warning information within the international relief system is analysed in Chapter 3. Chapters 4 to 8 present five country case-studies plotting the story of famine early warning and response in 1990–91 in each country. Barriers to, and opportunities for, timely response are identified in each case. The five countries reflect the diversity of early-warning and response systems in Africa. Some of the countries face endemic food crisis (e.g. Ethiopia), whereas others face only periodic episodes of food shortage (e.g. Mali). In some cases, relations between national government and international donors were good in 1991, as in Mali; elsewhere they were fraught with difficulty and tension as in Sudan and Ethiopia. Some systems operated in the context of decentralized government (e.g. Kenya), whereas others were highly centralized (e.g. Chad and Ethiopia). Such differences permit useful comparisons to be made and conclusions drawn about the particular set of circumstances which are most likely to ensure that a strong link between early-warning information and preventive action can be forged. Finally, Chapter 9 concludes with a set of practical policy recommendations about how to tackle the institutional, political and logistical constraints to realizing the benefits of early — if imprecise — warning, to inform the reversal of the current policy failure of famine prevention.

11

CHAPTER 2

What are Famine Early-warning Systems?

Introduction

Timely, accurate and appropriate predictive information has long been recognized as an essential prerequisite for famine prevention. People who are vulnerable to the threat of famine have their own indigenous information systems, but these *informal* sources are rarely exploited by outside decision-makers. Information in the public domain can also play a crucial advocacy role, leading some to argue that a free press is the surest way to prevent famine (Drèze and Sen, 1989). In the Sahel and Horn of Africa, however, such sources rarely make a central contribution. It is *formal* EW information which is increasingly demanded by decision-makers responsible for the allocation of resources to prevent famine. To this end, purpose-built information systems — or famine EWS — have been set up. Evaluations of their performance tend to concentrate on technical questions of data collection and analysis. In contrast, the emphasis here is on policy issues concerning ownership and use of information. Although models of information systems put the link between information provision and use at the heart of the system, the practice of EW shows that this relationship is frequently flawed.

EWS as information systems

Famine EWS are sub-systems of wider information systems used in agricultural and food-security planning, and frequently share components with other systems. Most EWS are quite clearly defined in an institutional sense — often originating as discrete projects — even though they may be located in statistical departments, agricultural planning units, or relief and rehabilitation commissions in which a range of information and/or decision-making tasks are undertaken.

Like any information system, most EWS are designed according to: information needs; where to draw the line between the system and its external environment; the minimum level of human and financial resources to meet system objectives; and what demands the system will make on the wider environment. Information systems are both processes (the provision of information for use in decision-making) and organizations (the actual structure and operation of a system which collects information). As organizations, they have the following basic elements: *components*, which can be physical or abstract, and objects or processes; a *structure*, comprised of the various components; an *environment*, or the context within which the system operates; a *boundary*, which divides the structure from the environment; and finally,

12

inputs and outputs, which determine how the system operates within its environment. Feedback loops, while conceptually important, are weak in practice in most EWS.[1]

The missing link between EW and response can only be partially understood by analysing the EWS as an information system. It is helpful to distinguish between data, information and knowledge, to clarify how information generated by such a system is used. The key distinction for famine EW is between the use of information and the use of knowledge. For the sake of simplicity, in the following chapters we revert to the more common terminology 'use of information', although strictly speaking this refers principally to 'use of knowledge':

- *data* are unanalysed facts and figures, at times collected by an information system;
- *information* is analysed data, often presented in a form designed for a particular decision-making task;
- *knowledge* is the absorption, assimilation, understanding and appreciation of that information;
- *use of data* is the process of transformation of raw data into information;
- *use of information* is the process of transmission and reception of information;
- *use of knowledge* is acting on the contents of the information received.[2]

Figure 2.1 shows the overall structure of a typical EWS and its component parts. The points at which data become information and information becomes knowledge are indicated on the diagram. The first component is *observation and measurement* which includes data collection and processing. All observation and measurement works through an *observational filter*, which defines how the world external to the system is perceived. This filter is the result of conceptualization (the way the real world is understood to work) and operational definition (how the world is agreed to 'be' by the system). Next, is the conversion of data into information or interpretation and analysis (involving *problem definition, synthesis of data* and *analysis of options*). Finally, *decision-making and implementation* processes are the conversion of information into knowledge.

EWS as information systems share a number of common characteristics.

Data
- EWS rely on multiple sources of information, many of which are collected for reasons other than famine EW, for example, agricultural production data used routinely by the Ministry of Agriculture.
- Measurement is often indirect via the use of proxy indicators of food stress.

From data to information
- Problem definition is relatively straightforward for most EWS, although this is no longer the case if the system shifts from a narrow focus

---

[1] These criteria are based on FAO's (1986:54) model of an information system.
[2] The categorization builds on Machlup (1979): see Davies, 1994, on which this section is based.

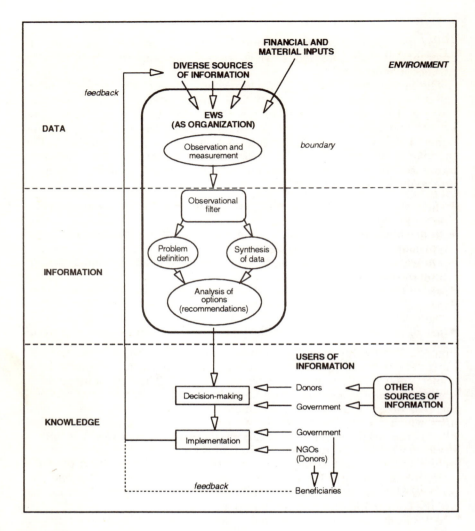

Figure 2.1 *An EWS as information system (as process)*
Source: Based on FAO's model of an information system (1986).

on famine prediction towards the broader concern of livelihood security.[3]

- Synthesis of data is most straightforward if the mandate of the EWS is limited to estimating aggregate food aid needs. Again, this becomes more complicated if disaggregation or more varied types of response are required.
- Analysis of options, leading to recommendations, tends to be limited to food aid requirements: few EWS have a wider menu of options.

---

[3] This, it should be noted, is distinct from problem identification (to predict famine) (see page 18). Problem definition relates to *how* famines can be predicted (e.g. by monitoring FAD and/or FED, see page 3).

14

From information to knowledge

- Decision-making (undertaken by donors, government and NGOs) tends to be deliberately separate from and external to the EWS, either to guarantee the objectivity of the information provided or in recognition of the other factors which decision-makers must take into account.
- Decision-making is influenced by sources of information apart from that provided by the EWS.
- Implementation is also separate from both the information system and from decision-making and tends to be undertaken by different groups (e.g. NGOs rather than donors, different parts of government).

Environment

- The boundary between the EWS and the rest of the government/donor bureaucracy is problematic. On the one hand it is quite clear, to wit, the explicit separation noted above; on the other hand, informal sources of information can mean that in reality the boundary between information providers and decision-makers is blurred.
- Integration of EWS into existing institutional structures is rarely achieved and frequently there is both geographical and institutional distance between producers and users of information.
- The environment within which EWS operate demands multiple and conflicting roles of the information system (the government may have one set of needs, donors another).
- EWS must be able to communicate with multiple actors, operating at different levels (international, national and local).
- Local people — who are both the source of much EW information and the beneficiaries of preventive action — are almost always geographically and institutionally distant from the EWS.

Inputs and outputs

- Inputs into EWS fall into two categories: financial, material and human resources; and information generated by other sources. EWS in most countries in the Sahel and Horn of Africa are characterized by a high degree of foreign (donor) funding.
- Outputs are usually restricted to published results of the information system and recommendations for action — the latter usually described in terms of food aid needs.

Information generated by EWS

EWS are concerned with three types of information. The first is positive information, describing the status and behaviour of conditions, situations and things (e.g. rainfall levels, size of the harvest). The second is normative information, which involves a judgement about how good or bad a condition, situation or thing is (e.g. household food-security status). The third is prescriptive information, indicating what goals and courses of action can be derived from the other two types of information (e.g. estimated food aid requirements).

15

There are a number of salient characteristics of information provided by EWS which affect its use in decision-making:[4]

- Supply-side indicators continue to predominate over demand-side ones, in spite of doubts about the accuracy of annual harvest assessments (and especially the overall food balance sheets which they are used to calculate).
- Socio-economic indicators are tracked by most systems, but these are less influential in decision-making than production indicators, except for targeting purposes. Critical determinants of local food security status continue to be left out (e.g. levels of household food stocks and indebtedness), often because they are the most difficult to monitor.
- Local people's coping strategies are rarely incorporated systematically, other than as a retrospective justification for the failure to respond in time ('people did cope' as in the case of Sudan in 1991). When they are cited as part of the evidence of crisis, it is often in an arbitrary way, not helped by the fact that the sequence and range of strategies used by local people are often changing. This kind of information is potentially very effective in famine mitigation when it signals the final stages of coping prior to destitution, but coping strategies are notoriously difficult to monitor and interpret accurately (see Davies, 1993).
- Nutritional surveillance data are often a key part of EWS. They are both influential with donors and frequently used as a 'trump card' to prove the existence of a crisis already under way.
- Many EWS, especially those which are donor-funded, are increasingly reliant on high-tech inputs using sophisticated information technology and satellite imagery.
- The tendency for information to be distorted in its transmission through bureaucratic layers is prevalent: at each level the message is filtered and ultimately reduced to a handful of straightforward, quantitative indicators which betray the complexity of the crisis.
- On the other hand, messages have to be simplified so that busy decision-makers are not inundated. This leaves little room to convey the uncertainty implicit in many of the indicators coming out of EWS: an estimate of those at risk of starvation is a good example because it is very hard to make accurately, yet it is also highly emotive and persuasive.
- The information generated by an EWS is highly temporally specific and rapidly loses its value to decision-makers.

For all the common characteristics shared by EWS, they nevertheless vary widely. Table 2.1 sketches a typology of EWS, showing two ends of the spectrum, from top–down, data-centred and famine-driven systems at one extreme to bottom up, more subjective and livelihood security-driven ones at the other. Most EWS fall somewhere between these two poles.

The scope of the EWS depends on its overall objective. If it is to save lives, it will focus on triggering (emergency) famine relief, usually food aid.

---

4   Details of the kind of information provided by EWS are not the central concern of this book and have been examined in depth elsewhere (see Davies *et al.*, 1991 for a review of the literature).

Table 2.1   Typology of early-warning systems

System characteristics	Famine early-warning system	Food and livelihood monitoring system
Scope	Famine-oriented	Livelihood security-oriented
Determinants of food security	Food production	Access to food
Level of operation	Macro, centralized	Micro, decentralized
Unit of analysis	Geographic, e.g. nation/ districts	Socio-economic, e.g. vulnerable groups
Approach	Top–down, often quantitative, 'objective' indicators	Bottom–up, participatory often qualitative, 'subjective' indicators
Response	Food aid	Diverse, flexible

Source: Adapted from Davies *et al.*, 1991.

If it is to save livelihoods, it will need to detect much earlier stresses which risk undermining not only people's capacity to consume today, but also to produce in the future. All the systems considered in this study, with the exception of the EWS in Turkana, fall into the first category. The Malian EWS, while recommending interventions in non-famine years, nevertheless restricts its response options to the distribution of free food aid.

Food production continues to dominate most indicators used by EWS, not least because annual harvest assessments are easy to understand and are believed to be the most directly comparable data between countries (despite widely differing methodologies and levels of accuracy) and the best starting-point for making inter-annual comparisons. Although EWS increasingly use socio-economic indicators to provide supporting evidence of different vulnerable groups' access to food, information about distribution rarely figures as prominently as levels of food availability in EWS assessments, especially in their recommendations for action. Most socio-economic indicators are used to facilitate domestic targeting of food aid, rather than to inform the earlier decision about overall quantities required.

Most of the systems covered in this book are macro-level and centralized, although some have complementary local-level systems which feed into the national EWS. In general, unless decentralized data are available for all at-risk areas, they can distort decision-making; for example, the availability of local-level information gives a particular area undue visibility, making it appear more vulnerable by virtue of the fact that information exists. In any case, it is usually the aggregate food balance which is used as the central planning tool for triggering and for deciding on the scale of response, however detailed the information provided by the EWS may be.

The preferred unit of analysis for decision-makers is administrative boundaries, drawn along geographic lines. Even though information may be provided about particular vulnerable groups (e.g. displaced people, pastoralists), decisions to respond rarely take account of differentiation within an administrative area. If targeting does take place, it is usually at a much later stage and conducted by the distributing agency, rather than by decision-makers responsible for triggering an early response. Moreover, it is generally based on pre-existing physical criteria (e.g. children under five years of age, pregnant and lactating women), on geographical differentiation, or on self-targeting mechanisms (most frequently food-for-work programmes), but rarely on the basis of what people do — their livelihoods.

The approach of most of the EWS studied tends to be top–down and geared towards quantitative data about a handful of apparently 'objective' indicators (e.g. the size of the harvest), although in some cases there is significant movement towards a more bottom–up, participatory approach, incorporating subjective indicators of food-security status. This tends, however, to provide data which are not readily used by decision-makers, either because they are qualitative and more complex, and/or because they fail to give a bottom line of how much food aid is needed. Decision-making structures and response systems have not evolved at the same pace or in the same way as the EW information which is fed into them. Consequently, much local-level information is never used.

Response options continue to be dominated by food-aid distributions, and the systems studied (with the exception of Turkana in 1990–91) are characterized by a dual food aid trap. The information system is designed principally to indicate food aid needs, while the response system (divorced from wider development initiatives) can offer only food aid, irrespective of how appropriate this is.

Use of EW information

Public policy decision-making can be conceptualized most simply and rationally as a continuous cycle of identifying problems, formulating alternative solutions, analysing options, deciding, implementing decisions, observing the results, evaluating the situation, and then continuing to deal with new or existing problems (FAO, 1986). Implicit in much information systems analysis is that this cycle is a purely technical process. According to this logic, the use of EW information in decision-making can be described in a relatively straightforward manner.

Problem identification is clear for EWS and done well in advance of the system being established: how to predict famine, in order to prevent it. Related to this, is the formulation of alternative solutions. If EWS are bounded by a narrow famine-prevention remit, solutions tend to be confined to the distribution of emergency food aid during the hungry season to prevent starvation. As mentioned in Chapter 1, most EWS in Africa were set up to service donor and UN food-aid institutions and this remains their *raison d'être*. Even when their scope is expanded, it is rare that alternative response options to protect livelihoods are developed systematically alongside. In the analysis of options — or the assessment of possible policy routes to be taken as a result of analysing available information — the issue is usually not what to do (food aid distribution is the most common, and often the only, option), but rather how much is needed, when and where.

18

The decision to respond is the next step, often requiring a second round of analysis when perceived needs are not met (i.e. inadequate quantities of food aid are pledged), and available limited resources have to be re-allocated.

The implementation of decisions is rarely carried out by the EWS or by donors (with the exception of the World Food Programme). Sometimes recipient governments will implement food aid distributions, but often it is foreign and local NGOs which are entrusted with this task (see Chapter 3). These may be — but are not always — contributors to the EWS. Observing the results tends to be the responsibility of the implementing agency, some-times backed up by donor and government observers. In emergency situa-tions, these are usually fairly crude exercises as logistical considerations of moving and distributing relief take priority.

Evaluating the situation in the aftermath of the relief operation again tends to be separated from many of the actors involved. The performance of the EWS itself is usually evaluated independently of any decisions which it has helped to inform; and often the performance of the implementing agency (the NGO) will be evaluated independently from the performance of the donor agency which supplied the resources for the response. The actual impact on beneficiaries is often inadequately evaluated because of lack of monitoring data during the emergency. Too frequently there is no evaluation of the response, despite the substantial resources consumed, because of sensitivities over failure in such a high-profile activity.

In the context of decisions about famine prevention, continuing to deal with new or existing problems takes two forms. In situations of chronic crisis, one relief operation is rarely finished before the next one begins. More commonly, the tendency is for a stop–go approach; once the crisis is deemed to be over, systems are frozen or dismantled until the next time around. This can have detrimental effects both from the point of view of institutional memory, and for the beneficiaries of relief.

Constraints to the use of EW information

Actual decision-making processes about response to EW have none of the elegance of this model. Due to the widespread belief that lack of informa-tion has been an obstacle to famine prevention, it is often assumed that if EW information *does* exist, it will be used in a manner consistent with stated policy objectives. This is rarely the case, especially with regard to *timely* warnings. There are a number of reasons for this. The quality of information provided obviously plays a part, as does its appropriateness (although each actor's definition of appropriateness will vary depending on the interests they seek to protect or pursue). Far more important are the barriers within the environment in which the EWS operates. There are three sets of environmental constraints to information use, summarized in Table 2.2 as institutional, political and logistical barriers, which operate at various levels, depending on the actor in question.

As far as institutional constraints are concerned bureaucracies are not usually well designed or adequately resourced to exploit EW information.

19

Table 2.2 Constraints to the timely use of early-warning information

| Actors | Institutional | Examples of constraints | |
		Political	Logistical
Government	Lack of human and financial resources. Inappropriate bureaucratic procedures and structures. Avoidance of responsibility. Lack of institutional memory. *Ad hoc* response arrangements.	Conflicting political objectives. Reluctance to accept aid conditionality.	Lack of financial resources with which to act. Lack of infrastructure and weak transport sector.
Donors	Distance from problem and failure to appreciate lag time in delivery of relief. Inadequate co-ordination between field and HQ, or with other donors. Inappropriate bureaucratic procedures and structures. Avoidance of responsibility. Lack of institutional memory.	Home country political agenda. Unwillingness to breach sovereignty. Lack of accountability to local beneficiaries.	Distance over which resources must be mobilized. Lack of infrastructure and weak transport sector in-country.
NGOs	Dependence on donors. Bureaucratic overload. Lack of institutional memory.	Difficulty in preserving neutrality. Lack of accountability to local beneficiaries.	Lack of financial resources with which to act. *Ad hoc* response arrangements.

At national government level famine prevention may be split between several ministries (e.g. Agriculture, Livestock, Health), all of which are competing for additional resources which the response may yield. The institutional location of the EWS, and of the responsibility to prevent famine, can be critical: if, for example, both are located in a powerful ministry (Finance or Planning), there may be a better chance of timely response than if they are located in a sectoral line ministry or inter-ministerial unit. Specially established planning units for EW/response can duplicate existing structures, encounter resentment from other ministries they are supposed to co-ordinate, be short of resources in years when there is no crisis, and suffer from lack of responsibility for action. A few EWS have sought to build on existing sources of information, such as in Mali, albeit with substantial donor support and the creation of additional bureaucratic structures. Systems which are wholly integrated into existing bureaucracies are rare, and most likely to occur when the system is not highly dependent on donor funding.

If set up as discrete projects, EWS can be isolated from the rest of the bureaucracy and resented because they are better resourced; if within donor agencies, they are looked on with suspicion by the recipient government; if part of NGO operations, their relationship with formal information channels is often ambiguous. Generally, formal EWS in Africa have tended to be set up as purpose-built units, often at the behest of donor agencies; the Relief and Rehabilitation Commissions in Sudan and Ethiopia are cases in point.[5] While donors do not suffer from resource constraints in the same way as national governments, they share many of the problems relating to inappropriate bureaucratic structures and procedures. For donors, the key constraint is the absence of mechanisms explicitly designed to respond to the timing and nature of EW signals. For example, despite the mandate of emergency departments, they may be prevented from reacting to signals which coincide with the last quarter of the financial year when budgets have been run down. The greatest cost of this is in speed of response. A related problem is inadequate understanding of the urgency of a situation. In most decision-making structures, it is those who receive information first (generally members lower down a bureaucratic hierarchy) who are entrusted with the task of selecting information to pass up. If this selection process is inadequate, decision-makers do not receive the information they need.

Avoidance of responsibility affects both donors and governments. Clay and Schaffer (1984:2) identify a number of 'escape hatches' which enable organizations practising development policy to shun responsibility. These include the separation of policy choice and implementation, the

---

5 It is interesting to note that this has not been the case in Botswana, which has not been heavily dependent on foreign aid to respond to food insecurity caused by drought. Instead, there are a number of co-ordinating committees, including an Early Warning Technical Committee, which encourage the integration of the administration of the Drought Relief Programme into existing institutional structures. And responsibility for preventing famine lies with the powerful Ministry of Finance and Development Planning, which ensures that it is given high priority (Buchanan-Smith and Tlogelang, 1994).

latter often being the responsibility of another organization. Inadequate information is frequently identified as a reason for poor implementation, implying the need for more information and more staff to provide it. Yet within this model, no amount of information can bridge the structural gap between choice and implementation, unless explicit mechanisms are developed within the bureaucracy to do so. In the case of food emergencies, Cutler (1985:15) has argued that:

> The establishment or strengthening of food crisis information systems becomes an escape route — agencies argue that they cannot act decisively until they have more and better information. Without being carefully linked to a defined and mandated response system, the EW information systems become ends in themselves.

Yet as the case-studies show, even defined and mandated response systems which exist on paper, and at times even in practice, can fail to trigger a timely response if there are political gains to be had from delay or none to be had from assuming responsibility. The need for certainty in the type of information which donors want reinforces the tendency towards lateness of the response (see Chapter 3).

Another dimension to avoidance of responsibility is that actors coping with an impossible overload of information and (latent) choices often deal with what they are forced to, in such a way as to minimize immediate effort and problems. In this 'garbage-can' view of decision-making processes 'intention is lost in context-dependent flows of problems, solutions, people and choice opportunities' (March and Olsen, 1989:14).

NGOs share some of these constraints, but are also prone to their own specific institutional barriers. First and foremost is their dependence on donors for resources to respond: NGOs can only lobby for action (but not respond) until donors have made the decision to release resources. This severely hampers strategic planning. NGOs face a dilemma: they are under pressure from donors to be their foot-soldiers in an emergency and are promised huge amounts of resources which are hard to refuse, but this in turn compromises their independent (non-governmental) status. Second, there is a tendency for NGOs to have light bureaucratic structures to reduce overheads, but these can rapidly become overloaded once an emergency is under way. Reliance then on temporary and/or untrained staff becomes almost inevitable.

Different potential users of EW information, with multiple objectives, present a further set of institutional barriers. Lack of co-ordination and duplication of effort is the most obvious problem; but also, within both government departments and donor agencies, bureaucratic parochialism can paralyse effective response (see Tabor, 1983). A further consequence is the tendency to bypass existing structures (see Hubbard, 1989, and Buchanan-Smith, 1990, for examples of this in Sudan). For example, a relief operation run by donors and NGOs may have the long-term effect of weakening government structures which play little part in the EW/ response process.

Lack of institutional memory is another barrier. Rapid changes of staff, a failure to document past experiences and to build up preparedness, and preoccupation with logistical constraints to moving large quantities of food during emergencies, all contribute to a sense of starting afresh each time around. There is no time to reflect on past experiences, even where these have been documented. Mistakes are frequently repeated.

Political constraints fall into two categories: those relating to conflicting political objectives of different actors (frequently labelled 'political will'); and those to do with wider relations of dependence between actors.

Information generated by EWS is not politically neutral. Agendas of governments and donors differ widely and information can do little to bridge this gap. A donor may be under domestic pressure to respond as a result of widespread media coverage of a crisis, or alternatively may wish to do nothing because of wider geopolitical interests. Recipient governments, while seeking to maximize aid flows, may also have clear domestic reasons for furthering the access of one group over another to food aid, irrespective of need. It is political interests rather than humanitarian motives which are most influential in determining the timing and nature of the relief response. NGOs, usually seen as the upholders of the humanitarian card, may also be subject to conflicting pressures, such as the desire to attract relief resources into those areas in which they are already working.

The second set of political constraints relates to the prevailing hierarchy between donors, governments and NGOs. Whereas data and information may be relatively objective, each decision-maker uses knowledge in a self-interested way. When it is Northerners who are using knowledge about Southern beneficiaries to inform public action (such as levels of food relief), the relationship is essentially hierarchical — Northern assumptions, values and analyses predominate. This is clearly the case in the international relief system. This hierarchy is repeated within developing countries between powerful elites and weaker groups. Knowledge is thus a political tool, reflecting existing hierarchies and playing a critical role in the allocation of resources between competing interest groups. People working in EWS are generally all too aware of the manipulation of the information they provide, but can do little to prevent it.

In terms of control over resources, the hierarchy is clear. Donors seek to use their resources to achieve a range of policy objectives which may have rather tenuous links with famine prevention (for example, trying to pressure a recipient government into improving its human-rights record). Similarly, for recipient governments, negotiations over response needs take place within the wider context of donor/government relations, characterized by the desire to minimize conditionality and protect sovereignty, while simultaneously maximizing aid flows. Governments are accountable to local interest groups and cannot afford to ignore them: these are rarely the same groups identified by the EWS as most in need of additional resources. NGOs sit somewhat uncomfortably between these two positions, trying to retain their neutrality and independence as they are drawn into the big business of donor relief money, as well as endeavouring to operate on the ground in an impartial way when often they are manipulated and their resources are misused by powerful interest groups in and outside government. This in turn undermines their credibility.

Logistical constraints refer to obstacles that are a function of the physical and infrastructural environment (for example, being a landlocked country, lacking roads, or having a weak transport sector). This affects implementation of decisions taken, but also has implications for the timeliness of decision-making, in recognition of the inevitable delays in delivering relief. Frequently donor headquarters implicitly assume that once resources have been allocated, the job is done even though it can be months before the food actually reaches the hungry. Poor infrastructure and often *ad hoc* institutional and logistical arrangements exacerbate the adverse consequences of late decisions.

Conclusions

Two sets of propositions arise from this review. These relate firstly to EWS as information systems, and secondly to the use of EW information in making decisions for response. It is these propositions which we explore in the subsequent case-studies and return to in the concluding chapter.

EWS as information systems

- All too often the implicit assumption made by EWS is that the ways in which food systems work or fail is self-evident. This tendency is further exacerbated by the need to simplify the complex processes which make up household food security for monitoring purposes.
- For those EWS concerned with saving livelihoods rather than lives alone, both the definition of the problem and the range of options become more complex.
- Much evaluation and analysis of the performance of EWS is preoccupied with the extent to which observation and measurement provide information which meets the criteria of accuracy, relevance, timeliness, consistency and accessibility, rather than the extent to which the information is used.
- EWS are critically influenced by the external environment in which they operate: some elements of this environment are common to all EWS (for example, donor decision-making procedures), whereas others are location-specific (for example, current relations between the government of a particular country and the main donors).
- EW practitioners are usually distanced from decision-making and not well integrated into other response structures.
- Beneficiaries are even further distanced from the system.

Use of EW information

- The capacity to generate EW information has far outstripped the potential of decision-makers to use it to trigger timely response to prevent famine. This is due to inadequate and inappropriate institutional arrangements at government and donor levels, and to unrealistic assumptions about the ability of information to resolve conflicting political objectives between governments and donors.
- Whereas collection and analysis of EW data are technical issues, the use of the knowledge gained from them is determined by institutional and

24

political factors. Questions of who owns and controls EW information, hence how objective it is perceived to be, are key determinants of its use.

- It cannot be assumed that any of the actors using EW information to trigger response has exclusively humanitarian objectives. All are influenced by wider political interests.
- The nature of EW information — particularly the rigid temporal boundaries within which it is valid — and the need to respond rapidly, make the logistical dimension (the actual relief operation) especially critical.
- Dependence on the international relief system by countries in the Sahel and Horn of Africa for resources to respond to crisis emphasizes the significance of donor decision-making, and the need for donors to be convinced by the *early*-warning information.
- There is an inconsistency between donors who demand certainty, and therefore evidence of a crisis before responding, and the need to respond early to often incomplete information warning of deteriorating food security.
- Many of the apparently obvious solutions to making response more timely and appropriate (for example, pre-positioning of resources) are inconsistent with the bureaucratic procedures and political objectives of donor agencies and recipient governments.
- Accountability to the victims of famine and the potential beneficiaries of relief assistance is weak and attenuated for some actors (for example, governments) and non-existent for others (donors, NGOs).

CHAPTER 3

The International Relief System[1]

Introduction

In each of the five African countries considered in this book, almost all the relief resources used to alleviate the food crisis in 1990–91 were provided through the international relief system. Lack of resources in each case constrained the national government's capacity to act. Decisions made by Western donors, the key players in the international relief system, about whether, when and how to respond to the crisis were critical determinants of whether timely preventive action was taken. This chapter investigates the kind of EW information the donors received and how they interpreted and used it. It focuses on four principal donor agencies: the Overseas Development Administration (ODA) of the British Government, the United States Agency for International Development (USAID), the Commission of the European Communities (now European Union, EU), and the United Nations World Food Programme (WFP). Within each agency decision-making about relief aid tends to be highly centralized. The chapter therefore focuses on decision-making processes at headquarters level — in London, Washington, Brussels and Rome, respectively.

Sources of early warning about food crises in Africa available to donor agencies have proliferated during the last decade. Yet the international relief system persists in responding to food crises after they have begun, and not in advance. The reasons for this have very little to do with information and prediction, and much more to do with internal institutional procedures, with political factors, and with logistical problems during implementation. This chapter identifies the principal constraints.

The beginning of the 1990s was a significant period in the evolution of the international relief system. First, Western aid budgets were stagnating or declining for domestic economic reasons. At the same time, the need for emergency relief escalated as widespread food crises in sub-Saharan Africa coincided with the high-profile Kurdish refugee crisis in northern Iraq after the Gulf War, and a cyclone disaster in Bangladesh. As emergency budgets proved inadequate to meet the demands made upon them, extra resources had to be found. Emergency expenditure has thus been increasing, and taking on a higher profile with Western electorates as the most public image of aid, and the most politically sensitive with respect to aid cuts.

---

[1] This chapter is based partly on an earlier draft entitled 'Case Studies of Four Donor Agencies', written by Celia Petty of Save the Children Fund with Margaret Buchanan-Smith in 1992.

Second, as the spotlight began to turn away from Africa towards eastern Europe in the wake of the collapse of the former Soviet Union, a new form of political conditionality was applied to aid for Africa, making a clear distinction between countries eligible for development aid and those eligible only for relief. Third, long-running dissatisfaction with UN agencies and their co-ordinating role crystallized around the Kurdish crisis and sparked off some reorganization within the UN. And finally, although beyond the scope of this book, the Kurdish operation established the important precedent that the international community was prepared to use force in support of humanitarian relief operations, which opened a lively debate about the issue of sovereignty and relief. The impetus for most of these changes originated outside the African continent, but they have implications for how international relief aid is provided to Africa, some of which this chapter explores.

Preventing famine: whose responsibility?

Who should be responsible for preventing famine, and for ensuring that relief is provided in time to those in need? The answer, of course, is the national government. But few African governments have the resources or capacity necessary to fulfil this role, including the governments of our five case-study countries. The international system is therefore relied upon to supply almost all relief resources and much of the capacity. This has the effect of shifting the centre of gravity in decision-making about when and how relief should be provided away from Africa towards Western capitals.

Although national government should be held accountable for famine prevention — for example, misguided and inappropriate macro policies have often created the conditions in which famine is likely to occur[2] — whether it is depends upon the political system, and the government's power base. Dictatorship can protect the government from having to listen to the concerns of all its people, until conditions deteriorate to such an extent that it is overthrown, as happened in Sudan during the famine of the mid-1980s when President Nimeiri's government was deposed. Even in more pluralistic political systems, those most vulnerable to famine usually have little power. The threat of famine in a remote rural part of the country where the local people carry little political clout is much more likely to be ignored than food shortages in the capital which can threaten riots and political instability.

If the government is impoverished, it can do little when large-scale famine threatens, even if it wants to. In this scenario, donors play a key role in determining whether or not famine is prevented. But they are not necessarily responding to the voices of the famine victims. The lines of accountability between Western donor governments and famine-prone people in Africa are extremely tenuous if, indeed, they exist at all. Ultimately,

---

[2]   For example in Sudan and Ethiopia, where exchange regulations and export taxes have had the effect of undermining rural growth, and policy failure is held responsible for domestic discrimination, in the worst cases exacerbating ethnic conflict (von Braun *et al.*, 1993).

Western public opinion has most impact on the international relief system. To some extent, it is lobbying on behalf of the victims of famine, but this is a very weak link, to a large extent determined by Western media coverage.

The prominent role played by Western donors raises some difficult issues, such as who controls the relief operation. Recipient governments naturally want to retain overall control over the way the relief is provided and distributed. But this may not meet the conditions of donors supplying it, who want the right to choose the most trustworthy channel in *their* opinion for distributing *their* resources, to the people that *they* want to help. Events in northern Sudan in 1990–91 illustrate well an extreme case of this (see Chapter 5).

What is the international relief system?[3]

So far Western donors have been mentioned as the key players, as they provide most of the resources flowing through the international relief system. But it is in fact a network of different actors (see Figure 3.1). The main flow is from donor agencies and the general public in donor countries, through NGOs and UN agencies directly to the affected population, or through the additional layer of government agencies and local NGOs. The humanitarian aid budget of most donor agencies has expanded substantially during the last decade. Extra relief destined for sub-Saharan Africa accounts for a large part of the increase. Within ODA, for example, emergency aid has increased from 2–3 per cent of the aid budget in the early 1980s to 11 per cent in 1991–2. In the EU, humanitarian aid was an average of 14 per cent of the development aid budget between 1986 and 1990, increasing to 21 per cent in 1991.

How the donor agencies decide to channel their resources largely determines the role played by the other organizations. Since the early 1980s, NGOs have played an increasingly important role as a channel for relief assistance (see Chapter 1). For example, between 1977–8 and 1980–81 NGOs handled less than 0.5 per cent of ODA's emergency aid; between 1988–9 and 1990–91 this proportion had risen to 28 per cent. Within the EU the proportion of emergency aid channelled through NGOs increased from zero in 1976 to 37 per cent in 1990 (Borton, 1993). This trend is most pronounced in Africa. In the Horn, NGOs were the implementing partners for some 65 per cent of ODA's bilateral emergency relief between September 1990 and January 1992 (House of Commons Foreign Affairs Committee, 1992).

During 1991, however, a number of donors developed their own operational relief capacity. An extra arrow should be added to Figure 3.1 going directly from the donor agencies to the affected population. This change was triggered by the Kurdish refugee crisis. In at least two donor agencies, ODA and the EU, it sparked off a reorganization of their emergency aid departments, one of the principal motivations being the desire to promote their

---

[3]   This section is based on Borton, 1993.

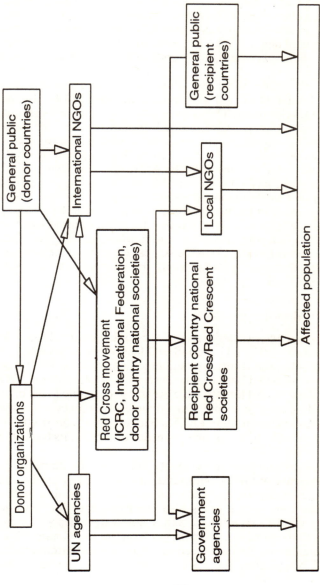

Figure 3.1 *The international relief system circa 1990*
Source: Borton, 1993.

29

visibility in relief work. Most relief was being channelled through NGOs, and because of their operational work on the front line they had enjoyed the highest profile during the crisis and had been given the credit for what had been done, rather than the donor providing financial support behind the scenes. At the same time, there was pressure to expand and improve the performance of the emergency departments in each organization.

Within ODA, an initiative from the Minister in 1991 created a new Emergency Aid Department and thus expanded ODA's disaster and emergency section; it also set up a register of personnel available for contracting for emergency work. The aim was to give ODA the capacity to carry out its own assessments of need, to take a more active role in co-ordination on the ground and, where necessary, to provide ODA relief teams of skilled personnel.

Within the EU Commission, the proposal to reorganize the system for administering humanitarian aid was similarly initiated in 1991, by the Commissioner for Development. The aims were to speed up disbursal of emergency aid by creating a more unified framework for managing and financing the EU's emergency aid activities, as well as to ensure that it was more closely associated with the EU than with implementing NGOs, and thus to promote the EU's visibility. In April 1992 the new EU Office of Humanitarian Aid (ECHO) was established, reporting directly to the Commissioner and working independently of any Directorate-General, including that for Development, according it high status and political profile.

In both cases, NGOs were worried that their operational role would be marginalized. So far, the increased operational capacity of these two donors has been most evident outside Africa, for example in former Yugoslavia, although there is a general trend among donors to promote their visibility in relief work.

Profile of four donor agencies

The four donor agencies under discussion include the three largest food aid donors in the world: WFP, EU and USAID (see Table 3.1). ODA is a much smaller donor, although it has a strong emergency focus. WFP is a multilateral agency, and the EU can best be described as 'plurilateral'. ODA and USAID are bilateral, and tend to have greater geographic focus in their aid budgets, including emergency aid. For example, emergency aid to the Horn of Africa figures prominently in ODA's budget, but it contributes little or no emergency relief to francophone countries except via its contribution to the EU's aid.

The bilateral programmes are strongly influenced by domestic political interests. In the case of ODA, ministerial approval is required for country allocations of relief resources. Accountability to democratic constituencies and to parliamentary structures is also much stronger for the bilaterals. This kind of pressure exists for the other donor agencies — for instance, the European Parliament can exert pressure on the EU Commission — but not to the same extent. Political accountability is most attenuated when it comes to the UN agencies. There are a number of relevant bodies to which

Table 3.1 Profile of donors' food aid programmes

	ODA[a]	USAID[a]	EU	WFP
Total food aid	148 000t (1990–91[b])	7 882 000t (1990–91[b])	1 579 770t (1991[b])	3 000 000t (1991[b])
As % of global food aid	0.1	40–50	15–20	15–25
Relief food aid (as % of total food aid)	N/a	632 000t (8%)	626 729t (40%)	1 606 000t (54%)
Relief food to SSA	N/a	577 300t	520 000t	1 101 700t
% of emergency food aid channelled through NGOs	Approx. 28%	Aprox. 50% for SSA	Approx. 37%	2–3%

Notes:

(a) There is some double-counting. For the bilaterals figures refer to their total contribution, but some of this is channelled through the multilateral agencies of the EU and WFP.

(b) The period differs because each agency uses a different financial year: ODA, April to March; USAID, October to September; EU, January to December; WFP, January to December. All figures quoted include January/February 1991, when most of the relief food distributed during the 1991 calendar year in the Horn of Africa and the Sahel was pledged.

UN agencies are accountable, for example, WFP is accountable to its governing body, the Committee of Food Aid Policy and Programmes (CFA), which is composed of civil servants of different member governments of the UN, but in practice accountability to member states' parliamentary structures is indirect.

Most relief is provided in the form of food aid, policies about which vary widely. ODA, at one end of the scale, does not favour food as a development resource; it tends to provide the minimum amount of food to which it is committed under the Food Aid Convention. Its bilateral food aid programme has a strong emergency orientation. Towards the other end of the scale are USAID and the EU, which both attach considerable importance to food aid as a development resource, not least because of their substantial domestic food surpluses. It is argued, however, that food aid donations are increasingly independent of surpluses, at least in terms of quantity if not of commodity composition (Uvin, 1994).

For USAID, food aid has been an important resource supporting its overall foreign policy. Hence Egypt received more than twice as much US food aid (none of it emergency aid)[4] during 1990 and 1991 as all recipient countries in the Horn of Africa and the Sahel put together. Even during 1990–91, a year of multiple disasters, emergency food aid represented only 8 per cent of the total US food aid budget (see Table 3.1). But to some extent the emphasis is changing. The 1990 Agricultural Development and Trade Act stresses to a much greater degree the use of food aid to promote food security and other development objectives (Shaw and Clay, 1993).

The EU has provided food aid for humanitarian purposes since 1968. Initially closely associated with the disposal of domestic farm surpluses, food aid has been increasingly linked to development objectives since the 1980s. A new food aid basic regulation was established in 1986 in response to parliamentary and public criticism, establishing food security as one of the main objectives of food aid policy, and extending the use of triangular transactions.

WFP was set up in 1962, specifically to channel surplus agricultural commodities into Third World development projects. During its first decade it handled very little emergency food aid. The tide started to turn after the Sahelian famines of the early 1970s, when an International Emergency Food Reserve (IEFR) was set up, to be drawn upon at short notice for emergency relief. The largest increase in WFP's emergency work, occurred during and after the African famines of the mid-1980s. Emergency food aid now accounts for approximately half of WFP's resources, most of which is currently destined for conflict-related emergencies (WFP, 1992). The role played by WFP in different emergencies depends very much on the response of the bilateral donors and how they wish to channel their resources (Figure 3.1).

---

[4] It was all provided under Title I of Public Law 480 (PL 480), which is essentially a concessional loan programme for countries unable to meet their food import needs through normal commercial channels. Priority is given to countries where there is the potential for commercially viable US agricultural exports in the future.

As stated above, almost all relief is provided in the form of food aid partly because of the availability of surplus food commodities in Western donor countries; it is usually much easier to obtain food than money. But it is also to do with the prevalent view that famine is caused by food shortage and in turn leads to death by starvation. Therefore the most appropriate response is to provide food to those threatened. As Chapter 1 explains, this is a stereotyped and over-simplified perception; the processes causing food crisis and/or famine are much more complex.

The political context of emergency aid to Africa in 1990–91

Aid budgets under pressure

By the beginning of the 1990s, aid budgets were under pressure in a number of donor countries (see OECD, 1994). In the US this was a direct result of the government deficit; US aid decreased in real terms by 2.7 per cent in 1991. The British Government has also been committed to reducing public expenditure; cutting back the aid budget is one of many targets for achieving this. In 1991, the UK aid budget increased marginally, but in 1992 aid spending fell by 4 per cent in real terms.[5]

This trend has had an impact on the orientation of aid programmes and on the profile of emergency relief. But there is no reason to suppose that the upward trend in emergency aid will change in the near future. Impoverishment and increasing civil strife in Africa are likely to increase the need for relief: the crisis in Rwanda is a case in point. Fighting and civil insecurity associated with political change in eastern Europe and the Commonwealth of Independent States are making unprecedented demands on emergency budgets, most obviously in the case of Bosnia. Emergency relief is the most public image of aid, more newsworthy than most other development issues. As long as the donor agency can prove that it is responding generously to publicized emergencies, the cuts in development aid will be less noticeable and less controversial to Western electorates.[6] The reorganization of the emergency departments in the EU and ODA, described above, to increase the donors' visibility in relief work is indicative of this trend. The emergency relief portion of Western aid budgets is unlikely to be subjected to the same financial constraints as the development portion.

As aid budgets are cut back, there is a simultaneous shift towards a more strategic focus together with greater accountability of development aid within some agencies to try and maximize its effectiveness. This is most explicit in the American case. Ronald Roskens, Administrator for USAID in 1991, stated that in future aid resources should be concentrated on those countries that 'utilize them most effectively', in a move towards 'results-oriented evaluation and performance-based programming' (Roskens,

---

5   The decrease in bilateral aid is even more significant; it fell by 10 per cent in real terms during 1992, while multilateral contributions increased by 5 per cent.
6   Lobbying against aid cuts in the UK, for instance, has tended to emphasize the humanitarian relief portion of ODA's activities (Borton, 1993).

1991:2–3). By targeting the potential winners, however, there is a real danger that conflict-ridden and famine-prone countries risk further marginalization, contributing to economic decline, impoverishment and further violence if they become ineligible for aid investment. USAID's programme will also have a tighter strategic focus. A recent decision has been taken to close nine out of 21 USAID missions in Africa, two of them in Sahelian countries.[7] The effects are yet to be seen, but could be serious. For instance, USAID is the largest food aid donor to Chad and the most important provider of emergency relief. The withdrawal of all USAID mission staff in 1995 raises questions about how well informed the agency will be in future when food crisis or famine threatens, and how willing it will be to respond if there is no local mission to exert pressure and to channel information to Washington (see Chapter 6).

Aid conditionality

The 1980s was a decade when economic conditions were increasingly applied to aid programmes. Economic conditionality was particularly associated with structural adjustment lending, 'to remove what the lender sees as fundamental policy-induced obstacles to economic growth', but also as an end in itself, as a way in which donors, and particularly institutions like the World Bank and IMF, can exert influence over policy-making in developing countries (Mosley *et al.*, 1991:67). This partly reflected donor disillusionment with the development process in many Third World countries, especially on the African continent.

The beginning of the 1990s marks a period when political conditions became much more explicit with respect to Western aid. Political conditionality was not new; the Cold War era had been characterized by aid allocations determined by political criteria. But with the ending of the Cold War political conditionality changed from being implicit to becoming a central plank of Western aid policy. The practice of applying conditionality correspondingly increased. Whereas Cold War political conditionality was motivated by the extension of East-West geopolitics into the South, the new conditionality is concerned to use aid to bring about local political reform, improved human rights and the pursuit of market-oriented economic policies (ODI, 1992).

Both economic and political conditionality have been ruthlessly applied to many African countries, especially by bilateral donors, but also by the EU. They tend to be least stringently applied by UN agencies, not least because of Southern representation in the UN. Although conditionality is supposed to provide positive encouragement to recipient countries to undertake political and economic reform in accordance with Western models, there is a punitive dimension. There are a number of examples in the 1990s of African governments which have not complied with the 'new' form of political conditionality, where aid has been suspended or terminated

---

7   USAID missions were to be closed in Côte d'Ivoire, Togo and Zaïre in 1994; in Burkina Faso, Botswana, Cameroon, Chad and Lesotho in 1995; and in Cape Verde in 1996.

Table 3.2   Food aid to case-study countries, by category, 1991 (cereals only)

	Total food aid (tonnes)	Relief food aid (tonnes)	Relief as % of total
Chad	75 899	26 792	35.3
Ethiopia	923 436	818 164	88.6
Kenya	50 922	6 162	12.1
Mali	48 650	1 411	2.9
Sudan	579 764	557 733	96.2

Source: WFP data.

(Robinson 1994). Thus, the Belgian and French governments suspended aid to Zaïre following reports of human-rights abuses and President Mobutu's resistance to democratic reform. Somalia and Sudan were both ineligible for US and UK development aid in 1990 and 1991 for similar reasons. In Ethiopia during the Mengistu regime, the British Government channelled development aid only through NGOs and British Council training programmes; US development aid had been terminated altogether.[8] Table 3.2 shows the percentage of total food aid carrying the emergency (humanitarian) tag in 1991 for each of the five countries considered in this book. Sudan and Ethiopia stand out for the very high percentage which was relief food. Humanitarian aid is officially exempted from political conditions.

Such sharp distinctions have long-term implications. There is little aid-assisted investment in development processes designed to protect vulnerable people from drought and other food shocks in the long term. Relief needs are likely therefore to increase in such countries. Of course this may be exacerbated by national policies which do little to improve the conditions of the poorest. The Sudanese Government continuing to fight the civil war in the south of the country is an obvious example. This poses a dilemma. Western donors may be reluctant to provide development aid to a government whose politics and policies they are opposed to, and in the Sudan case fearing that indirectly they are helping to finance the war.[9] But at the same time, they may have to provide ever-increasing quantities of relief aid because nothing is being done to improve the standard of living of those most vulnerable to famine and because they cannot ignore domestic constituents' demands to provide relief. Once again, northern Sudan (which is not war-torn) illustrates this point well. Large-scale relief operations have become an annual event during the 1990s. But in the 1980s north Sudan was the recipient of large quantities of development aid, and only in 1985 and 1986 were there major relief operations.

---

[8]   In the US case, conditionality is enshrined in legislation. The Brooke Amendment (passed before the Cold War ended) prohibits the donation of US development aid to a country where a military coup has overthrown a democratically elected government. Thus, both Sudan and Ethiopia were ineligible for US development aid during 1990–91.
[9]   For example, an overvalued exchange rate poses a 'tax' on aid, and aid expenditure may simply relieve government of its commitments so that it is free to spend more money on the war.

Sources of EW information used by donor agencies

In addition to the numerous sources of formal EW information about food crises in Africa available to donor agencies, informal sources of EW information are also significant. One agency official has commented that they are now swamped with 'too much information'. A common sight in the offices of an emergency-aid department is an 'in-tray' piled high with different early-warning reports. Although each bureaucracy has its own established system and procedures, which on the surface appear to favour formal communication channels, the importance of personal contacts and trusted information sources which may not be part of any formalized information system should not be underestimated. Table 3.3 summarizes the principal sources of EW information on Africa for each of the four donor agencies considered in this chapter.

Famine is a process, and has been characterized as a downward spiral in Chapter 1. But agency officials concerned with preventing it often regard famine as an event, distinguished by large-scale population displacement and an 'obvious' increase in mortality. Information which provides proof that this kind of event will occur is what decision-makers seek. But there is a fundamental mismatch between what donors want from an EWS and what is available as genuinely *early* warning (Field, 1993b). Decision-makers are looking for certainty of fact on which to base their decisions, which may involve allocating thousands of tonnes of relief food aid. It may indeed be possible to detect deteriorating food security with certainty, to warn of the likely consequences of a drought or series of drought years, and to alert donors to the need for public action. But to predict with great accuracy the exact processes which will result in famine and precisely how much relief is needed is impossible.

UN assessments

Of all the different kinds of EW information available, the FAO and WFP assessments come closest to the donors' notion of certainty. FAO's GIEWS, set up in 1975 after the Sahelian famines of the early 1970s, focuses mainly on monitoring food security at national level, balancing production and imports against consumption needs and exports. It also draws attention to localized pockets of acute food insecurity. Based in Rome, GIEWS depends for its information on data supplied by over 100 member governments, about 60 NGOs and by FAO country representatives; it has a close relationship with those national EWS supported by FAO. GIEWS produces a series of regular EW reports throughout the year; if it wants to draw attention to a crisis which requires an urgent response, it will issue a Special Alert. By far its most influential activity is its annual harvest assessment. A mission is fielded from Rome to work with the respective national government. In countries in the Horn and Sahel, the assessment usually takes place in October/November, and the results are published in November/December.

The needs-assessment mission fielded by WFP is carried out at the same time as the FAO assessment (since 1991, they have been combined into

Table 3.3 Response to early warning: ODA, EU, USAID, WFP

	ODA	USAID	EU	WFP
Own EWS	No	FEWS	No	Annual needs assessments in selected countries reported as most 'at risk'.
Funding of early-warning projects	Limited. E.g. funded rainfall monitoring using satellite imagery in some African countries.	Limited. Mainly through FEWS support to national early-warning capacity in countries where field representatives are located.	Funds SAPs in Chad and Mali[a].	Limited. Funded risk-mapping exercises in 1990–91.
Principal sources of early-warning information for Africa	NGOs; UN assessments; UK embassy/high commission.	FEWS; US mission/embassy; ICRC; UN assessments; NGOs.	NGOs; UN assessments; country delegations.	Own needs assessments; WFP field representatives; NGOs; Other UN agencies, e.g. FAO; National EWS.
Most influential source(s) of early warning	FAO harvest assessment; British NGOs.	FEWS; Information from missions.	FAO harvest assessment.	Own needs assessment.
Influence of the media	Very strong.	Very strong.	Strong.	Not so strong.

Note: (a) In Mali SAP now funded by consortium of donors.

one mission), but it is more micro-level, focusing specifically on food needs, with a view to targeting areas and groups requiring assistance. WFP carries out a needs assessment only if it receives a special request from its field office or if it is alerted, for instance by GIEWS or by NGOs, that there is a particularly serious food problem and need for a large-scale relief operation. In 1990–91 needs-assessment missions were sent to Sudan and Ethiopia, but not to Chad, Mali or Kenya.

The results of the FAO harvest assessment are regarded as a key source of information for both ODA and the EU, neither of which has its own EW capacity. In the words of one agency official, the FAO assessment is regarded as the 'gold standard'. It is often the trigger to start the main round of relief pledging, while the WFP assessment is used for relief planning and targeting.

Donor agencies attach so much weight to the UN assessments because, first, they are seen to possess the critical requirement of the international stamp of credibility. The irony is that their information is usually only as good as that of the national EWS upon which they depend for data. But the international agencies are given the benefit of the doubt, whereas national EWS are not. Second, busy decision-makers swamped with information tend to gravitate towards simple, straightforward messages. Quantitative estimates of aggregate production are believed to be non-controversial, and a good basis for cross-country and inter-annual comparisons. The harvest assessment provides administrators in agency headquarters with a single, authoritative figure for a country's food needs, often necessary to convince politicians. (Agency representatives in-country, on the other hand, are usually monitoring all kinds of different EW data throughout the year.) Finally, it is also used in-country as the focal point around which consensus can be built about relief needs between donors and the national government. The critique of the harvest assessment in the Ethiopia, Sudan, Chad and Mali case-studies implies that the exercise is actually more problematic than is widely assumed by officials in donor headquarters. It appears to carry disproportionate influence compared with the validity of its quantitative estimates and with its advantages relative to other sources of EW information.

USAID, on the other hand, attaches much less importance to UN assessments, not least because of its own EW capacity (although its Famine Early Warning System project, FEWS, itself uses some of the UN data). One senior official in USAID headquarters in Washington ranked the FAO and WFP assessments as low as fourth on his list of the most important EW sources. USAID is less trusting of the UN assessment missions, concerned that they are not entirely objective because of their association with the host government.

NGOs

These have become an increasingly significant source of EW information for most donor agencies. In countries where a donor has cut its development programme, and has limited presence, the information role of NGOs is particularly important, as was the case for both ODA and USAID in Sudan in 1990 and 1991. Greater reliance on NGOs as the implementing agents in relief operations has led to close donor/NGO relations being forged. The EU, for instance, depends on information supplied by NGOs to its local delegation, but has also developed direct lines of communication between the headquarters of the main European-based NGOs and the Commission in Brussels, especially the Food Aid Division and more recently ECHO. This communication is often informal; personal contacts are highly influential, especially where a relationship has been built up between the individuals concerned. ODA has developed a close relationship with the major relief NGOs in the UK. This was regarded as critical to the flow of information into ODA during the African famines of the mid-1980s (Borton *et al.*, 1988). Since then the relationship has, if anything, strengthened. Throughout 1990 and 1991, the Minister held regular meetings in London with British NGOs, which helped to formalize the relationship and with it the flow of information into ODA.

One of the advantages of this close relationship is the link it provides between headquarters-based bureaucrats and conditions on the ground in remote parts of Africa; NGOs have the benefit of being able to talk from direct field experience. Since the famines of the mid-1980s, some NGOs have taken seriously their potentially powerful role. They have developed their own information systems and have invested in surveys and studies which contribute to a better understanding of the food economy and of local conditions. Their analysis has often become more sophisticated as a result.[10] But this is not always the case. Sometimes in an emergency inexperienced and junior staff are recruited rapidly and put in charge of information systems. One of the disadvantages of donor dependence on NGO information is that it tends to be very fragmentary, usually covering only the small area where the NGO is operational. NGOs can suffer from 'tunnel vision' (Cutler, 1993), which can in turn distort the donor agency's perspective.

NGOs have considerable lobbying power and have usually developed links with politicians and with the media. In the UK, British NGOs were a strong lobbying force towards the end of 1990, urging ODA to respond promptly to the food crisis in Sudan. As a result, approximately 15 000t of relief food were provided by ODA *before* the FAO harvest assessment, to British NGOs for distribution in Sudan during the last few months of 1990. This is a very small amount compared with total needs, but it is none the less significant that ODA was prepared to release this food while negotiations with the Government of Sudan were still deadlocked. European NGOs were a powerful lobbying force on the EU during 1991. A close liaison between some NGOs and members of the European Parliament put political pressure on the Commission which resulted in extra relief resources being made available for Africa, and the launching of the EU's Special Programme for Africa (see below).

---

[10] For example, Save the Children Fund (UK) carried out detailed surveys in Ethiopia, in the Ogaden Region in 1991 and in the north-east highlands in 1992, where there was a dearth of good information and limited understanding of the respective food problems. These surveys provided useful information about relief needs in the case of the Ogaden, and about the food economy more generally in the north-east highlands (see Chapter 4).

Donor agency representatives in-country

Information circulated within a donor agency, from its country representatives to headquarters staff, is taken very seriously. In USAID's case, information received in Washington from the country mission was ranked as the number one EW source by one senior official. ODA receives frequent reports from the British Embassy or High Commission, usually compiled by the Aid Secretary. The EU Commission relies on its country delegations, described by an official in Brussels as the most important channel for EW alerts, with NGOs coming second. Similarly, WFP in Rome is in regular and close contact with its field representatives, who often play an important coordinating role in-country in terms of pooling EW information.

Each country representative has his or her own trusted sources of EW information. As mentioned above, regular contact with NGOs, especially in the most famine-prone countries like Sudan and Ethiopia, is one of the most important sources. The national EWS in each country invariably distributes its bulletins to representatives of all the main donors, but this information does not often percolate back to headquarters, although of course it does help to inform the local representative's view about food conditions. The different national EWS do not figure prominently as EW sources used within donor agency headquarters, partly because of a lack of trust in information emanating from government — an issue explored in the case-studies.

The system for feeding information back from country offices to headquarters is most formalized in USAID and WFP. The USAID missions send monthly Food Security Operations Reports to Washington, as well as regular country situation analyses. WFP receives weekly situation reports from its field offices. ODA and the EU operate more *ad hoc* systems. Reports may be filed monthly, weekly, or every few days if the situation is critical. Neither agency assigns one of its staff in-country to carry out regular reporting,[11] a reflection of their reliance on a wide range of other outside information sources. Inevitably the type and quality of reporting varies from one country to another. In the British case, the Aid Secretary in the embassy is usually a diplomat with a fairly limited knowledge of food aid and emergency issues, rather than an ODA staff member. USAID and WFP, on the other hand, have well-developed internal information systems.

USAID and FEWS

The only agency to have its own formal EWS is USAID. Its Famine Early Warning System project (FEWS) was launched in 1985 in the wake of the African famines of the mid-1980s on the grounds that inadequate information had prevented the agency from managing emergency operations effectively. The project was in its second phase during 1990–91, with field representatives based in six of the seven countries covered by FEWS in the

---

[11] Sudan and Ethiopia are exceptions in the EU case. Relief consultants have been assigned to the Delegation in each case.

40

Sahel and Horn of Africa.[12] FEWS' principal role is to provide EW information to USAID officials within missions and in Washington.

FEWS is at the 'high-tech' end of the EW spectrum, making extensive use of satellite imagery and computer applications which are affordable only by Western donor agencies. It relies almost entirely on secondary data, analysing and collating them into an eye-catching and concise form usable by busy officials at USAID. This reduces duplication, but means that FEWS' assessments can only be as good as the data already available. FEWS has made important progress in some EW areas, however, for example in its work on vulnerability assessments. In addition to its monthly (every ten days during the crop-production season) one-page bulletins, FEWS also produces three more detailed reports during the year: a pre-harvest assessment of cereal production in October, a harvest assessment in January, and a vulnerability assessment in June.

FEWS' remit has been strictly confined to providing information, *not* to making recommendations, the fiercely defended domain of decision-makers within USAID. To some extent it has afforded them protection from having to justify why they failed to react to a recommendation. But as FEWS field representatives who have analysed and interpreted the data are usually the best informed about the most appropriate relief action needed, some of this experience is wasted. FEWS staff also interact closely with officials in Washington, and in the country missions. The FEWS representative usually plays a key role in preparing the monthly Food Security Operations Cable, which does include recommendations to Washington. However, there has been no formal link between EW and response, at least during the first and second phases of the FEWS project.[13]

FEWS has built up credibility over the years. Its information is widely used in Washington, occasionally even in Congress and by the Select Committee on Hunger. But the emphasis USAID places on having its own filter for interpreting EW information is indicative of its distrust of other sources, even sometimes of the UN. It depends upon FEWS to provide a commentary on other assessments, and sometimes to come up with a single reliable figure on relief needs when different sources conflict.

Influence of the media

It was the Western media, *not* conventional EWS, which triggered an international relief response to the Ethiopian famine in 1984–5 in which one million people lost their lives. Some EWS, including Ethiopia's own national EWS, had provided timely warnings that relief was urgently needed, but these were not heeded by Western governments until their own electorates

---

12 FEWS field representatives were based in Mauritania, Mali, Niger, Burkina Faso, Chad and Sudan. Because of the Brooke Amendment, the Ethiopia representative was based in Washington until early 1993, since when the Sudan representative has been removed from Khartoum.

13 This is changing during the third phase of the project, which began in early 1995. For the first time FEWS' remit is expanded to include recommendations.

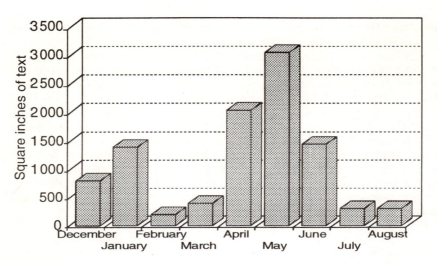

Figure 3.2 *UK newspaper coverage of African famine, December 1990 to August 1991*
Source: SCF (UK).

demanded action when presented with harrowing scenes on television from Ethiopia's famine camps. The public's reaction to this media coverage was responsible for eventually turning the tide within donor governments, from a reluctance to help an African government closely aligned to the Soviet Union, to the launching of one of the biggest relief operations the African continent has ever seen. Screening of the now famous BBC television report by Michael Buerke and Mohammed Amin marked the turning point. Donor agencies were publicly criticized for not responding in time.

The legacy left by this episode is of much greater sensitivity among Western donors to media coverage of famine. The media again had some influence on the donors' response in 1990–91, but the impact was much diluted by coverage of the Gulf War; Africa's problems were overshadowed. After the end of the Gulf War the spectre of famine began to hit the news once again, especially in Sudan and Ethiopia where the scale of the food crisis was greatest. It is interesting to note that after ODA's main pledging season at the beginning of 1991 (when the results of the FAO harvest assessment had been announced), there was a second wave of pledging for Sudan and Ethiopia in April and May. This coincided with intensive lobbying by British NGOs for a more generous response to famine in Africa, with increased press coverage in the UK as illustrated in Figure 3.2.

The EU and USAID are also sensitive to the threat of a 'media disaster'. For all three agencies, decisions to pledge large quantities of relief in 1990 and 1991 were always accompanied by press releases and sometimes press conferences; for example, USAID held a press conference in Nairobi in December 1990 to announce its first major relief commitments to Sudan. The UN is not subject to quite the same pressures because of its looser links and accountability to the general public. Nevertheless, it has learnt the lessons from its well-publicized mistakes of the mid-1980s, when FAO and WFP received very bad press over their report on relief needs in Ethiopia.[14]

The case-studies confirm the significance of the Western media's influence, but it is by no means a source of *early* warning. Famine is only newsworthy when it is full-blown and the pictures are guaranteed to shock. Editors of newspapers and producers of television programmes are not interested in predictions of what *might* happen. Pre-famine situations where livelihoods are under threat before lives are at risk, are not sufficiently dramatic to make the news, nor if the country concerned is of little political interest. The criteria for guaranteed media coverage are extreme: shocking visual images of human suffering, on a large scale, and preferably in an area well known to Western people.[15] In short, media coverage of famine which triggers a relief response is usually late, selective and often sensationalist.

Influence of formal political channels

Responding to famine attracts more media attention, and more debate and interest within formal political channels than other forms of international aid. For a Western government there is political capital to be gained, especially where the electorate is aware of the suffering and hunger of the people in need. There is also a political cost in being seen not to act where there is a humanitarian disaster. Major announcements about emergency food or humanitarian aid are usually declared with some ceremony in the parliament of the donor government. This was the case in the UK in 1991 whenever relief aid was committed to Sudan or Ethiopia.

For USAID, Congress's Select Committee on Hunger is one of the main sources of political pressure. It has no legislative authority but can stimulate congressional hearings with a view to gaining press and media coverage. It was set up with this role in 1985, at the time of the well-publicized African famines. During 1990 and 1991, congressional hearings were held on both Sudan and Ethiopia, with witnesses from the State Department and from USAID being questioned on the current relief situation and on the level of grants being given by the US Office of Foreign Disaster Assistance (OFDA).

Within the EU, the European Parliament, through its budgetary powers and its Parliamentary questions and resolutions, played a significant role in mobilizing EU emergency aid during 1991. It was apparent from early in the year that the regular food aid budget would be inadequate to meet exceptional emergency demands. Some European NGOs requesting food

---

[14]   Although they agreed that estimated relief needs were in the region of 600000t, they appeared to endorse an appeal for only 125000t for the year, on the erroneous assumption that this was all that could be handled logistically in the Ethiopian ports (Goyder and Goyder, 1988; Cutler, 1993).

[15]   The extensive media coverage of the war and its consequences in Bosnia, which is on the doorstep of Western Europe, compared with the very limited coverage of the civil wars and their consequences in Angola and Sudan are examples of this.

aid resources from the Commission were told informally of the budget con-straints, and that the only route to change the situation was a political one, via MEPs. This is how the EU's Special Programme for Africa came into being, accompanied by a shower of letters from MEPs urging action. The Commission's timing for its initiative was crucial. The Commissioner for Development first raised the idea of a Special Programme in mid-March 1991, after the end of the Gulf War, when Africa's food problems once again received media attention. In April, the European Parliament passed a res-olution on famine in Africa, supporting the Commissioner's proposal. In May, the Council, Parliament and Commission came to a tripartite agree-ment to launch the Special Programme and a supplementary budget was approved. If political interest and questions about relief for Africa had not been raised in the European Parliament, it would have been much more difficult for the Commission to find the extra relief resources it needed. Thus, it worked with the political channels which can exert pressure on member states to increase its emergency response capacity.

For WFP, the influence of formal political channels is weak and tenuous. But for the other three donors considered here, formal political channels can exert a great deal of influence on emergency aid programmes. There is a close and circular link with the media. Politicians may ask questions about a donor agency's humanitarian aid response before news of the particular crisis hits the press and they may subsequently try to stimulate press coverage to mobilize public support. But pressure through political channels is undoubtedly greatest when there has already been media coverage of a particular disaster, and public opinion already supports a relief intervention. In the examples shown here of how the British Parlia-ment, Congress and the European Parliament exerted influence over the emergency aid programmes of ODA, USAID and the EU, respectively, in 1991, it is no coincidence that the problems of Sudan and Ethiopia were most frequently raised. Chad's food crisis, for instance, which was on a much smaller scale, was given no public airing in any of these three fora. Once again, relief needs must be large, the crisis severe, and the country of political importance before Western politicians will fight for its cause.

Making decisions about the relief response

Since the beginning of the 1990s, most drought-related food crises in Africa are foreshadowed by EW, from formal information systems set up specifi-cally for this purpose and from other sources, including NGOs and the field staff of donor agencies. But there is no guarantee that donors will act on the basis of this information. Some of the most common constraints are spelt out below. The institutional system for making decisions about relief within each of our donor agencies is described in Table 3.4, which indicates the number of different departments and divisions involved.

Institutional constraints
A common characteristic in almost all bureaucracies is the tendency for staff to practise risk avoidance. To prevent famine the least risky act would

Table 3.4 Relief decision-making within donor agencies

	ODA	USAID	EU	WFP
Departments involved in relief decision-making	EU and Food Aid Dept; Emergency Aid Dept; Geographical Depts	Regional desks within Bureau for Africa; Food for Peace Office; Office of Foreign Disaster Assistance[a]	Food Aid Division; Emergency Aid Division; Geographical Services Division[b]	Operations Dept, which comprises Regional Bureaus and the Disaster Relief Service; Resources and Transport Division
Main decision-making body for releasing food relief	Ministerial approval of proposals made by departments listed above	Development Co-ordination Committee (subcommittee of Food Aid Committee) until 1991[c]	Food Aid Committee of member states, chaired by Commission	Disaster Relief Committee; Horn of Africa Co-ordinating Committee (*ad hoc*, set up in mid-1991)

Notes:
(a) FFP and OFDA were incorporated into the new Bureau for Food and Humanitarian Assistance in 1991.
(b) Since 1992, also EU Office of Humanitarian Affairs, ECHO.
(c) Subsequently Food Assistance Policy Council.

seem logically to be the provision of relief assistance *early* in a food crisis, before lives are threatened, to ensure that there are no famine deaths. Unfortunately this is not how risk avoidance works in practice within the main donor bureaucracies.

Within all four donor agencies considered here, certain procedures must be followed before humanitarian aid can be released. Proposals usually have to be drawn up and discussed before decisions are taken. All actions have to be justified. Inaction does not have to be justified, apart from exceptional circumstances when, sometime later, there is a public or political outcry and questions have to be answered by senior members of the bureaucracy through political channels and in the media, defending why nothing was done. The nature of bureaucratic procedures usually means that there is more risk involved in a staff member precipitating action than not. This only serves to reinforce the quest for certainty, described above. Decision-makers within the bureaucracies must be convinced about the severity of a crisis, and that relief is really necessary before they will take action. Field (1993b:257) goes so far as to say that the 'quest for certainty as the key to decision converts early warning into late warning, and even later response'. It certainly influences how donors use EW information.

Using Clay and Schaffer's concept of the 'escape hatch' (1984:2), there are plenty of excuses which can be used to explain why a donor agency is not yet able to take a decision to provide relief, even though EW information provides indisputable evidence of a food crisis. Two of the most common procedural escape hatches are: 'we cannot act because the government has not declared an emergency', and 'we must await the report of our fact-finding mission before action can be taken' (Cutler, 1993:74). Both were used to justify delayed relief responses in 1990–91; the first in the case of Sudan, the second in Chad where the fact-finding mission awaited by donors was the FAO/CILSS harvest assessment. When it is politically expedient to act, and there is greater risk associated with not responding — for example when the media publicize a story of suffering and inaction — it can be surprising how the 'escape hatches' suddenly vanish. If a lack of resources was the problem, then extra resources miraculously appear. The politically motivated EU Special Programme for Africa in 1991 is an example.

Timing of decision-making
In most donor agencies decisions about providing relief to countries in the Horn of Africa and the Sahel are not made until January. As EW information has usually poured in for many months beforehand, an agency view will have been formed about the severity of the crisis, but the results of the FAO harvest assessment (and WFP needs assessment), available in November/December, are awaited before main pledges are made. Although some relief aid may have been released earlier for NGO distribution, this is usually a very small percentage of total needs, and of what the agency finally commits. In the EU's case, the timing of the financial year has a bearing on when relief aid is made available. Aid may be earmarked before the end of the calendar year but it is not released until January, the beginning of the new financial year.

46

This schedule presupposes that the time to respond once decisions have been taken is less than six months, if food is to be shipped and then distributed in-country before June/July, when the hungry season in most countries in the Sahel and Horn is well under way in a crisis year. As explained below, the time-lag for most donors is much longer. The case-studies of Ethiopia, Sudan and Chad provide convincing evidence that decisions made in January are simply too late to ensure that the relief reaches beneficiaries in time, especially if the destination is far inland. In short, bureaucratic procedures in donor headquarters are rarely geared to the needs of recipient governments or people. Indeed, there is an implicit assumption in most donor headquarters' planning and timetabling that once the food arrives in-country, the job is complete. In fact, distribution to remote rural areas can take at least a further three months.

Bureaucratic procedures for mobilizing relief

In 1990–91, the EU had the most cumbersome set of bureaucratic pro-cedures for mobilizing relief. First of all, DG VIII had to request the Directorate-General for Agriculture, DG VI, to publish a regulation in the EU *Official Journal*, in nine Community languages, inviting tenders for the contract to purchase and ship the food. This could take between six and eight weeks, with a further two weeks for the submission of tenders. Purchasing and transporting the food would normally take another eight weeks. Thus, the absolute minimum time for the whole procedure was four months; often it would take longer. In short, there were *no* emergency procedures for waiving the normal lengthy tendering process. This was not helped by the fact that the EU was legally bound to put to European tender all relief commodities for which there was a surplus within the Union. This carries an opportunity cost in terms of speed of response and the financial cost of the operation, if a cheaper and faster alternative of local purchase exists. It is interesting to note, however, that in the case of the Special Programme for Africa in 1991, which received the highest political backing within DG VIII, normal tendering procedures were waived. In the best-case scenario, this halved the delivery time. Since then, with the establishment of ECHO, at-tempts have been made to speed up the EU's response time in an emergency.

ODA and USAID can also suffer from lengthy bureaucratic procedures, although in each case there are ways in which these procedures can be circumvented. For example, in the interests of speed, ODA's Disaster Unit does not have to go through competitive tendering. Within USAID in 1990–91, the timing of the response depended upon the department re-sponsible. OFDA had its own independent rapid-response facility, for the 'real' (often high-profile) emergencies, where it was exempt from federal law and the procedural requirements of the Foreign Assistance Acts. In other cases, including relief for Chad in 1991, the Bureau of Food for Peace was responsible for mobilizing relief food. This was where bureaucratic delays were most likely to occur (see Chapter 6).

One of the main constraints facing WFP is that it must wait for an official request for relief from the recipient country before it can begin to move.[16] The Disaster Relief Service must then make a recommendation that an emergency operation should be launched, which has to be approved by WFP's Executive Director, and is followed by the circulation of emergency telexes among other UN agencies, the donor community and the major operational NGOs. Since WFP's status with respect to FAO has been elevated, FAO's Director General no longer has to approve *all* WFP's emergency operations, only those over $1.5 million. As described below, the main constraint WFP faces is lack of immediate access to relief resources.

Political constraints

Whether a donor decides to act on the basis of EW information or not, has much to do with the political context. In effect, the information is filtered through the political interests of the donor state. Is this a government it supports? How closely does it want to work with the government in a relief operation? What are the political consequences of not responding and of a serious food crisis developing? Donors' willingness to work with the government in Mali to develop a programmed response mechanism, compared with their reluctance to provide relief to Sudan, illustrates this point particularly well (see Chapters 5 and 7). Although humanitarian aid is supposed to be isolated from political conditions, the willingness of donors to respond is rarely neutral, but depends upon the political relationship that exists with the recipient government.

Executing decisions: the relief response

The next step in the process is implementing the decision to launch a relief operation. Time is of the essence. How quickly can each agency mobilize relief and access resources? Who will distribute on the ground? What is the time-lag for each donor agency between a decision being taken to provide relief, and resources arriving in-country? These are some of the logistical issues which determine whether or not EW is translated into timely preventive action.

Exceptional demands were made upon the international relief system in 1991. Did lack of access to resources constrain the donors' response? In the EU's case the 1985 Dublin Plan, in response to the African famines of the mid-1980s, had created a special reserve for future emergencies which could draw upon resources within the food-aid budget. In 1991 this proved inadequate to meet demands. An exceptional case had to be made to launch the Special Programme for Africa to unleash extra resources. This worked well, and enabled the Commission to act with flexibility and speed. But it is significant that the Special Programme had such strong political backing, without which the EU's response would certainly have been constrained.

In 1990–91 ODA had a notional allocation of £10m set aside for unforeseen disasters and emergencies, out of its contingency reserve. Its food aid

---

16 In practice, however, it may start the ball rolling before an official request is received, although no food will arrive in-country until it is requested. This has been the case in Ethiopia, where the emergency has been more or less 'permanent' (see Chapter 4).

budget was also boosted in 1991–2 by transferring unspent funds from the Sudan budget, which had been suspended, for emergency expenditure. But when both these measures proved inadequate, applications for extra humanitarian aid resources had to be made to the Treasury, for the Kurdish crisis and for Africa. The applications were successful. An extra £20m was allocated for Africa, mostly for the Horn. UK media coverage of both emergencies was undoubtedly a factor encouraging the release of extra funds.

USAID in theory has considerable flexibility to switch resources from the regular to the emergency food aid programme, especially under Title II of Public Law 480.[17] USAID has a 'waiver authority', which means that it only has to advise Congress officially that it is switching resources from the regular to the emergency programme because of extraordinary emergency needs; it does not require congressional approval. In practice, however, the waiver authority can get bogged down, for example by management problems or because of shortages of a particular commodity. This mechanism was used during 1990–91. OFDA, which can make a request for extra dollar resources in exceptional circumstances, more or less doubled its emergency budget in 1990–91 through additional funds. An extra $27m was allocated to the Kurdish refugees and $40m to Africa. There tends to be greatest flexibility in the budgetary and allocation system early on in the financial year.

Ironically, WFP had most difficulty in getting hold of extra food aid during 1990–91, despite having access to many potential sources because of its multilateral nature. The main reason was the lack of resources pledged in advance to the IEFR. This has a target level of 500000t, but donors, in particular the US, have rarely pledged more than 150000t at the beginning of each calendar year (WFP, 1994). This is mainly because of a reluctance to commit resources in advance and lose control over how they will be used. WFP must therefore rely on special appeals, a slow and cumbersome procedure. It made a number of these during 1991, but donors were often slow to respond.[18] This robs WFP of its multilateral character if it is constrained by bilateral donor prioritization. Its rapid response capacity is jeopardized and its flexibility to access resources quickly is limited to its capacity to 'borrow' from its own development programmes and from national security reserves in Africa and from other donors. This occurred in two-thirds of emergency operations in 1990. Commodity borrowing capacity is now stretched to the limit.

All four agencies considered in this chapter, but especially ODA, the EU and USAID, have become increasingly dependent on NGOs as the distributors of relief. If the recipient government agrees with this arrangement

---

[17] The Title II food aid programme provides emergency and non-emergency food aid through Private Voluntary Organizations (or NGOs), through multilateral agencies such as WFP and through bilateral government-to-government programmes.

[18] To try and overcome the shortfall in advance commitments to the IEFR and to increase its flexibility, WFP sought permission in 1991 from its governing body, the CFA, to supplement the food reserve with a cash reserve which would facilitate commercial purchases. An Immediate Response Account (IRA) was approved, with a target level of $30m. Contributions have consistently fallen short of the target to date.

there is unlikely to be any delay in releasing relief resources, for example in Ethiopia in 1991, and similarly where there is a well-established institutional framework for handling relief food, as in Mali.

But if there is no such consensus, the dispatch of relief resources can be seriously delayed. The situation in Sudan at the end of 1990, and the delays in launching the much-needed relief operation illustrate this point particularly well, and also the danger of NGOs becoming too closely associated with a particular donor. The Sudanese Government became suspicious of foreign NGOs which appeared opportunistic: when it suited them they were seen to assert their independence from their home government's policies, at other times they appeared to follow donor government relief policy and to act as agents of donors. This can trigger a backlash, whereby African governments seek to exert excessive control over NGO operations, again compromising their non-governmental status.

The minimum time between a decision being taken to provide relief and the relief arriving at its African port of destination is usually four months. This is the average response time reported by ODA staff.[19] The EU's procedures for mobilizing relief food take an absolute minimum of four months to complete, as described above. In practice, the time-lag is usually much longer — often six months or more — and the EU has earned a reputation for being one of the slowest donor agencies to respond. WFP has made a great effort to reduce the lead time since the mid-1980s, but the whole process still takes an average of six to nine months, and WFP staff are not optimistic that this could be reduced. Only in exceptional circumstances, with immense political backing and the waiving of 'normal' bureaucratic procedures, can the response time be shortened. The EU's Special Programme for Africa is a good example.

All these figures refer only to delivery to the African port of entry. It can easily take a further three months to transport relief to beneficiaries far inland, especially where the infrastructure is poor. If decisions to release relief resources for the Sahel and Horn of Africa are not taken until the beginning of the calendar year, and if delivery schedules to Africa are routinely four to six months, followed by a further two to three months for internal transport, the relief will fail to reach beneficiaries by the start of the hungry season. This is borne out in most of the country case-studies. The food relief is simply arriving too late. Once again, bureaucratic procedures in donor agency headquarters are not geared to the needs of recipient governments or people.

Donor co-ordination

This is important at all stages of the response to an emergency: from the initial assessment of needs, to organizing food aid pledges, delivery and

---

[19] A detailed evaluation of ODA's relief operations in Africa in the mid-1980s showed the average response time to be 18.4 weeks, although there was a wide variation around the mean (Borton *et al.*, 1988). In a comparison with other donors during the same period, however, ODA fared rather well.

distribution on the ground. This role naturally falls to the UN. It fulfils it most successfully at the first stage, in co-ordinating needs assessments through WFP and FAO. The majority of donors look to these exercises to confirm the scale of the crisis before they take action. Thereafter, co-ordination is more problematic.

The UN Disaster Relief Organization (UNDRO) was set up in 1971 specifically to co-ordinate relief activities within the UN system, and between the UN and bilateral donors. There has long been dissatisfaction with its performance; it has been hampered by a lack of resources, by an unclear mandate and by a long-running dispute about whether it should in fact be operational (Borton, 1993). Bilateral donors criticized its failure to co-ordinate relief activities in Africa during 1990 and 1991. WFP was similarly seen to fail in co-ordinating food aid pledges. Midway through 1991, the UN set up a Special Emergency Programme for the Horn of Africa (SEPHA), within the office of an Under-Secretary General, to co-ordinate appeals, but an overview of food aid commitments was still felt to be lacking.

Eventually it fell to the EU to host a co-ordination meeting during 1991 not only of its member states, but also with six other bilateral donors and a selection of UN agencies and NGOs attending, principally to clarify food aid commitments and the shortfall in pledges. There was a sense of exasperation that the UN had been unable to fulfil this role, which hampered some donor agency officials in their efforts to make a case to the politicians for releasing extra relief resources.

In-country responsibility for donor co-ordination should lie with the UN Resident Representative. In practice, personalities can exert a great deal of influence and there is little consistency. In Sudan, for example, WFP played the main co-ordinating role. The effectiveness of, and structures for, donor co-ordination on the ground vary from one country to another, as illustrated in the case-studies.

The UN's failure to co-ordinate its own agencies adequately, and to provide leadership to the rest of the international relief system attracted most criticism not in Africa, but during the Kurdish refugee crisis in 1991. This provoked an unusual and high-level political initiative from the G7 Summit in London in July to strengthen the UN system. Following a UN General Assembly Resolution later in the year, the new UN Department of Humanitarian Affairs (DHA), absorbing UNDRO, and headed by a newly appointed Under-Secretary General for Humanitarian Affairs, was created, with a principal objective of improving co-ordination. The DHA is in charge not only of co-ordinating consolidated appeals but also of an inter-agency standing committee, a central emergency revolving fund, and in-country relief operations. In practice, however, its role has once again been constrained by a lack of resources.

Conclusions

In most African countries, the international relief system plays a critical role in all major relief operations. This is certainly true of the case-studies in this book. Typically, Western donors provide most of the relief resources and international NGOs play a key role in implementation on the ground. Inevitably this shifts the locus of decision-making away from Africa towards Western capitals, although this partly depends on the extent to which the recipient government is prepared to let it happen.

An effective famine response system was defined in Chapter 1 as one which intervenes early, to protect livelihoods before the point of destitution is reached when famine threatens lives. This implies that a range of interventions is appropriate, not just the provision of food aid. The practice of the international relief system does not fit this model. In very few cases do donor agencies respond early to protect livelihoods. This is not considered part of the terms of reference for emergency relief, which is geared to the more limited objective of saving lives. However, donor agencies still pay little attention to ensuring that the food aid arrives before the start of the hungry season in the recipient countries: the relief assistance almost always arrives months later.

The institutional establishment and procedures within most donor agencies are not geared to timely response. Although donors are now provided with ample EW information from a variety of sources, it can rarely provide them with the level of accuracy and precision that their 'risk-avoiding' bureaucracies demand. Therefore, delayed decisions can almost always be justified by the absence of a certain type or piece of information. The assessments carried out by FAO and WFP come closest of all formal EW sources to the donors' notion of 'certainty'. Carried out late in the agricultural season, they synthesize the information into a straightforward quantification of relief needs, and carry the international stamp of credibility. Indeed, credibility and trust are key determinants of which EW sources will be taken most seriously by each donor. Thus, USAID has created its own in-house FEWS; all donors rely on their own field representatives; and most have built up close relationships with certain NGOs, where trusted personal contacts can play a significant information role. The donors' quest for certainty causes them to wait until the harvest is almost over before pledging significant quantities of relief, usually in January/ February for countries in the Sahel and Horn of Africa, which, with the long time-lags in release procedures and delivery, make it impossible for the relief to be distributed in time. The onset of the rains can delay delivery even further.

Response time can be speeded up, but only when there is strong political pressure within donor countries to do so. This is most powerful when high-profile media coverage combines with pressure exerted through formal political channels. This combination was effective in 1991 from March onwards, when the Gulf War had ended and food crisis in Africa re-emerged as a topical issue. It was influential in the launching of the EU's Special Programme for Africa, releasing extra resources and in some instances halving the delivery time for relief. But there is unlikely to be this kind of political pressure until the emergency becomes newsworthy, which means that there must be evidence of human suffering on a large scale. The crisis must already exist, and must not coincide with a more newsworthy one. Media coverage and political pressure rarely work as a form of *early* warning for *timely* response.

On the other hand, political obstacles can delay the launching of a relief operation even further, especially where there are political differences between donor and recipient governments. Although humanitarian aid is exempt from political conditionality, in practice political differences can be played out in disagreements about the *modus operandi* of the relief operation which can result in serious delays.

In the early 1990s significant changes were taking place within the international relief system. This occurred against the background of stagnant or declining Western aid budgets, while expenditure on relief aid was increasing in response to the rising number of humanitarian emergencies. Some of these changes were triggered by the most high-profile of all relief operations in 1991: the international response to the Kurdish refugee crisis. The clearest manifestation of change was the reorganization of the emergency departments within some of the principal donor agencies, including ODA and the EU, and of the UN's co-ordination capacity. A principal aim of the reorganization was to improve emergency response capability. But there was also a political motivation, to increase the donor's profile in relief work, as this is the most public image of aid, and hence the most politically sensitive part of the aid budget to cut. At the same time, the amounts of development aid available for certain countries, especially in Africa, were declining, usually because of new and explicit forms of political conditionality which rendered the country ineligible. This situation may be exacerbated in the future as some donors, notably USAID, adopt a tighter strategic focus in their aid programmes.

There is already a sharp distinction between relief and development aid within most donor agencies, especially in terms of the type of aid available, its objectives, and the procedures for releasing it. Hence, relief is normally food aid geared to saving lives; protecting livelihoods is regarded as more of a developmental objective. The ideal model of *early* response implies a blurring of the distinction; the scope of relief should be broadened to include saving livelihoods, recognizing a continuum of livelihood insecurity rather than a clearly demarcated threshold which rigidly separates development from emergency needs. Although a number of donor agencies have recently become interested in the notion of linking relief and development, partly because of concerns about rapidly growing emergency budgets and the disruptive effect emergencies can have on longer-term development processes,[20] Western aid policy is evolving in ways that create new obstacles to the idea. As some donors strive to raise their profile in emergency work, there is little incentive to blur the distinction between relief and development in practice: the creation of ECHO within the EU has raised concerns that its allocation criteria sharpen the distinction between relief and development work, and that this could constrain an effective response to chronic, complex emergencies such as those in the Horn of Africa.

---

[20]   See, for example, Buchanan-Smith and Maxwell, 1994; WFP, 1992.

Meanwhile, the new political conditions applied to aid mean that there are limited prospects for linking relief and development in countries where the development aid budget has been slashed. If little is done to reduce vulnerability in the long run, there is a danger that the need for relief will intensify in the short term, and unless the boundaries of what constitutes relief are widened, little will be done to protect livelihoods even during a crisis.

CHAPTER 4

Ethiopia

Introduction

The image of famine in Ethiopia has become synonymous with the failure of national and international humanitarian relief systems. The scale of the famine in 1984–5, when an estimated one million people lost their lives, will go down in history as one of the greatest disasters on the African continent this century. It could have been prevented. The haunting memories live on, amid promises that it should never be allowed to happen again. In the aftermath, money and skills were invested in systems designed to prevent famine in the future, particularly EWS. Has this made any difference? This is the question this chapter attempts to answer by focusing on how prevention mechanisms functioned during 1990–91.

The crisis in 1990–91 was not a repetition of drought, war and famine on the same scale as the mid-1980s. However, it was a year of localized and severe food insecurity — indeed, in some areas reaching famine proportions. Parts of the country had suffered drought, some for the second consecutive year, and the security situation gradually deteriorated as the Tigray People's Liberation Front (TPLF) consolidated their territorial gains, finally marching into the capital, Addis Ababa, and overthrowing the Mengistu government in May 1991. This introduced new demands on the relief system as large numbers of soldiers were demobilized and civilian populations displaced. But eventually it had the effect of restoring peace to most of the north of the country after many years of war. Meanwhile, political instability and insecurity in neighbouring countries caused large influxes of refugees and returnees to pour over the borders into Ethiopia, particularly from Somalia. The relief system was put under great pressure. It is within this context that this chapter assesses the performance of the EW/response system in place in Ethiopia.

Since the mid-1980s, Ethiopia has become one of the largest recipients of food aid in the world, over 80 per cent of it carrying the emergency label. Yet the country has continued to suffer from recurrent episodes of acute food insecurity, even famine. It is estimated that more than half the population is food-insecure, and the proportion is growing as poverty intensifies. All the evidence points to the endemic nature of the country's food crisis, yet problems have been treated on an emergency basis for at least the last decade. Some of the principal reasons are to do with the politics of aid.

Ethiopia was caught in the cross-fire of Cold War politics for a number of years. It was starved of Western development aid as most donor governments took a hard line towards the socialist Ethiopian Government of

President Mengistu.[1] This had the effect of perpetuating 'emergency' reactions, and sharpening the already marked distinction between development and relief aid within Western donor bureaucracies. It also resulted in Western donors setting up their own parallel systems alongside government, in terms of EW and decision-making for relief and its distribution. Western donor/government relations were characterized by distrust and suspicion: yet, the government was prepared to tolerate this duplication of systems by donors — which sometimes went as far as to threaten its sovereignty — because of a coincidence of basic objectives: to get food relief into the country. In the absence of other development aid, the government wanted to maximize food-aid receipts; allowing donors to act with some independence was the most likely way of achieving this. And Western donor governments wanted to ensure that there was no repetition of the 1984–5 famine and their embarrassing failure to prevent it; they are particularly sensitive to media coverage of food crisis in Ethiopia. This correspondence of basic objectives against a backdrop of antagonistic relations is what differentiates the Ethiopian story of EW/response in 1990–91 from the Sudanese one, and from events in the mid-1980s.

A similar pattern emerges to that of the other case-study countries in terms of how the international relief system used EW information about Ethiopia in 1990–91. FAO and WFP assessments were the trigger for donor pledging, rather than assessments by the national EWS. Evidence of food crisis under way was one of the most effective indicators. But in some ways the pattern was exaggerated in the Ethiopian case, because of strained donor/government relations. The outcome was relief delivered too little and too late, mostly after the start of the hungry season. Although since the mid-1980s Ethiopia derives some benefits from a relief food pipeline which flows from one year to the next, there are still breaks, and delivery schedules drawn up in the early planning stages of the 1991 operation were not met. The national EW and response system was highly centralized, efficient in terms of producing annual assessments of numbers of people in need and food aid requirements, but necessarily simplifying very complex food-security problems in a large country with poor communications and a population of over 50 million.

The change in government in May 1991 marks a turning-point. It has ushered in a new political and economic climate, with a significant improvement in international relations between the Transitional Government and Western donors. This has brought the promise of a more flexible approach to emergency relief and important new injections of development aid, although the overall timing of relief deliveries remains little changed so far. An ambitious programme to decentralize government has been introduced, with implications for how the EW and response system will operate in future. Whether, and when, this new era will turn around the trends of deteriorating food security and increased vulnerability to famine remains to be seen.

---

[1]   In the US case, development aid was blocked by legislation: the Brooke Amendment (see Chapter 3, note 8).

Food security

Food insecurity

Ethiopia is one of the poorest countries in the world, consistently at or near the bottom of any development league.[2] Estimates of the percentage of the population who are food-insecure in an 'average year', combining both transitory and chronic food insecurity, have ranged from 46 per cent (World Bank, 1988), to a more recent and higher estimate of 55 per cent (Maxwell, 1993), or around 27 million people. In parts of the country people are living on a knife-edge, where very little would precipitate a slide into famine.

One of the fundamental problems is the large structural food deficit. Ethiopia was last able to feed itself in 1982. In 1993–4, which was not regarded as a particularly bad year for the country as a whole, there was an estimated one-million-tonne grain import requirement, only half of which could be classified as emergency needs (FEWS, 1993). This reflects the continuing failure of agricultural productivity to keep pace with population growth. At current annual population growth rates of 2.9 per cent, FAO has estimated that cereals and pulse production must increase annually by 320000t to keep pace. Instead, cereal production has risen by only 1.2 per cent per year, and, since the 1960s, has declined per capita by an average of 4kg/year (Webb and von Braun, 1994). The seriousness of this lies in the country's inability to earn the foreign-exchange requirement to make up the deficit (Belshaw, 1990).

The economy is highly dependent on the agricultural sector, which employs 85 per cent of the population and is, in turn, highly dependent on annual rainfall patterns. There are two growing seasons, the main *meher* from June to October, and the shorter *belg* from February to May. Research by IFPRI has shown that a 10 per cent decline in rainfall results in a 4.4 per cent decline in national production (of about 300000t), and average price increases of 14 per cent (Webb *et al.*, 1991).

There is concern that worsening poverty is exposing much greater numbers of people to chronic food insecurity every year, but especially to the risk of acute food insecurity and famine after only one drought year. Although there have been at least 10 serious droughts and food crises this century, the incidence has increased during the last 25 years. Drought has often been the trigger causing famine, although in parts of the country, especially the north, war and conflict have played a major role. There was civil war in Eritrea for over 20 years and in Tigray, which provided the backdrop to the devastating drought-related famine in the mid-1980s.

The picture is very uneven across the country. The most food-insecure regions tend to be in the northern, central and eastern parts of the highlands, where subsistence farming systems have come under increasing pressure from growing human and livestock populations, and from

---

2   In 1990, GNP per capita was $120, second lowest in the world (World Bank, 1992). With a large and rapidly growing population, GDP per capita growth rates have been negative during recent years. The estimated population in 1991 was 53.3 million.

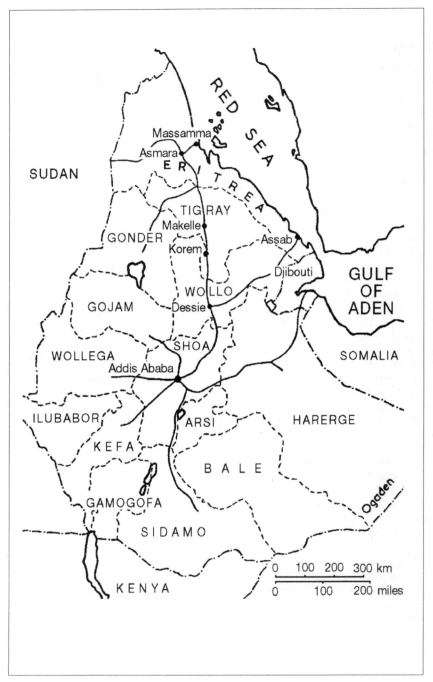

Figure 4.1 *Map of Ethiopia*
Source: Curtis *et al.*, 1988.

58

Table 4.1   Ethiopia: annual food aid donations (imports and local purchases) (thousands of tonnes)

	Total food aid	Emergency food aid	% of total
1985(a)	1261	1107	88
1986	1098	941	86
1987	425	307	72
1988	1255	1099	88
1989	487	404	83
1990	908	822	91
1991	988	898	91

Note:
(a) Date for 1985 refer to cereal food aid only. Data for other years refer to all food aid.
Source: WFP Interfais; except 1985, WFP, Addis Ababa.

environmental degradation (Belshaw, 1990). See Figure 4.1 for a map of Ethiopia. A recent study into how the population 'makes ends meet' in the north-eastern highlands has described farmers as 'walking coping mechanisms' in a very marginal rural economy (Holt and Lawrence, 1993:6).

For years, the method for alleviating the food problem has been short-term: the annual provision of emergency food aid through large-scale relief operations (see Table 4.1). More progress has been made in improving EW and food-relief operations, geared specifically to the short-term objective of preventing famine, than in formulating and implementing successful policies to improve food security in the longer term.

In the wake of the famine of the early 1970s the Relief and Rehabilitation Commission (RRC) was set up in 1974, and in 1976 the EWS was established. So far it is the RRC which has been at the centre of most efforts to tackle food insecurity. As the main conduit for emergency relief resources, the RRC's expansion over the years has reflected the growth of the donor-funded emergency industry.[3] Despite these measures, Ethiopia experienced one of the worst famines ever in the mid-1980s. It happened because of a fatal failure to respond early to warnings about the developing crisis; because of inappropriate estimates by international agencies of relief needs, based more on logistical capacity than actual requirements; and because of the response delays even when a relief operation was launched.

According to Goyder and Goyder (1988:90), the explanations are mainly political, and responsibility lies both with the international aid community, for whom Ethiopia was seen to be of little political importance within the Soviet sphere of influence, and with the government which did not give adequate support to the RRC's request for massive aid to combat the famine in 1984, being more preoccupied with its tenth-anniversary celebration of the military takeover. Ultimately, 'TV secured a response where the RRC's figures had failed' (Goyder and Goyder, 1988:93). As noted in Chapter 3, the media played a key role in arousing the demand for action,

---

[3]   This has sometimes been a source of tension with other impoverished ministries which did not get access to Western donor funding.

and embarrassed Western governments for their failure to respond in time to prevent massive loss of life. Since then, there has been greater public awareness in the West of famine in Africa. And Western donors now keep a watchful eye on the media, keen not to be caught out a second time for failing to do enough to prevent famine.

There has been much analysis of the principal causes of famine in Ethiopia. Whereas Sen's (1981) analysis of famine in the early 1970s strongly emphasized food *entitlement* decline, subsequent studies have redressed the balance, drawing attention to the significance of food *availability* decline as a result of drought, compounded by logistical constraints because of poor infrastructure and lack of transport (Kumar, 1990). This last point is particularly important as it militates against private sector trade relieving food shortages, and has implications for the provision of relief, especially in the famine-prone north-eastern highlands, such as Wollo and Tigray.

Food policy

The emphasis on emergency aid does not mean that there has been no long-term food policy in place. Under Mengistu, the socialization of agriculture was pursued, with a concentration of resources on state-owned farms and producer co-operatives, and tight controls over marketing. There was a strong rhetorical commitment to food self-sufficiency, and an effective urban public distribution system funded by quotas levied on surplus producers. This policy did little to improve the country's food-security status, however, in many ways causing it to deteriorate further (Maxwell, 1993). In 1987, a National Food and Nutrition Strategy was formulated but never finalized.

During the early years of the 1990s, this interventionist approach was rapidly dismantled. Since March 1990, there have been a number of major reforms, marking the beginning of the transition from a centrally planned socialist economy. Grain markets were liberalized as well as agricultural labour markets, and land tenure was reformed to give greater protection to small farmers. The change in policy direction initiated in the final year of the Mengistu government has been accelerated since the change of regime in May 1991. As significant pledges of development aid are now being made, the prospects for new policies to tackle food insecurity look more promising.

Similarly, the National Disaster Prevention and Preparedness Strategy (NDPPS), drawn up in 1989, signals a new approach. It is an attempt to link relief and development more closely with the long-term aim of reducing vulnerability to future drought. The design of an Emergency Code, drawing on the approach and experience of the Indian Famine Code, is the principal instrument for implementing the strategy. The Transitional Government has given renewed impetus to the NDPPS, and in 1993 approved a revised version of the Emergency Code, renamed the 'Directives for Disaster Prevention and Management'. These represent a determined attempt to move away from dependence on free food aid as the principal form of relief. They propose a much wider range of relief options, designed to contribute to long-term development objectives as well as to meet short-term relief needs. For instance, an Employment Generation Scheme, based on food- and cash-for-work, is a central component of the new plan. It also introduces a more decentralized approach to disaster management, which has been given particular emphasis since the Transitional Government embarked on a radical programme of regionalization.

In an impoverished country with very weak local administration, this new approach cannot be implemented overnight. It must be an iterative process, safeguarding the old system until a tried-and-tested alternative is in place. In a country scarred by famine, the cost of failure is too high to contemplate. The success of the policy changes overwhelmingly depends on continued peace and political stability — conditions that are not yet assured.

The EW/response system

Early-warning system

The national EWS in Ethiopia[4] was the first to be set up in Africa, in 1976. It is run by the Early Warning and Planning Services (EWPS) within the RRC. It has been supported by donor funds during most of its existence, but has been very poorly resourced compared with most other national EWS in the Sahel and Horn of Africa — a reflection of the unfavourable aid climate during the Mengistu regime. There are now better prospects for donor support, which is much needed as the system adjusts to a more decentralized system of government.

In a country characterized by a lack of success in long-term food security policies and where most aid has been food relief, the EWS has, not surprisingly, been geared to triggering and directing food-relief operations year after year. According to the typology presented in Chapter 2, Ethiopia's national system falls squarely into the category of conventional, famine- and food aid-oriented, top–down system of early warning. It was designed to cover two broadly defined production systems: an agricultural and a pastoral one. It does not monitor food security among the urban population. The design has evolved from the 'Food and Nutrition Information System' on which it was initially based in the 1970s, to a methodology emphasizing agricultural and socio-economic indicators. Now the EWS monitors most conventional EW indicators, based on a three-phase monitoring sequence: first, food-supply indicators; second, social stress indicators such as migration and market data; and third, individual stress indicators such as nutritional status and disease.

The EWPS has depended on other government departments for information, especially the Central Statistical Authority (CSA) for crop-production forecasts and market monitoring, and the National Meteorological Services Agency (NMSA), which has particular prominence because drought is usually regarded as the biggest threat to food security

---

[4] This section is based on Buchanan-Smith *et al.*, 1991; People's Democratic Republic of Ethiopia, 1990.

61

Table 4.2   Ethiopia: outputs of the national EWS in 1990–91

Report	Perspective	Date of publication
Food-supply Prospect	Assessment of numbers and location of people requiring relief assistance during following 12 months	October/November
Synoptic Food Supply	Assessment of harvest and population in need of assistance following *meher* and *belg* seasons	January/February = *meher* August = *belg*
Food-supply Situation of the Pastoralist Population	Assessment of relief needs for pastoralist population	Usually twice a year
Monthly Bulletins	Regular early-warning update	Monthly
Special Flash Reports	Assessment of particularly serious and localized problems	As needed
Relief Plan of Operation	Record of relief requirements and commitments	March/April

each year. The EWPS (before regionalization) also used to carry out its own primary data collection at *awraja* (district) level through informal early-warning committees of key local government officials, and it fields teams from Addis Ababa to carry out twice-yearly surveillance of pastoral areas, and disaster area assessments as needed.

A wide array of reports and publications is usually produced by the EWPS each year (see Table 4.2). Its most important output has always been the annual forecast of the numbers and location of people regarded as at-risk, plus an assessment of the food aid required, normally provided in October, at the end of the *meher* season, and revised the following February.

While data collection was based on the old administrative unit of the *awraja*, all data analysis was carried out in Addis Ababa. Relief allocations were decided in the capital, and decisions regarding relief interventions were communicated from the centre. It was a highly centralized system, with little contact between collectors and analysts of data. Inevitably, this meant that the data were highly aggregated. The system was ill-placed to monitor coping strategies and to be sensitive to the complexity and diversity of local livelihood systems. It could report on the overall picture but easily overlook acute localized problems, one of its greatest shortcomings. With the process of regionalization under the new Transitional Government, relief and rehabilitation bureaux have been set up around the country, taking over some of the responsibilities of the RRC in Addis. EW staff are being appointed at regional and local levels and it is envisaged that they will eventually have greater powers and responsibility, although this requires a substantial investment in training.

A number of NGOs and international agencies are also active in the field of EW. Save the Children Fund (UK) has been running a Nutritional Surveillance Programme in Wollo, Harerghe and Shewa, since the mid-1970s. This is closely linked to the RRC's EWS, and provides most of its data on nutritional surveillance. In 1992, CARE started to produce bulletins based on a household food information system for Borana, Harerghe and Shewa. Meanwhile, the Christian Relief and Development Association (CRDA) has for a number of years provided a conduit for most of the informal EW reporting of the churches and NGOs.

On the donor agency side, the most important components of the international EWS are the annual FAO harvest assessment and the WFP needs assessment, described in Chapter 3. Ethiopia is also covered by the USAID-funded project, FEWS, although the Brooke Amendment prevented the FEWS representative from being based in Addis Ababa until June 1992. The UN's Emergency Prevention and Preparedness Group (EPPG) based in Addis Ababa also provided fairly regular monitoring during 1990 and 1991 of some of the most food-insecure and inaccessible parts of the country, including Eritrea and Tigray, through its small network of field officers. However, since the Transitional Government came to power and donor agency and government information systems have been better integrated, the EPPG has been scaled down into a UN Emergencies Unit.

Finally, in the rebel-held territory of Tigray and Eritrea, the respective liberation fronts were running their own informal EWS (see Buchanan-Smith et al., 1991) until the war ended in 1991. In Tigray, the TPLF worked in conjunction with the Relief Society of Tigray (REST). In Eritrea, the Eritrea Relief Association (ERA) was responsible. Neither of these was an official EWS, and obviously had no links with the Government of Ethiopia. Both systems were based on a relatively well-developed structure of local administration, and were geared to monitoring the impact of war, including the disruption of production and restrictions on population movement.

There have been many players in the EW process in Ethiopia, both from within the country and outside (see Figure 4.2). This is because of the scale of food aid needs, as well as the distrust between donors and government. Large amounts of information and numbers of reports were produced as a result. Indeed, some donor missions in Addis Ababa, like the Canadian International Development Agency, employed their own information officers to synthesize the information provided in order to form a coherent view.

All components of the EWS have been driven by a concern to prevent large-scale famine ever happening again. In a country where such a large proportion of the population is vulnerable to acute food insecurity if the rains fail or if their livelihood systems are disrupted by conflict, this has been their main point of reference. But it should be the job of the EWS to monitor conditions all along the continuum of food security to famine, to detect pockets of localized food crisis, and to provoke action which is geared not only to preventing big famines but also to alleviating less acute and more common episodes of food insecurity. This wider remit has not been adopted by the EWS.

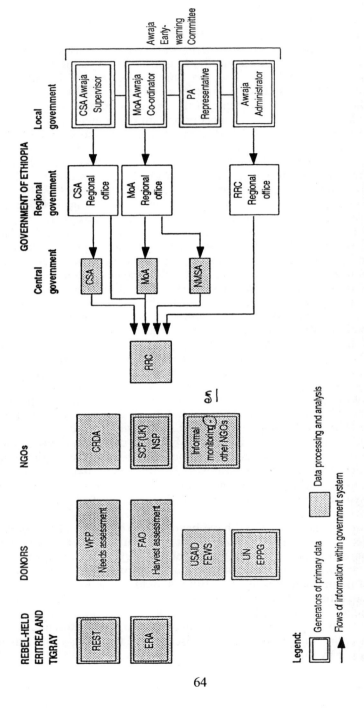

Figure 4.2 *Ethiopia: main components of the national and international EWS in 1990–91.*
Source: Adapted from FAO, 1991b.

Response system

After a bad harvest, the need for relief is greatest in June/July; this is the hungry season when reserves from the previous year's harvest are exhausted. Transport difficulties during the rainy season mean that an effective EW/response mechanism in Ethiopia is one which succeeds in delivering relief before the months of June/July when the main rains begin.

Despite the fact that emergency relief operations have continued on an annual basis in Ethiopia since the mid-1980s, no formal programmed response mechanisms have been put in place. Nevertheless, a tried-and-tested system for receiving EW information and for making decisions about relief allocations and to some extent for its distribution, has been established over the years. As international donors provide almost all the resources to respond to EW of food insecurity, they have been key players.

In Addis Ababa a well-established timetable of meetings within the donor and NGO community had been set up by 1990–91. Under the Mengistu regime, the government was excluded from most of these meetings. In fact there was a remarkable lack of regular contact between government and the international aid community; each had its own system and there was little communication between them, reflecting the antagonistic and suspicious nature of relations. Where there was co-ordination, it was provided by the EPPG and WFP; WFP usually informed the government about donor food aid commitments and allocations. Otherwise, the only formal government procedures were those requiring NGOs to submit project proposals for food aid distributions for RRC approval. The donors were fully aware of the government's objective of maximizing food aid, and were suspicious of some of its means of achieving this. They were therefore keen to set up their own independent decision-making and relief systems over which they felt they had some control, consigning relief to NGOs to distribute, rather than to the RRC. Under the Transitional Government the situation has changed considerably, and there is now much closer consultation between government and donors and NGOs.

The UN has usually played the main co-ordinating role within the donor community. This was particularly important where sensitive political negotiations were required to set up relief operations and relief corridors into contested regions in the north of the country under the Mengistu regime; for example, the Southern Line operation between the port of Asseb and communities in northern Wollo and Tigray in 1990.

The way in which the international community interprets EW information is particularly important to the timing of decisions to respond. The donor spotlight turns on the EWS once the annual WFP and FAO assessments have been carried out in November, and major relief decisions for the following year are usually made in January. This rarely allows sufficient time for food to be shipped from Europe or North America and distributed to those in need in remote parts of the country before the hungry season begins.

For many donor agencies, and certainly for those discussed in this book, Ethiopia is one of the largest recipients of food aid. Decisions about the

65

total quantities of relief allocated are taken at donor agency headquarters. Because of the large amounts being pledged, and because of Western media interest in the plight of Ethiopia, its food aid needs and the pledging process have tended to have a high profile within agencies.

Government decision-making in response to EW is not easily mapped out, particularly for the Mengistu period. Over the years various government committees have existed, to pull together different sources of EW information at key times of the year. Generally, the RRC has played the key role in the decision-making process on the government side, especially regarding how much relief assistance should be requested from the donor community.

The story of EW/response in 1990–91

EW signals and decisions to respond
The crop season in 1990–91 illustrates the complexity of Ethiopia's food problems. There was a record harvest in some of the more productive regions such as Shewa, while other areas, especially in the north-eastern highlands and in the Ogaden, were facing a second consecutive year of drought and serious food shortages. The security situation was also changing rapidly. With the overthrow of the Dergue government the relief system came under immense pressure, and its flexibility was put to the test of whether it could adjust to varying (and increasing) estimates of need throughout 1991.

From early on it was obvious that, with the late, and poor, rains in many parts of the country, the relief operation would have to continue into 1991, the norm in Ethiopia since the mid-1980s. Continued pledges of financial support were solicited to keep the airlift to Asmara going, long before the results of the annual relief assessments appeared. WFP issued an appeal for 100 000t of food aid as early as October 1990, in order to keep the pipeline flowing.

Figures 4.3 and 4.4 summarize the results of the main EW assessments made in 1990–91. Between October and December 1990, two parallel exercises estimating food-relief needs were under way. The CSA Statistical Bulletin in November published estimates of 5.6m tonnes, revised upwards in December to 5.8m tonnes (CSA, 1990a and b). The FAO harvest assessment then came up with estimates for total production of cereals and pulses of 7.47m tonnes,[5] not greatly different from the FEWS prediction in October of around 7.2m tonnes (FEWS, 1990). These aggregate figures conceal large regional differences. The northern parts of the country — especially Eritrea and Tigray — were singled out as severely drought affected. When the food balance-sheet exercise was finally completed, the food aid requirement was estimated to be 985 000t, for approximately 4.44 million people in need (FAO, 1990).

On the demand side, the RRC's EWPS published its first estimate of numbers in need (4.3 million) and food aid requirements (840 000t) in

---

5   If the figures are adjusted to be comparable with the CSA November estimate, the two forecasts are consistent at 5.6m tonnes.

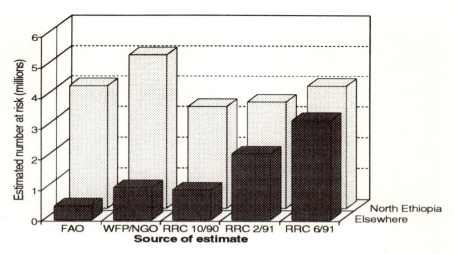

Figure 4.3 *Ethiopia: number of people at risk, 1990–91 – comparison FAO, WFP/NGO and RRC*

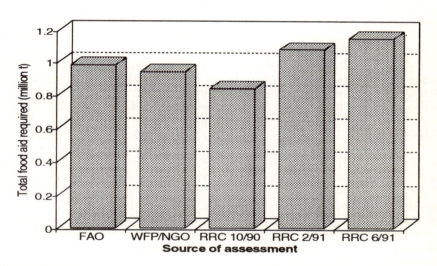

Figure 4.4 *Ethiopia: assessments of relief needs, 1990–91 – comparison FAO, WFP/NGO and RRC*

October (EWPS, 1990b). Concern was reiterated about the situation in Eritrea, which, it was claimed, had 'experienced one of the worst ever droughts, even worse than 1984/85', for the second successive year (EWPS, 1990b:1). The WFP/NGO assessment in December came to a final estimate of 941 600t for six million people, higher than the RRC mainly because of the inclusion of beneficiaries in rebel-held or war-affected parts in the north, not covered by the EWPS. Again, there were quite big regional differences, and each assessment used different ration rates to calculate food aid needs. Meanwhile, early FEWS estimates were rather lower at 615000t, although a worst-case scenario of needs rising to over one million tonnes was cited as a possibility (FEWS, 1990).

Donors used the WFP assessment as the basis for making decisions about how much food aid to pledge; it had the necessary international stamp of credibility, and provided a breakdown of relief needs to regional level. WFP appeals were launched periodically from January 1991, initially using the December requirement figure, against which the rate of pledges and commitments by different donors throughout the first half of 1991 was measured.

During 1991, the RRC gradually increased its estimate of numbers in need, first in February, to 5.59 million people in need of over one million tonnes (EWPS, 1991b). By this time there had been an assessment of the famine developing in the Ogaden, where no relief operation was in place. The EWPS issued a Special Release on the Ogaden in early 1991 (EWPS, 1991a), adding an extra 524000 to the total of those in need, and this was followed up by a special government appeal in March. Additional relief needs for other regions suffering from severe malnutrition were identified. Acute malnutrition[6] in east Harerghe and north Omo had been detected, where the mean weight for length of children under five years had dropped below 85 per cent of reference. This was taken as an indicator of severe food insecurity so soon after the harvest; feeding programmes were set up. In January, FEWS had already commented on the severity of the drought in eastern Ethiopia: 'major parts of the new East and West Harerghe and Dire Dawa regions appear to have experienced the worst agro-climatic conditions of the decade over the past two years' (FEWS, 1991:46). The revised RRC figures had no immediate impact on relief planning. WFP continued to use its original figure of 941593t until July, when, together with other UN agencies, it raised its estimates to over one million tonnes for an estimated seven million vulnerable people (including the drought-affected, refugees and returnees) (UN, 1991). As time wore on, there was a growing awareness that the scale of the food-security problem had still been underestimated in some drought-stricken areas. In April, SCF (UK) published a report based on the Nutritional Surveillance Programme monitoring, estimating that 370000 people were in need of relief assistance in Wollayita alone, higher than the RRC's assessment in February for the whole of north Omo. Concern was also expressed about the deteriorating situation in east Harerghe and south Shewa: 'A problem which only a few months ago seemed to be confined to specific villages has abruptly changed to threaten whole districts' (SCF (UK), 1991:2).

The security situation was also changing rapidly during 1991, having a direct bearing on relief needs. With the TPLF advance, some areas became inaccessible for relief distributions, for example, the Sudanese refugee

---

[6] The trigger point for nutritional intervention in Ethiopia is when the mean weight for length for children under five drops below 90 per cent.

camps in western Ethiopia. Moreover, with the overthrow of the Mengistu government in May, large numbers of demobilized soldiers and displaced civilians eventually converged on Addis Ababa, requiring immediate relief assistance. Meanwhile, the increasing hostilities in Somalia led to large influxes of refugees and returnees, mainly into drought-stricken eastern Ethiopia. Few of these security-related factors had been predicted, being beyond the remit of the national EWS. Their consequences were mostly reported upon as they happened. The WFP appeal in April warned that 'the drought . . . is parallel in its potential effect to the tragedy of the 1984–85 famine, exacerbated by the massive refugee presence'.

In June, after the overthrow of the Mengistu government, the RRC raised its estimates once again, to 1 149 480t for 7.47 million people. By now the number of drought-affected people had increased, most notably in north Omo, Harerghe, and especially in northern Ethiopia, and 750 000 extra people were added to the list as displaced in Addis Ababa, together with 340 000 returnees from Somalia. The UN's Consolidated Appeal for the Horn of Africa in July also increased its estimate of relief needs to 1.2 million tonnes, a figure close to the RRC's (UN, 1991). In early June, an explosion at an ammunitions depot, which killed hundreds and destroyed the homes of thousands, compounded relief problems in the capital.

The relief response
Despite clear and early indications of the need for another large relief operation during 1991, food aid pledges were slow, especially during the first six months of the year, and well below estimated requirements. This is a

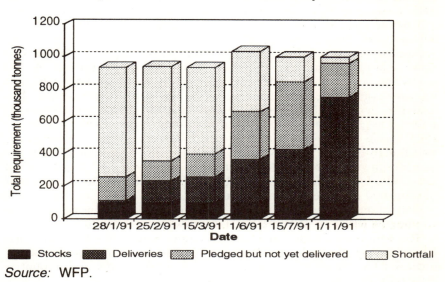

Source: WFP.

Figure 4.5 *Ethiopia: Emergency food aid 1990–91 – record of availability and deliveries*
Source: WFP.

69

Table 4.3 Ethopia: Timetable of food-aid pledges and deliveries, 1991 (thousands of tonnes)

Food aid	Date					
	28/1/91	25/2/91	15/3/91	1/6/91	15/7/91	1/11/91
Requirement						
(as per WFP)	941.6	941.6	941.6	1037.2	1006.2	1006.2
Available						
(a) 1990 stocks	94.4	94.4	94.4	94.4	94.4	94.4
(b) 1990 pledges	31.2	31.2	31.2	31.2	31.1	31.1
(c) 1991 pledges	134.6	232.9	277.8	541.1	728.5	838.8
Shortfall on						
availability	681.4	583.1	538.2	370.4	152.2	41.9
Deliveries to date	19.2	137.6	164.5	273.7	334.2	661.8
Shortfall on						
deliveries	922.4	804.0	777.1	763.4	671.9	344.4
Availability as % of						
requirements	28	38	43	64	85	96
Deliveries as % of						
requirements	2	15	17	26	33	66

Source: WFP.

common pattern in Ethiopia, even though it is widely accepted that food aid is needed year after year. More rapid pledging to make up the shortfall was urged again and again by WFP, while a number of NGOs expressed their concern about the empty food aid pipeline. By the beginning of June, only half the estimated needs had been pledged (see Figure 4.5 and Table 4.3).

This was more serious when translated into deliveries. By the middle of July only one-third of the revised estimate of relief needs had been delivered in-country — still less to final beneficiaries — despite the fact that by now the hungry season had started. By November, only two-thirds of total needs had been delivered. Although stocks left over from 1990 helped to improve availability, the slow delivery rate had serious consequences. For example, in SCF (UK)'s feeding programme the supplementary weekly under-fives' ration had to be halved in March/April to make stocks last (SCF (UK), 1991). From March to July, CRDA reported increasing malnutrition in east Harerghe (CRDA, 1990/91b). The Ogaden was the worst case; despite evidence of deteriorating food security in 1990, highlighted in the EWPS famine alert in January 1991, by mid-July less than 10 per cent of estimated relief needs had arrived.

Only about 12 per cent of total food aid distributed during 1991 was handled by the RRC (EWPS, 1992). Most was consigned to international NGOs for final distribution and monitoring. Since 1984–5, donors and NGOs had set up their own transport systems; local capacity was inadequate for the task of moving huge quantities of food around the country. Four different transport fleets existed during 1991. The principal one, with more than 250 trucks, belonged to the WFP Transport Operation for Ethiopia; CRDA had about 70 trucks, which helped to service the Joint Relief Partnership on the Southern Line; Oxfam and SCF (UK) had a Joint

Transport Operation; and there was a separate fleet supported by German aid for refugee operations. By 1991 some of these were showing signs of wear and tear and their capacity was reduced. The main problem was fuel shortages, as Ethiopia no longer had access to cheap Soviet supplies.

The changing security map posed its own challenges to maintaining the relief flow. The re-opening of the port of Massawa in January 1991, after much negotiation, was a major breakthrough for delivering food to Eritrea, and ended the costly airlift to Asmara. Shortly afterwards, a new airlift had to be organized to bring food into the Ogaden. The Southern Line operation from the port of Asseb to destinations north of Dessie managed to keep going, despite deteriorating security, apart from a temporary break in March.

Evaluating the EW information

The food balance sheet and needs assessment

Remarkably, the FAO annual harvest assessment (resulting in the food balance sheet), and the WFP needs assessment carried out in 1990–91 arrived at very similar conclusions about the total quantity of food aid required: FAO, 985000t; WFP, 941593t. But there were substantial differences in their estimates of numbers of people requiring assistance: 4.44 and 6.06 million, respectively. In order to make a fair comparison between the results of the FAO, WFP, and RRC/EWPS (October) assessments, the regions of northern Ethiopia have been excluded.[7] The WFP and RRC figures for total food aid needs for the rest of the country are fairly close, but the FAO figure is much larger. The estimates of numbers in need also differ sharply (see Table 4.4).

Both the food-balance-sheet and the numbers-in-need approaches are based upon key assumptions about consumption requirements or relief ration rates. There is very little consistency in this respect between the various assessments as each use different consumption requirement values (see Table 4.5). This highlights the rather dubious accuracy of some of the main parameters on which the exercises are based, and the difficulties of estimating food security in terms of quantitative measures of 'enough food'. It also calls into question the 'objectivity' of these assessments.

The figure for annual consumption requirements per capita of 162kg, used by FAO (and by FEWS), is based on the results of baseline nutrition surveys carried out by the Ethiopian Nutrition Institute, to establish 'normal' consumption levels (and relates to kilocalorie requirements of approximately 1710kcal/day), the underlying assumption being that relief assistance is supposed to relieve transitory (and acute) food insecurity, rather than tackle underlying structural food insecurity.[8] On the other

---

7   Both the FAO and WFP assessments take rebel-held territory in the north of Ethiopia — Eritrea, Tigray, north Wollo and Gondar — into account, having access to various reports not available to the RRC.
8   By comparison, the per capita consumption figure used by FAO in Chad in the food-balance-sheet exercise, also based on past nutritional surveys, is only 127kg. This highlights the problem of making direct comparisons between the results of harvest assessments (and food-balance-sheet calculations) in different countries. The parameters are not consistent.

Table 4.4 Ethiopia: comparison of the final results of the FAO, WFP and RRC (October) assessments, 1990–1

Agency responsible for assessment	Total food aid needed (t)	Number of people in need (millions)
1. Total		
FAO	985 000	4.44
WFP/NGO	941 593	6.06
RRC EWPS[a]	840 000	4.29
2. Excluding n. Ethiopia		
FAO	235 000	0.44
WFP/NGO	154 903	1.04
RRC	163 294	0.96

Note: (a) RRC assessment figures are based on the EWPS report of October 1990.
Sources: FAO, 1991a; WFP, 1990; EWPS, 1990b.

Table 4.5 Ethiopia: relief ration rate, or annual consumption rate, on which different agencies' assessments are based

Agency		Relief ration rate (kg/month)	Implied or explicit consumption rate (kg/capita/year)
FAO		15.4[a]	162.0
WFP/NGO	Drought-affected:	14.1	169.2[a]
	Displaced:	14.7	176.4[a]
	Northern population:	14.7	176.4[a]
RRC		17.0	204.0[a]

Note:
(a) Denotes implied rate, deduced from other parameters used in the respective assessment, e.g. in the FAO assessment, total relief food aid needs (excluding structural food aid) amount to 850 000t, for an estimated 4.44 million people, implying an average relief ration rate of 15.4kg/month.
Sources: FAO, 1991a; WFP, 1990; EWPS, 1990b.

hand, the WFP figure for the relief ration rate of 14.1kg is based on a daily requirement of 1 755kcal, which gives a per capita annual consumption rate of 169.2kg. The RRC's ration rate assumes a 2 000kcal/day requirement, and translates into a much higher per capita annual consumption rate of 204kg. This highlights the difference in views about what relief food is supposed to achieve: in the first case, maintaining the *status quo*, even if this perpetuates high rates of malnutrition; in the second case, meeting some notion of basic nutritional requirements.

Historical precedent plays an important role in determining the final figure for the total amount of food aid needed for the forthcoming year. FAO tries to ensure that at least some of the members of its harvest assessment team have carried out the exercise in Ethiopia before, and 'have a feel' for conditions in the country. There is a strong element of learning by doing, retrospectively reviewing the accuracy of the previous years' food-balance-sheet exercises, and comparing the conditions of the current year with those in previous years. Thus, to some extent, each exercise works back from what appears to be a reasonable and realistic final estimate of relief needs. The finer details are conveniently overlooked.

In the words of one donor representative, it has been a process of 'consensus building amongst the experts'. This seems to be a pragmatic approach to a very difficult task, nevertheless giving it the air of a scientific approach by using food-balance-sheet or ration-rate calculations. It was by this process that the UN agencies finally agreed a figure for relief food aid for Ethiopia in 1991 of around one million tonnes.

When the figures and assessments are examined and compared at regional level, there is much less consistency (see Figure 4.3). This has important implications for the targeting of food aid between regions. If northern Ethiopia is excluded from the two assessments so that they are comparable, WFP recommended that 20 per cent of total relief needs be allocated to Harerghe, while the RRC assessment recommended only 14 per cent. In the end, the allocation was often decided according to the operational location of the different NGOs charged with distribution, rather than according to estimated need.

The challenges of carrying out a nation-wide survey in Ethiopia are huge, especially under a system that is heavily centralized. Rather crude methodologies have been used to come up with aggregate estimates of relief needs. In order to arrive at a final figure of numbers in need, the EWPS has usually asked each Peasant Association to make its own estimate, without specific guidelines; inevitably bias has crept in. It is hard to see how the methodology behind these calculations could be improved in a highly centralized system of EW in a country of great diversity. Under the new Disaster Directives the planned direction for EWS is towards decentralization, which is probably the best option for strengthening EW. But to make it work, and to devise a more accurate and location-specific method for calculating annual relief needs will require a substantial amount of training and capacity building at local level.

Are the assessments accurate?

How accurate is the notional baseline (or historical precedent) which is being used as a reference point in the annual assessment calculations? Some donor representatives have argued that food aid deliveries have consistently fallen behind requirement targets in the last few years, yet devastating famines do not appear to have developed as a result. Can people 'cope' better than we think? There is certainly a very poor understanding of coping strategies in Ethiopia, and very little monitoring of them in regular EW data collection.

At the same time, it is not evident that food aid needs have consistently been overestimated, for two reasons. First, cases of acute food insecurity and even famine may have developed on a localized basis due to failure to deliver food aid, and gone undetected. In Wollayita, in north Omo, SCF

(UK) detected rapidly deteriorating food security, and roughly a threefold increase in mortality, in March 1991, which can at least be partly attributed to food shortage (SCF (UK), 1991; Lawrence *et al.*, 1994). The extent of this problem was not picked up by the regular RRC monitoring system.[9]

Second, the events of 1984–5 have been imprinted firmly in people's memories, in terms of what to look for as evidence of famine — specifically, large population movements. Yet, how people behave in one famine situation may not be repeated in another, when both underlying and proximate circumstances are different (Walker, 1989:95). Also, it is by no means clear that evidence of famine should be the benchmark against which success or failure to deliver food aid is measured. There are clear indications that poverty is increasing and becoming more severe in many parts of Ethiopia. The asset base of many households has been depleted, people are becoming progressively more food-insecure and certainly more vulnerable to drought as their capacity to withstand external shocks has been eroded (Webb and von Braun, 1994; Dagnew, 1993). In the absence of development aid reaching these people, the role of relief food aid needs to be reviewed. Food aid may be playing a very important social-security role in the face of intense poverty, beyond simply saving lives. This has been confirmed in a SCF (UK) survey in the north-eastern highlands in 1993, where it was concluded that food aid had had an important impact in alleviating poverty and protecting nutritional status (Holt and Lawrence, 1993). A failure to deliver food may simply contribute to the downward poverty spiral, as people use up their already depleted assets to survive.

Donor agencies have often been sceptical of the government's own estimates of the amount of relief aid required, which they have regarded as a political exercise to maximize food aid receipts. Government officials have acknowledged that under the previous regime they were sometimes under political pressure to change their EW figures. The national EWS was not free from political manœuvrings. Yet the extent to which food aid needs were exaggerated has probably been overestimated by donors. At the end of 1990 the WFP assessment came up with a higher figure than the RRC for the number of people in need of assistance, both in total and even when northern Ethiopia was excluded (see Figure 4.3).

Use of EW information

Two sets of decisions have to be taken to ensure timely response in Ethiopia: the total amount of food aid (or other resources) to be committed to the relief operation; and where and how the relief should be allocated. The government's view of the need for a relief operation determines the latitude given to the international donor community to intervene but the government does not have its own resources to respond with — it provided only 5000t from the Food Security Reserve in 1991 for the Ogaden. Because the international relief system provides almost all the relief resources

---

[9] It has caused SCF (UK) to question whether the trigger for nutritional intervention of the *mean* weight for length dropping below 90 per cent is appropriate (see Lawrence *et al.*, 1994).

used in a crisis, how the donors interpret EW signals and data is particularly relevant, and is the focus of this section.

The most influential indicators

FAO and WFP end-of-year assessments are much more important in triggering a response, and in determining the scale of that response, than any of the RRC's reports — as was demonstrated in 1990–91. National EW information was regarded with deep suspicion; a commonly held view was that the RRC assessments were 'as dramatic as possible' (pers. comm., donor representative in Addis Ababa). Ethiopia's EWS has always suffered a credibility problem among donors. This was never more evident than in 1984, and was one of the reasons why response from the international community was so fatally late. With hindsight, it was acknowledged that the information provided had in fact been timely, reasonably accurate and efficient[10] (Goyder and Goyder, 1988). Nevertheless, the RRC's EWS continued to be disbelieved, and its methodology and reporting system have been poorly understood by many donor agency representatives in Addis Ababa.

Recently, and certainly during 1990–91, the FAO and WFP assessments have differed very little from government assessments. Indeed, they have drawn heavily on government data sources. On the one hand, they have been required to verify government early warnings; on the other hand, they have provided the international imprimatur necessary to give national data credibility. The WFP figures for the quantity of food relief and the number of people in need were those used for planning throughout the year. No donors required the government to issue a formal appeal for assistance before they responded, unlike Sudan (see Chapter 5). They were entirely guided by the WFP appeal.

Donors are more or less resigned to Ethiopia's continuous need for relief aid, and budget on that basis. What is less clear is their responsiveness to the scale of the need. During 1990–91 there seemed to be a waiting game to see how the situation developed, especially the security situation, before large commitments were made. This meant that many potential benefits of an EW system were lost. Some donor representatives were even sceptical of the UN agencies' assessments, expecting them to be overestimated. Because there was no evidence of people dying despite failure to deliver the required amount, it was argued that the UN assessments were not totally independent of government influence, upon which they depended for basic data. This helps to explain why pledges did not meet requirements.

It also confirms that evidence of acute food insecurity is required to trigger response; mere forecasts of what 'might' happen are not enough. Nutritional surveillance data are particularly influential in this respect, playing an important advocacy role as a late indicator by showing how conditions have deteriorated, thereby justifying earlier assessments of

---

[10] For example, as early as 1981, the RRC warned of deteriorating weather conditions, appealing for international aid assistance in 1983 (Kumar, 1990).

needs. During 1991, these data were often reported in agency telexes and memos justifying or recommending interventions, as clear evidence of human stress. In launching and re-launching its appeals for food-aid assistance, WFP made dramatic comparisons with 1984–5: 'The drought . . . is parallel in its potential effect to the tragedy of the 1984–85 famine' (WFP appeal of April 1991). These kinds of statements seemed necessary to inject a sense of urgency to get the response system moving.

Political factors
The segregation between donor and government decision-making processes was stark. In such an environment of antagonistic and suspicious relations, the relief system could easily have foundered. The government could have put its foot down in protest against the unilateral decision-making of the international agencies. Instead, the existence of a common objective to get relief resources into the country, and to prevent famine, seemed to work in favour of relief food being provided and distributed around the country, despite difficult donor/government relations. The Ethiopian Government had no choice but to allow the international aid agencies to set up their own systems, and not to interfere with them, as long as this ensured the delivery of relief aid. The long-term consequence was that government structures were often bypassed, and sometimes weakened and marginalized.

As a consequence, the role of international NGOs became significant. They provided an important and often informal channel of EW to the donor community, usually for the particular localities where they operated. Their information seems to have enjoyed high credibility: for example, reports on the situation in Harerghe, provided by CARE to USAID; and SCF (UK)'s report on evidence of famine in April (SCF (UK), 1991) supported by lobbying of certain donor agencies, helped to ensure that pledges were stepped up.

NGOs were most influential in determining where food aid was allocated. Once an agency had decided how much relief it was prepared to commit, it was up to the NGOs to bid for it, usually on a geographical basis. There was little reference back to the original distribution plans for each region which had been drawn up. The disadvantage of this was that allocations were decided in a very haphazard way, and coverage could be extremely patchy without reference to areas prioritized according to need.

The RRC had no real involvement in these decisions. It was simply required to approve project agreements with different NGOs for free food distribution. On its own admission, the RRC was usually reluctant to try and change these allocations, for fear that the food would be withdrawn.

The legacy of 1984–5, when the media exposed a full-blown famine largely neglected by the international relief system, has been a key factor influencing donors' willingness to respond to appeals for food aid for Ethiopia since. When pledges were made to meet Ethiopia's needs during 1991, they were often given a high profile by the agency concerned, and accompanied by widely publicized press releases.

76

1991: a very slow response

Despite this, pledges were very slow. This was due in part to the particular circumstances, especially at the end of 1990 and beginning of 1991 when the Gulf crisis dominated foreign policy and aid considerations and certainly drew attention away from the plight of African countries. However, slow bureaucratic decision-making within donor agencies, described in Chapter 3, was another reason. Some NGOs have complained that it took up to four months to get a decision on a proposal. Despite the fact that Ethiopia requires food aid every year, there are still delays in pledging. In 1991, this was exacerbated by other demands on the international relief system, not least that large-scale relief operations were being launched in other countries in the Sahel and Horn of Africa. There was a lot of competition for limited resources.

Implications for the final response

In its first appeal of January 1991, WFP stressed the need for food aid to be pledged and delivered 'prior to the onset of the lean season between May and October'. The outcome was very different, as illustrated in Figure 4.5. It usually took at least four months from the moment a decision was taken to the food arriving in one of the Ethiopian ports, even longer for it to get to its final destination inland. In some cases NGOs experienced an eight-month delay between hearing that their proposal for a food aid distribution had been approved, and receiving the food in-country. The only consolation was the late arrival of food pledged in 1990, which could be put towards the 1991 operation. However, this contingency measure was not always straightforward; there were sometimes considerable delays in approving the diversion of food from its original destination.

Fortunately, threats of another 1984–5 were not realized, as some food kept trickling through. But there were serious consequences of the delayed arrival of food aid and sometimes the drying up of the food aid pipeline: it posed severe problems for NGOs responsible for distribution, and most importantly, for the recipients who suddenly found the rations on which they depended were cut.

On current timetables for donor pledges, imported food aid is arriving too late. The alternative is to promote pre-positioning of relief stocks. For a number of years, the idea of establishing and maintaining a national food-security reserve in Ethiopia has been discussed and studied, specifically to improve the timeliness of the response system, so that there is a readily available source of food in the initial stages of an emergency. The proposal for a food-security reserve was first studied in 1974, by FAO, which recommended a 50000t reserve. Subsequent studies increased the target size to 205000t in 1987 (ODNRI, 1987). It never came near its target level: the maximum it reached was 102500t. This was partly because recurring emergencies never permitted enough extra food aid to be imported to build up the reserve. But it was mainly due to lack of donor support for the reserve. They did not feel they had adequate control over its use, justified by actions

77

such as the government emptying the reserve's warehouses at Nazareth in order to house the military, in 1989.

Since the change in government, interest in the reserve has been resuscitated. An Emergency Food Security Reserve was established as an autonomous organization under a legal directive in October 1992, with donor support. As the likelihood of a 'food emergency' occurring every year is now accepted, the newly stated objective of this reserve is to provide a readily available food stock in strategic locations, which can be loaned to relief agencies in an emergency until such time as other sources of supply can be mobilized. Only in exceptional circumstances, when the loan function proves inadequate, will free draw-down be possible. The short-term target level of the reserve stands at 205000t, increasing to 307000t in the medium term.

At the time of writing, the environment seems more conducive than before to a reserve being established and maintained. The food-security reserve could play a valuable role in ensuring more regular and timely delivery to beneficiaries, and certainly improve on the response record of 1991. Analyses of past famines which emphasize the logistical constraints, in terms of topography and lack of infrastructure and transport, to private-sector food marketing and to the timely provision of relief (Kumar, 1990) lend further support to pre-positioned food reserves, ideally part of a decentralized network.

Insecurity and the EW/response process

Early warning
The war in Tigray and Eritrea was of such long standing that in the rebel-held regions entirely separate EWS were set up by the humanitarian/relief wings of the respective liberation fronts. Neither system, however, had much international recognition before the mid-1980s, when their warnings were ignored with fatal consequences. Famine developed in both Eritrea and Tigray, leading to large influxes of refugees into Sudan (Clark, 1986; University of Leeds, 1988). Thereafter, both REST and ERA received more attention, and cross-border relief operations from Sudan became an institutionalized channel for providing international relief to rebel-held territory.

Of greater concern during 1990 and 1991 were the contested regions which neither the government nor the TPLF or EPLF monitored. The EWPS of the RRC carried out some long-distance monitoring of inaccessible areas using satellite imagery. These data alone, when unverified with ground truthing, sometimes showed contradictory information: for example, during the 1990 *belg* season meteorological reports of rainfall estimates contradicted satellite imagery of vegetation cover in parts of Wollo (EWPS, 1990a). The UN also played a role in monitoring conflict zones, mainly through the EPPG, whose field monitors regularly visited certain areas, like Eritrea.

In other places, like parts of Wollo during 1991, food security and EW monitoring simply broke down until peace was restored. The implications of this were serious. The EW/response system is geared to one forecast of relief needs per year, in December/January, based on the assumption that the performance of the agricultural season is the main determinant of food-security status. In 1991 this forecast quickly became outdated as the fighting and political events preceding the overthrow of the government created a new group of 'at-risk' people needing relief. It would have been very difficult, and politically unacceptable, for the national EWS to have tried to predict the likely *consequences* of political change in the country. It is a 'technical' system, geared only to monitoring drought and the consequences of insecurity, like displacement and refugee influxes. Thus, the RRC's final revised estimate in June 1991, of over seven million people in need, was not a prediction or a forecast, but a report on the actual situation (RRC, 1991). International components of the EWS, less constrained by political sensitivities, similarly provided no EW of food insecurity caused by the fighting.

The other important political factor affecting estimates of emergency needs during 1991 was the influx of refugees and returnees from Somalia into the east and south of Ethiopia. There was little warning or preparation for this, and again it would have been a difficult situation for the national EWS to cover, as it was heavily preoccupied with keeping up to date with internal developments. Once again, the international components of the EWS could have provided some warning, in view of the escalating conflict across the border in Somalia, but failed to do so.

So far, very few EWS are given the remit to warn of political events which may cause suffering or displacement. Yet this is an issue which needs urgently to be addressed as conflict is increasingly a cause of food insecurity in Africa, not least in the Horn (Duffield, 1991).

Providing relief
On the relief side, the conflicts raging in Ethiopia during 1991 posed major challenges. There were times when the relief systems broke down because of insecurity. Both Wollega and Illubabor regions received less than 10 per cent of their planned distributions, mainly because of insecurity and therefore inaccessibility; almost no relief reached these areas before July.

Some systems had been set up during the previous year, like the Southern Line relief operation, set up in March 1990 between the port of Asseb and communities in Northern Wollo and Tigray, and run by the Joint Relief Partnership. Contingency arrangements in other places had to be made rapidly as conditions changed, including the Ogaden airlift. All arrangements for relief operations which passed through contested and insecure areas had to be preceded by lengthy political negotiations. The UN played a major role, both through its Addis representatives, and sometimes aided by visits from high-level officials from headquarters, as for the airlift to Asmara, the Massawa–Djibouti shuttle which eventually superseded the Asmara airlift, and the Southern Line operation. Experience has thus been gained in Ethiopia in how to run relief operations in conflict zones.

Carrying out relief operations in very insecure conditions is extremely expensive, especially when airlifts are involved. They require a high and continued level of financial support from the international aid community, a commitment which is often unsustainable.

Conclusions

Different agencies and the RRC warned that parts of Ethiopia could experience 'another 1984–5' unless adequate quantities of relief were provided in 1991. Fortunately, these threats were not realized. Does this mean that the EW/response system worked, or that the predictions were exaggerated? The answer is not clear-cut.

The system certainly did work better than six years previously, partly because there was actually a system in place by 1990, which had been ticking over for several years. Large quantities of relief were provided in 1991 and had an impact. But the amount of relief distributed was much less than necessary, it arrived late, and there was considerable human suffering as a result. There are data to show that mortality increased significantly in parts of the country, confirming the need for *earlier* relief intervention. It is also possible that some of the most dire threats of famine were exaggerated. But in view of the donor agencies' reluctance to respond until there is evidence of a food crisis, there is an in-built incentive for EW practitioners to paint as severe a picture as possible in order to provoke a reaction.

What is remarkable about the EW/response system in Ethiopia is how it developed in an environment of strained and distrustful relations between the government and Western donors. The lack of co-ordination and communication between the two sides had major implications for the type of system which developed. The international aid community effectively set up a parallel system to government, from EW through to decision-making and even food aid distribution within the country. This could have been disastrous if the government had been unwilling to give the donor agencies such a free rein, in which case the donors would probably have been reluctant to commit large quantities of relief aid to a government which it did not trust, fearing its misuse. The result could have been stalemate, akin to the situation which developed over the border in Sudan during 1990 and 1991. The difference in Ethiopia was due to the fact that both donors and government shared one objective, albeit for slightly different reasons — to get food relief into the country. The government was prepared to pay the price of having less control than it would ideally have liked, as long as this meant that the relief kept flowing.

Of course, the legacy of 1984–5 has improved the chances that EW of famine in Ethiopia will be heeded in future years. The threat of media embarrassment still lingers. There are vested interests in ensuring that it does not happen again. Famine and relief operations in Ethiopia have a much higher international profile than in many other African countries, although in 1991 other events diluted this 'media effect', particularly the Gulf War which diverted attention away from Africa.

Food crisis in Ethiopia is endemic: there is severe and increasing poverty and a huge structural deficit in years of drought. A large proportion of the population is chronically food-insecure and highly vulnerable to any shocks to the food economy. Yet, because of the way the international relief system is structured, Ethiopia has been treated as an emergency year after year. Relief food has certainly provided a valuable safety net, and played some kind of social-security role. But EW and relief interventions have been geared to the extremes of food crisis. It has used famine as its reference point, at the expense of understanding and dealing with some of the underlying food-security problems.

There has been doubt in parts of the donor community about the projected scale and intensity of food insecurity in Ethiopia. Is it as bad as the EWS predicts every year? Evidence of acute food insecurity and sensational language are often required to speed up a sluggish response process. The answer lies in looking at the links between poverty and vulnerability to famine. The two cannot be separated, and the evidence points to a trend of worsening poverty, which may go unnoticed in conventional EW geared to famine.

The national EWS, which has been highly centralized since its inception, has been diligent in providing the key information required for relief planning, namely the annual needs assessment in October/November. Despite limited resources, it has continued to function and produce regular reports. It has provided wide coverage of a vast country through its network of local EW committees. However, the indicators have been highly aggregated, and this is mirrored in the main international components of EW: the WFP and FAO annual assessments. The system has been simplified to a few key indicators: harvest assessments and the food balance sheet, and estimations of numbers of people at risk. This is the information the response system has sought, not least in 1990–91, to form an overview in order to plan relief assistance each year. The system has been geared to a macro-level response.

What has been missing has been a real understanding of the local food economies around the country, their sensitivities and resilience, and of local coping strategies. This is a major challenge. The population of Ethiopia is large, and rural livelihoods complex and diverse. Only a more decentralized and locally based EWS could reach a better understanding of vulnerability and the nature of food insecurity from one year to the next. This is critical to support a successful change in direction away from the emergency approach. A decentralized system is suited to a more flexible and varied response system, beyond straightforward food aid hand-outs. The NDPPS offers many ideas in this respect. However, it will take time to implement, above all making local government strong enough to implement the strategy. There must be a genuine commitment on the part of donors to support a more disaggregated 'non-emergency' approach. Change should be slow and gradual. In the short term, annual injections of large amounts of food aid are likely to continue, and to be needed, until an alternative decentralized, and more flexible and appropriate, system is properly in place.

The RRC's EW information has not counted for much as far as the international donor community has been concerned. The response system has been heavily oriented to the FAO and WFP assessments. These have provided the trigger for donor agency decision-making about the amount of food aid they are prepared to commit each year. The national EWS has had very little *direct* influence in this respect, and has been poorly understood by many donor representatives. The irony is that the FAO and WFP assessment teams have drawn on it extensively for information to complete their exercises, especially the WFP needs assessment. Unlike the national EWS of the RRC, they have enjoyed the credibility accorded to an international agency and have generally been seen to be free from political interference.

The outcome of waiting for the end-of-year assessments has been the same in Ethiopia as in other countries in the Sahel and Horn of Africa dependent on the international relief system: too often an operation which brings food in too little and too late. The time-lag between decisions being made and relief arriving in-country is too long to ensure that the food reaches beneficiaries inland before the hungry season begins. At least in Ethiopia there is a food aid pipeline which flows from one year to the next. Thus, 1990 pledges of food were still arriving in 1991; a completely new system did not have to be set up from scratch. But the international delivery system is not doing justice to the objectives of EW, by failing to provide a *timely* response to timely warnings, lending weight to the argument for pre-positioned food reserves.

Food crisis and famine have been closely linked to war and conflict in Ethiopia. Where conflict has been protracted, relief corridors and special arrangements were negotiated to deliver humanitarian assistance. The situation was much more difficult where conditions were changing rapidly, as happened in the months before the government was overthrown. Relief routes were suddenly disrupted before contingency measures could be set up. Formal EWS have never tried to predict political events or the consequences of civil insecurity: it is certainly beyond the remit of the EWPS in the RRC. This is a sensitive topic. But the time has come for EW to be linked to regional monitoring of conflict in the Horn to try and provide advance warning, at least of refugee influxes so that preparatory measures can be taken. International components of the EWS are best placed to provide such forecasts of disruptions to food security caused by political instability.

The policy and aid environment in Ethiopia has changed considerably under the new government. There are better prospects for long-term food-security planning, for more constructive donations of development aid, and for more decentralized disaster management with a longer-term perspective. Above all, there is a need for investment in infrastructure, especially roads, in famine-prone parts of the country. But there are still many challenges to the new order, the most serious being political and civil insecurity.

The following areas deserve attention if the link between information about deteriorating food security and response is to be strengthened, and if more appropriate response options are to be developed in the future. First, while the EWS must certainly be able to predict the threat of a major famine, its remit should be extended to monitoring chronic food insecurity and detecting localized pockets of acute food crisis as well. In a country where there is a serious and endemic food problem, it is not appropriate that famine should always be the reference point. An approach is needed that identifies and tries to deal with the underlying causes of food insecurity as well.

Second, the new 'Directives for Disaster Prevention and Management', implemented by the Transitional Government, introduce a very different approach to disaster management, to some extent trying to tackle the underlying problems of vulnerability as well as immediate short-term relief needs. In particular, they provide the opportunity for developing a more decentralized EWS, which in time should be better placed to monitor local coping strategies and localized pockets of crisis, as well as developing more flexible response options. But in a country the size of Ethiopia, a decentralized EWS must remain under the control of a national unit, for the purposes of co-ordination and standardization, and for making regional relief allocations and international appeals.

The proposed changes to the EW/response system require considerable investment of resources and training if they are to work, especially to strengthen the capacity of local-level personnel. After years of a highly centralized system, the local administration is weak and under-resourced. The change in direction must be supported by a long-term commitment of aid.

The third point concerns speed. The above changes are likely to be (and should be) slow and gradual. In a country where many people are highly vulnerable to acute food insecurity, it is important that one system is not dismantled before another is in place. Food relief will be required for many more years. It is important to try and speed up the current system, which is too slow to make use of the benefits of *early* warnings. There are three options:

- Decision-making by donor agencies should be speeded up, so that major pledges of relief are made in September/October, and all the required food is pledged by January, giving enough time for the delivery system to bring in food before the hungry season begins.
- The EWS should provide earlier signals, in particular the annual harvest and needs assessments must be carried out earlier, with less certainty but allowing more lead time for food deliveries to be made. There is room for some merging of the two-track EWS of government and donors.
- Most importantly, more resources should be pre-positioned in-country to cut down on the lead time for delivering food from Europe or the US, and in view of the extreme logistical constraints to distributing food within the country. The food-security reserve should tackle this. In view of Ethiopia's annual relief needs there is no doubt that the reserve would be used frequently and its stocks turned over. The proposed rules, that the reserve should perform a loan function, to bridge the gap until imported food aid arrives, could make a major contribution to more timely deliveries of relief. But for it to work, a commitment from donors to resource the reserve is critical. Ideally, the locations of the reserve should be decentralized.

Some combination of all three options would be the best solution.

CHAPTER 5
Sudan

Introduction

This case-study provides an extreme example of how a hostile political environment can thwart the smooth running of an EW and response system, with reference to both the politics of donor/government relations, and internal domestic politics. In 1989 the government of Sadiq el Mahdi was overthrown by a military coup. By 1990–91, relations were at an all-time low between the new government, led by Lt-General al-Bashir, and Western donor governments. As a result, the relief operation launched in north Sudan in late 1990 and early 1991 was surrounded by tense negotiations and antagonism. EW information became a pawn in political wrangling, made worse by the government's reluctance to acknowledge the scale of the food problem, for fear of undermining its well-publicized policy of food self-sufficiency. A delayed and inadequate relief operation and the outbreak of famine in parts of the country resulted.

The case-study focuses on north Sudan, and in particular on Darfur, the westernmost state in the north, widely agreed to be one of the most food-insecure (see Figure 5.1). This is not to deny the unparalleled scale of the food crisis, displacement and suffering in south Sudan, where directly and indirectly the civil war has claimed the lives of hundreds of thousands of people over the last decade. However, this study is principally about drought-related food crisis, where the particular problems of EW and relief in a war zone cannot be held responsible for failure to prevent famine.

Widespread drought triggered a major food crisis in 1984–5. In 1990–91, drought triggered a crisis once again. The difference between these two episodes is that by the early 1990s, poverty and chronic food insecurity had escalated in north Sudan. There had been rapid economic decline, the war had drained national resources, and many households had been unable to rebuild assets since the 1984–5 famine. Thus, by the time the crisis hit the country at the beginning of the 1990s, the population was considerably more vulnerable than in the early 1980s. Eventually, just over 400000t of relief food were delivered to north Sudan by the end of 1991. But this was only about 50 per cent of estimated requirements for the year. In the remote state of Darfur, the delivery rate was even worse; barely one-fifth of estimated needs was distributed. In many parts of the country malnutrition rates soared, and there is some evidence of famine-related deaths.

This case-study of north Sudan is a story of weak EW capacity associated with the withdrawal of donor funds, complex and opaque decision-making processes, a lack of consensus between the government and donors about the scale of the food crisis, and a sorely inadequate relief response. Above

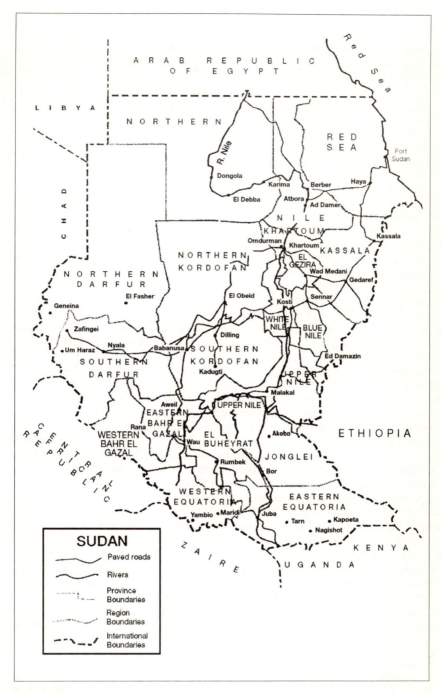

Figure 5.1 *Map of Sudan*
Source: Maxwell, 1991.

85

all, it is a story of soured political relations between Western donors and the Sudanese Government which seriously impeded the smooth running of the relief operation.

Food security in north Sudan, focusing on Darfur

In 1989, in north Sudan alone, it was estimated that over half the population was vulnerable to food insecurity.[1] The proportion has certainly increased since, due to an interaction of trends and shocks.

The 'trends' include, first, general weakness of the macro-economy. Between 1984 and 1990 per capita income had fallen by 25 per cent in real terms, the debt burden had reached crisis point, the budget deficit was 50 per cent of expenditure, and inflation was running at over 100 per cent. Second, the food system has become unstable and inequitable. Domestic sorghum prices were running at close to three times the import parity price in September/October 1990, even at the shadow exchange rate, and many of the poorest people did not have access to cheaper rations of sorghum. Third, the increasing commercialization of agriculture has favoured the growth of large-scale mechanized farming in the centre of the country, at the expense of the traditional rainfed agricultural sector which has been sorely neglected. While the economy performed so poorly, the population has been growing at about 2.8 per cent a year, and urbanization at more than twice that rate.

The most important 'shocks' are drought, the influx of refugees, and war.[2] The population has become more vulnerable to food insecurity as a result of the negative long-term trends, and hence less well equipped to cope with the short-term shocks, like the drought in 1990–91. During the 1990s, the pace of economic decline has simply accelerated. Sudan used to be self-sufficient in cereals, until the mid-1980s when the rate of increase in population and consumption needs outstripped production. In 1990–91, the figure for annual cereals consumption was believed to be about 3.3 million tonnes, of which 2.8 million tonnes were for northern Sudan. The cereals deficit in north Sudan was estimated to be a record 1.1 million tonnes (FAO, 1990c).

The food-security problems of north Sudan are amplified in the case of Darfur. The state has a population of 3–4 million. It covers a huge area, the size of Kenya, with a broad range of conditions from arid desert in the north to savannah woodland in the south. It is also one of the least-developed states in the country, due to its marginal geographic, economic and political status. For example, it received less than half the average per capita financial support from central government of other regions in the north during the first half of the 1980s (ILO, 1987).

There are few economic alternatives to rainfed crop production and livestock herding, but Darfur's full agricultural potential is severely

---

[1] Most of this section is based on Maxwell, 1989.
[2] Arguably, the prolonged civil war in the south of the country is no longer a 'short-term shock', because of its duration. There is a direct link between increasing impoverishment in parts of the country and the growing incidence of conflict, often based on long-standing tribal enmities.

constrained by its remoteness, and hence lack of access to markets outside the region. It is connected to Khartoum only by sand tracks, an inefficient rail link and irregular air services. Communications within the state are equally difficult, and during the rainy season often hazardous and impossible (Buchanan-Smith and Mohammed, 1991).

In 1989, it was estimated that about 60 per cent of the population in Darfur were food-insecure (Swift and Gray, 1989). The most vulnerable groups have been identified as the resource-poor, with little or low-quality land, pastoralists with too few animals to remain viable, female-headed and elderly households; those located in marginal areas, or unable to adapt their livelihoods to changing conditions; and those located in areas of high civil insecurity.

Famine has persisted in Sudan throughout the 1980s and beginning of the 1990s. In the south, where the scale of human suffering has been greatest, there is an unequivocal link between war and food insecurity. In the north, famine is usually triggered by drought, against the backdrop of the negative economic trends described above.

Because of the remoteness of Darfur, inadequate production due to drought can quickly translate into a serious regional food shortage, as there will be no compensating trade flows from outside. Drought is not uncommon, and people have well-developed strategies to cope with large inter-annual variations in rainfall. The problem is that these strategies have come under increasing pressure in recent decades: over the last 30 years there has been a declining trend in rainfall (Clift-Hill, 1987), combined with a growing population and very limited economic growth, leading to increased vulnerability within the Darfur population.

There have been more than 20 famines in the last 100 years in Darfur (de Waal, 1989). In the last decade the incidence has increased. In 1984–5 there was a 'famine that kills' (of which there have only been two during the last 100 years), the culmination of a series of consecutive drought years in the early 1980s, ignored by the Nimeiri government. For political reasons the response was very late. Eventually, over 170000t of food aid were delivered, between 1984 and 1986, but too late to prevent deaths of up to 150000. In 1987–8 there were again localized food crises. The smaller-scale Western Relief Operation was launched, using in-country resources of just over 14000t of food aid for Darfur (Buchanan-Smith, 1989). In 1989–90, localized food crises recurred and relief assistance of 17000 to 20000t was requested for North Darfur (APU, 1990) — but to little avail; only the very limited resources of the regional strategic food-security reserve were distributed, about 1700t. This lack of response intensified the consequences of a second poor agricultural season in 1990–91.

Relief operations in Darfur have been continuous between 1990–91 and 1994. An 'endemic crisis' is emerging in Sudan, especially in the west, similar to Ethiopia. What were once coping strategies for mitigating the effects of famine have often become integral parts of regular livelihood systems. Food entitlements are becoming weaker, and are closely linked to food production.

The impoverished economy has exaggerated the impact of international aid as a source of much-needed investment in development, and to shore up the most food-insecure groups in times of crisis. But international aid is closely tied to political relations between Western donor governments and the Sudanese Government.

After the famine of the mid-1980s, Sudan enjoyed a period of generous aid donations. The severity of the famine in Darfur in 1984–5 gave it an unprecedented prominence with donors: more than 20 new projects were either planned or being implemented in Darfur in 1986, a number of them focusing on food security, including the Darfur Regional Government Project funded by the ODA. This project supported the Agricultural Planning Unit (APU) within the regional government, which emphasized food-security planning, both for the long term and to strengthen short-term disaster preparedness and famine response.

By the end of 1990 and beginning of 1991, few of these projects remained. In the changed political environment of Sudan, and under increasing pressure from ethnic conflict in parts of Darfur, many projects closed prematurely and expatriates were withdrawn. ODA suspended all development aid to Sudan from January 1991, as did the US, and the EU suspended negotiations on Lomé IV. Sudan became a victim of the new form of political conditionality applied to Western aid, as its new Islamic government was seen to abuse human rights and to fail to comply with criteria of good governance (see Chapter 3). By 1991, humanitarian relief was virtually the only international aid resource available to the country.

The EW/response system

Early warning
Before 1984–5, no formal EWS existed in Sudan. It had a weak, or non-existent, relief infrastructure. Insufficient information was seen to have been a major impediment to the smooth running of the mid-1980s relief operation, a lack both of *early* warning and of information for planning and targeting once the operation was under way. During the second half of the 1980s there was a flurry of activity to set up EWS, as in many other countries in Africa.

Sudan enjoyed a particularly well-funded 'rehabilitation' phase after the 1984–5 emergency; setting up EW information projects was often part of the package. In 1990–91, however, the EWS in Sudan was less developed than in most of the other countries considered in this book. It, too, had fallen victim to the politics of aid. EW in Sudan has been characterized by a 'stop–go' approach: systems have been set up, run for a couple of years, collapsed when international funding stopped, and then, with a further food crisis, a new system has had to be installed. This has disrupted the evolutionary process of developing an information system of 'learning by doing', and has inhibited the accumulation of baseline data.

The national EWS, set up in 1986 in the Relief and Rehabilitation Commission in Khartoum, was supported by the Nordic Countries Trust Fund through the UNDP-UN Emergency Office of Sudan. Barely a year later the technical advisers' contracts were abruptly terminated because of a disagreement with the government and donor funding was withdrawn. The

EWS continued to function, but was poorly resourced, and as a result, carried out no primary data collection and became heavily centralized and oriented towards central Sudan. In 1990, donor support was restored through UNDP, with technical assistance from FAO. This strengthened the EWS, but support has focused on monitoring physical production indicators rather than socio-economic ones. Meanwhile, there has been a rapid turnover in personnel within the national EWS associated with the change in government.

During the mid-1980s SCF (UK)'s relief operation set up a monitoring and information system in Darfur, principally to plan and target the ongoing relief operation. In 1986 donor funds were withdrawn and the system was wound down; new national monitoring programmes were regarded as adequate replacement. In a country as large, diverse and with such poor communications as Sudan, this was unrealistic. In 1987 the APU of the Darfur regional government, supported by ODA, set up a new monitoring system, combining market monitoring with an annual pre-harvest survey. The latter — a joint effort of regional government and NGOs — formed the backbone of the system. Meanwhile, the Sudanese Red Crescent Society (SRC) was running a Drought Monitoring Programme (DMP) based on its network of branches in North Darfur and in 1988 Oxfam launched a nutritional surveillance project. With this diverse range of EW sources, the APU started to produce a two-monthly *Food and Agriculture Bulletin*, effectively the EW bulletin for the region.[3]

By the end of 1990, the regional system was crumbling, at precisely the moment when it was most needed. With the withdrawal of donor funding and expatriate advisers[4] in the climate of deteriorating Government of Sudan/donor relations, only Oxfam's nutritional surveillance programme was left intact. The food security and EW monitoring system in Darfur was thus substantially weakened by the time the 1991 relief operation got under way. As the main NGO involved in running the relief operation, SCF (UK) had to set up a new state-level information system once again, picking up the pieces of what had been so rapidly destroyed by the abrupt withdrawal of donor support. Inevitably, it takes time to install an information system. Initially SCF's system was geared to information needs within Darfur, for monitoring and targeting the relief operation. By 1992 a more comprehensive EWS was running, and regular bulletins were being produced once again.

Sudan has long been covered by components of the international EWS. First, FAO's GIEWS carries out an annual harvest assessment, and was influential in alerting the world to Sudan's food problems in 1990, by

---

[3] Harvest surveys and market monitoring were carried out in South Darfur by Western Savannah Development Corporation and Jebel Marra Rural Development Project.

[4] The ODA-funded expatriates were withdrawn from El Fasher in August 1990, and the British Embassy would not allow them to return, although other British expatriates who had been evacuated were reinstated in Darfur. Indeed, SCF (UK) was in the process of setting up a programme with new expatriate staff for the relief operation in Darfur.

issuing a number of Special Alerts. Second, WFP has usually carried out an annual needs assessment, at the end of the calendar year, since 1991 combined with the FAO harvest mission. Third, the FEWS project of USAID has covered Sudan since 1985–6. There was still a FEWS representative in-country in 1990–91, although north Sudan has since been dropped from the project in line with US policy which bars the government from receiving any development aid. Within Khartoum, a number of aid agencies — WFP, UNICEF and the UN Emergency Unit[5] — started to produce their own information bulletins during 1991.

Decision-making to respond

The wide range of EW reports is matched by the numerous decision-making fora. In 1991 there was an intensive schedule of nine regular meetings in Khartoum, all relevant to information exchange and decision-making about the relief operation. But unlike some other countries, such as Chad, decision-making was not a joint donor/government exercise, and was not executed in a transparent way.

A key high-level donor group met every week, plus weekly meetings arranged by the UN Emergency Operations Group for UN agencies and donors, and by WFP for NGOs and donors, mainly geared to the logistics of the relief operation. The EU Delegation, British Embassy and USAID mission each held regular meetings with the main NGOs involved in the relief operation, usually those contracted by the respective donor to distribute its food aid. None of these meetings involved the government. To a large extent, parallel donor and government systems were set up. There were only three meetings when donors, NGOs and government came together: an Operations Supervisory Group meeting, chaired by the RRC Commissioner; a Relief Allocations Committee at a somewhat lower level;[6] and the weekly Technical Co-ordination Committee (TCC), chaired by the RRC. This last committee had been important during the 1980s for information exchange, but its role became less significant as EW information became more politically sensitive, at which point the committee focused more on logistics.

This intensive timetable of meetings disguised the fact that decision-making was actually very opaque. Many key meetings relating to the relief operation were held off the record, particularly in the case of donor/government negotiations and agreements. The numerous meetings also reflect the complexity of the political situation and of the relief operation in 1990–91. Many actors were involved, and there was a lack of clear division of responsibilities between different 'co-ordinating' agencies, with the result that some meetings overlapped. There were numerous obstacles to transporting large quantities of food around the country, and to allocating

---

[5] The UN Emergency Unit had initially been set up in 1988 as the co-ordinating unit for Operation Lifeline Sudan (OLS). In February 1990, its remit was expanded to cover north Sudan.
[6] This committee proved somewhat redundant in 1990–91 because most decisions about geographical allocations of food aid had already been made in donor agency headquarters.

responsibility for different parts of the relief operation. The lack of freely circulating information meant that donor agencies were particularly dependent on NGOs working in the field to keep them informed about conditions in different parts of the country; hence, the 'closed' series of donor/NGO meetings.

By the end of 1990, the Bashir military government had put in place a much stronger regional administration in Darfur. In the past, regional structures had been unable to cope with running relief operations, for example during the Western Relief Operation of 1987–8 (Buchanan-Smith, 1989). The Darfur Regional Emergency Food Security Committee was established in April 1990. Area and Rural Council Food Relief committees were set up in 1991, following a Relief Planning Workshop organized by SCF (UK) in January. Although the function of these committees was to facilitate the relief operation rather than to take strategic decisions, this network greatly strengthened state-level relief administration.

The story of EW/response in 1990–91

There were two phases: the lead-up to the relief operation being launched, when assessments of needs were being made, and modalities were being negotiated and planned, lasting from approximately July/August 1990 until January 1991, and the period after an official appeal had been made in early January 1991, some food aid had been pledged, and the relief operation was under way. The emphasis at this stage was on monitoring to detect the impact of the relief being delivered and any deterioration in food-security conditions, rather than on EW.

EW signals and decisions to respond

The 1989–90 harvest had been poor, especially in Darfur, but little relief assistance had been provided. The population was particularly vulnerable to drought in 1990–91, not only because of deteriorating economic conditions, but also because they had no grain reserves from previous harvests. There were many forecasts of 'another 1984–5' (e.g. FEWS, 1990b; APU *et al.*, 1990; Graham, 1990). The 1984–5 scenario was not, however, re-enacted. In particular, there was much less population displacement. But nevertheless there were high rates of malnutrition, depletion of assets and impoverishment on a scale impossible to quantify, and there was evidence of excess mortality (Kelly and Buchanan-Smith, 1994).

Because the 1989–90 harvest had been poor and relief unforthcoming, it was not hard to predict that a second inadequate harvest could be disastrous. The APU issued such warnings for Darfur, in its *Food and Agriculture Bulletin* in 1990. In June 1990, FEWS (1990a) estimated that over one million people dependent on traditional rainfed agriculture in North Darfur were particularly vulnerable as they entered the 1990 agricultural season with depleted reserves and resources. As early as April 1990, GIEWS (FAO, 1990a) had recommended that 100000t be made available for Darfur and Kordofan; it gradually intensified its warnings in the absence of a

91

donor response and as the prospects of a poor agricultural season became apparent from about July/August 1990 onwards.

Everything hinged on the performance of the 1990–91 harvest. FAO took the unusual step of carrying out two assessments before the final harvest assessment, in July to monitor planting and in September to carry out a mid-season assessment. Both reported unfavourable prospects, mainly because of late and uneven rains. FAO first forecast a national grain deficit of one million tonnes in September: advance allocations of food aid were urged, especially because of the shortfall in donor pledges during 1990; cereals stocks were exhausted in several vulnerable areas, and prices had risen to levels deemed unaffordable by large sections of the population (FAO, 1990b). The national EWS bulletin in mid-July 1990 had reported millet prices at three times their level in June 1989. By October grain prices had again risen by over 300 per cent.

In Darfur, the APU co-ordinated a 'Rapid Assessment' on food security at the end of September, with RRC, SCF (UK), WFP, Oxfam and SRC. They made the first quantified assessment of food-relief needs for the state: a provisional estimate of 144000t, 35 per cent of it required immediately, and concluded that:

> The results are extremely disturbing, confirming the worst expectations raised by last year's poor harvest and inadequate relief response, compounded by the even worse harvest now expected for this year. The overall picture shows clear signs of a developing famine (Sharp, 1990:1).

This assessment was endorsed by the Darfur Food Security Committee and the results were reported in the national EWS bulletin in October. A pre-harvest survey in Darfur in October followed, showing that cereals production would meet only 11 per cent of consumption needs. Even in South Darfur only 60 per cent of consumption needs were expected to be met. An estimated 1 655 000 people were affected.

The definitive word on food aid needs was eventually provided in December, with the FAO and WFP assessments. Using the food-balance-sheet approach, the FAO team estimated a national deficit in north Sudan of 1.1 million tonnes, mostly concentrated in the west (Darfur and Kordofan) where the deficit was estimated to be 700000t. Commercial imports were not expected to exceed 100000t. Food aid needs in north Sudan were estimated to be a record one million tonnes. North Darfur was picked out as particularly badly hit (FAO, 1990c).

The WFP mission came up with a slightly lower figure for total food aid needs, of 859000t for north Sudan for 7.68 million people, and 274000t for Darfur for two million people. They concluded that a food crisis was already in progress, and therefore food aid should be requested by government and pledged by donors immediately (WFP, 1990).

The national EWS produced its own note on Sudan's food balance in January. With some very minor adjustments, it reiterated the deficit of 1.1 million tonnes and recommended an immediate contingency action plan to transport food to the west, to North Darfur and to North Kordofan in particular (EWSU, 1991).

Despite these numerous reports, the government made frequent public statements, from September 1990 onwards, refuting the seriousness of the crisis. In mid-September the Minister for Agriculture stated that high crop yields were expected and that rumours of impending famine were unfounded; in October, the Embassy in London issued a statement saying that relief work would be largely unnecessary due to increases in food production, and the Minister of Finance, also speaking in London, denied there was a famine, rather a 'manageable' food gap.

There were a number of contradictions. Despite these public statements, the Darfur Food Security Committee, chaired by government officials, drew up food aid distribution plans as early as October 1990, although the governing Regional Salvation Committee refused to pass the APU harvest assessment on to Khartoum until mid-December. Some government ministers were privately admitting the need for relief, despite the intransigent position taken in public. At the end of October the government issued its first request to donor agencies in Khartoum, asking for 'urgent delivery . . . of 75 000t . . . because of the acute food scarcity that prevails'. This was a small percentage of the total estimated need predicted at the time. Eventually, when the FAO harvest assessment was completed, the government endorsed its figure of one million tonnes of food aid needed, and at the turn of the year the Minister of Finance formally requested this level of assistance. Nevertheless, tension continued between the government and the donor community about the need and nature of the relief operation. President al-Bashir accused foreign relief agencies of defaming Sudan by begging on behalf of the Sudanese people.

The government did take some action independently in response to the crisis. In Darfur in April 1991 the state government arranged for the importation of 48 000t of wheat flour from Libya, to be bartered for Darfurian livestock and sold at cost price. In central Sudan irrigated land was being taken out of cash-crop production and sown to wheat instead, to reduce the large national grain deficit;[7] an increase of about 80 per cent in area planted to wheat produced a record harvest of 621 000t in April (FAO, 1991b). Most of these actions, however, made only a small impact on a very large problem.

On the donor side, despite the early calls to action by the UN and intensive lobbying by NGOs, the first food aid pledges were not made until November/December 1990, and then only for very small amounts in response to specific NGO requests. For example, in November ODA made 10 000t food available to CARE for Kordofan, and in December 5 000t to SCF (UK) for Darfur. The EU and USAID also pledged some food to different NGOs, mainly for western Sudan. It was not until the results of the FAO and WFP assessments were available that Western donors started to make larger pledges; USAID eventually pledged 100 000t, and the EU 110 000t. By late January just over 300 000t had been pledged. Thereafter, pledging was slow and far behind estimated needs. Even though the

---

[7] Although increased wheat production helped to improve food availability, the employment and income effects of switching from cash crops to wheat are usually negative, which affects food entitlements.

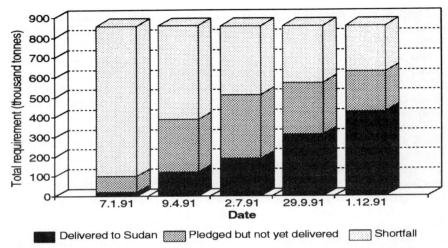

Figure 5.2 *Sudan: emergency food aid, 1990–91 – record of availability and deliveries*
Source: WFP.

EU launched its Special Plan for Africa in May 1991, providing an extra 117 000t to Sudan, by early July still only two-thirds of Sudan's requirements had been committed (see Figure 5.2).

The EW signals had certainly created an awareness of the impending crisis among donor representatives. In late September 1990 a draft *aide-mémoire* on relief assistance was circulated among them, stipulating certain conditions to be met by the government before they would assist in launching a relief operation. These included a requirement that the government should publicly declare an emergency and make a formal request for assistance; that it should recognize the neutrality of humanitarian assistance; that NGOs should be facilitated in their operations; and that a favourable exchange rate should be applied. The exchange-rate condition was accepted at the end of October, but lack of agreement on the other conditions became a major stumbling-block.

The deadlock was eventually broken with government acceptance of the results of the FAO harvest assessment in December. Relief assistance was formally requested in a letter of 24 December. But the conditionality *aide-mémoire* was never agreed. In January it was overtaken by a Logistics Coordination Plan drawn up by WFP, agreed first with donors and NGOs and then with the government, outlining the modalities of the relief operation and the division of responsibilities between the different institutions. This marked a turning-point towards a more pragmatic approach to launching the relief operation.

The relief operation

Under the logistics agreement the UN was to be the umbrella agency, working with the government on behalf of the donor community. This arrangement was fraught with difficulties. The donors' mistrust of government and the possible abuse of food aid for military and other non-relief purposes meant that all food was allocated to NGOs for distribution, and none to WFP. This led to a prolonged stand-off between government and donors over internal transport arrangements, exacerbated by increasing hostility between donors and the WFP field representative, who was felt to be too close to government and not sufficiently supportive of the donor/NGO case. Eventually NGOs were obliged to play a major role in the transport operation.

Late aid pledges, combined with internal transport problems, translated into extremely late deliveries to the final destination. By the end of 1990, very little food had arrived in Sudan, apart from 19 000t of WFP wheat. USAID had about 30 000t of food in store in Kosti. The balance was arriving in a trickle. In February 5 000t of ODA food aid for Darfur were delivered to Port Sudan. The first EU shipments reached the port in April. By July — the start of the hungry season — only about 30 per cent of total food needs had arrived in Port Sudan (see Figure 5.2).

The hardest part of the journey was still to come. The food had to be transported far inland to Darfur, more than 2 000km away. Experience has shown time and again how difficult and slow it is to transport relief food to the west. Even in the Western Relief Operation in 1987–8, when food was being transported only from central Sudan, it took nine months to distribute a small fraction of the total planned amount, well behind schedule. Slow transport was one of the principal reasons (Buchanan-Smith, 1989).

Many of the same transport problems were encountered in 1991: fuel shortages; insecurity and banditry on the roads which meant that contractors were unwilling to make the journey; competition with more attractive contracts for distributing food to more-accessible Kordofan; and the onset of the rainy season. Other factors unique to 1991 compounded the problem. The trucking market in El Obeid in Kordofan, which was chosen as the hub for trucking food into Darfur, proved inadequate. In June the transport hub had to be brought back to Omdurman, where the market is better served with trucks and contractors. In May, the government's withdrawal of large-denomination currency notes caused a serious cash shortage, adversely affecting transport operations. In August, just as the trucking operation was beginning to function better, the governor of Darfur annulled all transport contracts into the state, installing a single contractor instead who failed to fulfil requirements.

The effects of the late arrival of food into Port Sudan, and the subsequent transport difficulties, are summed up in Figure 5.3. By the beginning of July, only 13 548t had arrived in Darfur, a mere 5 per cent of estimated need. Yet this was the start of the hungry season. Eventually an airlift was launched during the rainy season to Geneina, the westernmost Area Council in the state, and to El Fasher. Even by early December 1991, less than one-fifth of Darfur's total requirements had arrived.

In Darfur there was a serious information gap during 1991 because of the disarray in the EW and food-monitoring system. Oxfam's nutritional surveillance project provided greatest continuity, although with limited

95

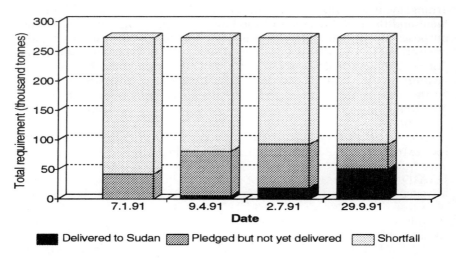

Figure 5.3 *Sudan: emergency food aid to Darfur, 1990–91 – record of availability and deliveries*
Note:
Some figures on pledges and deliveries to Darfur are approximate. Figures from different sources sometimes contradict.
Source: WFP, SCF (UK).

coverage. Results from its spot surveys are presented in Table 5.1. There was growing concern over the high and rising rates of malnutrition; for example, the malnutrition rates recorded in Dar Zaghawa were three times as high as those recorded in the previous year. One of Oxfam's reports in April concluded that the tiny amounts of relief distributed had had very little impact and that the situation was worse than in 1984–5 (Oxfam, 1991).

In the vacuum of systematic monitoring, many of the reports about conditions in Darfur were contradictory. For example, GIEWS reported deaths from starvation as early as February 1991 and continued to issue alarming accounts of conditions: in June 1991 that 'many families in Darfur are completely dependent on wild food (mainly *mukheit*)' and that food prices were well beyond the purchasing power of many people (FAO, 1991b). Meanwhile, in May, a high-level donor mission to the state reported that the situation was more or less under control and that the new rainy season had started. At a UN Emergency Operations Group meeting in Khartoum in July it was reported that the worst impact of famine had been averted and that there was sufficient emergency food for two to three months' relief operation. Later that same month, a USAID Food Security Cable gave a much more alarming account: 'Possibly thousands of Darfur residents are in imminent danger of starvation due to slowness of emergency relief commodities into the region'. This put the Darfur operation high on the agenda once again, and for a while dispelled complacency.

Table 5.1   Sudan: malnutrition rates reported by Oxfam in North Darfur during 1991

Location	% of children under 5 < 80% weight for height	% of children under 5 < 70% weight for height	Month
Malha	22	2	Jan./Feb.
Mareiga	31	1	Jan./Feb.
Cuma	17	2	Jan./Feb.
Dar Zaghawa (5 VCs)	17	2	March
Umm Keddada RC (5 VCs)	18	3	March
Mareiga	38	7	March/April
Fuda VC (Mareiga (RC)	19	0	March/April
Shakhakha VC (Mareiga RC)	14	0	March/April
Kebkabiya RC	19	2	May
El Sereif RC	18	1	May
Seraf Umra RC	20	2	May
El Fasher town	25	2	July

Note:
RC = Rural Council; VC = Village Council.
Source: Oxfam.

By the end of 1991 the picture of what had happened in Darfur was still very confused. A tiny fraction of estimated needs had reached the population. The widely held view in Khartoum was that somehow people had 'coped', and there had not been famine or food insecurity on the scale predicted. Others disputed this. There was a lack of information to provide unequivocal evidence in support of either case.

Evaluating the EW information

Different components of the EWS had exaggerated the severity and scale of the famine expected in north Sudan in 1991 in the view of many donor agency representatives (pers. comm., various aid agency representatives, Khartoum, December 1991). Despite the fact that little relief had reached beneficiaries, especially in Darfur, there was apparently no evidence of famine on the scale predicted, in terms of the conventional indicators of excess mortality and population displacement. The truth of the matter was that there were few monitoring systems which were able to detect famine-related deaths. Many NGOs and other monitoring agencies felt that it would have been politically unacceptable to do so in 1991. Yet these were the data donors were requesting — some kind of 'body-count' to convince them that the shortfall in relief deliveries really had been a failure.

In an analysis of the data that are available for 1991, Kelly and Buchanan-Smith (1994) have challenged the donors' assumption that there was no famine. Their argument is based on two key points. First, that the predominant view of famine held by Westerners is over-simplified and bears little resemblance to what actually happens. Famine is rarely a case of visible mass starvation. Instead, it is usually a much more complex process whereby an episode of acute food insecurity leads to social disruption and excess mortality among some groups of the affected population — a process which may be difficult to detect without detailed monitoring and careful analysis. In 1984–5, de Waal (1989) carried out this kind of analysis of famine in Darfur, which led him to conclude that there had been around 95 000 excess deaths. Without this investigation, it is almost certain that the scale of the excess mortality would have gone unnoticed and unrecorded. In 1991 there was no such investigation.

Second, just because excess deaths were not documented in 1991 does not mean that they did not occur. Malnutrition among children increased significantly, not only in Darfur (see Table 5.1). Kelly and Buchanan-Smith suggest that a rise (from 7 to 15 per cent) in the proportion of malnourished children less than 80 per cent weight for height can translate into a mortality increase of 25 per cent, or 40 per cent if the proportion rises to 20 per cent. But this could easily go unnoticed if the relevant data are not collected. On this basis they conclude that data from the anthropometric surveys carried out in 1991 strongly suggest that child-mortality rates did increase in north Sudan, by at least 20 per cent. For example, in El Fasher town a rate of malnutrition of 25 per cent was found in July 1991, compared with 13 per cent in July 1992 once relief was finally reaching Darfur in significant quantities (SCF (UK), 1992, July). In camps of displaced drought victims in Kordofan, data collected by the Ministry of Health (between late December 1990 and early March 1991) confirm that children under five were dying at a rate of more than 10 a week, which suggests a mortality rate almost double the expected level.

Rather than 'coping' successfully with drought, many so-called 'coping strategies' had serious and even fatal consequences. Cutting back on food consumption in order to preserve productive assets for the future causes malnutrition rates and the risk of death to rise, babies are born underweight, children's growth is stunted, their mental development impaired and their immune competence reduced. This is all the more serious for communities which have experienced acute food insecurity year after year.

The conventional wisdom within the aid community at the end of 1991, that there had been no famine in Sudan, has major and potentially dangerous implications for the credibility of EW information and for how aid agencies plan their relief response in the future. Careful analysis of the data suggests that there were substantial excess deaths in 1991, almost certainly of greater proportions than is generally assumed, and this occurred despite deliveries of half a million tonnes of relief food. The original needs assessment was probably of the correct order of magnitude. Rather than proving the inaccuracy of the early warnings, the failure of the relief response contributed to real suffering in 1991 and to leaving the population more vulnerable to future droughts.

One of the reasons for these ill-informed assumptions was a lack of adequate and detailed information. Of the five country case-studies in this book, Sudan had the least-developed EW capacity in 1990–91, despite the fact that it became one of the most food-insecure countries in sub-Saharan Africa during the 1980s and has had significant, but patchy, EW investment.

The scale and severity of the food crisis in 1990–91, after two consecutive bad harvests, meant that a sophisticated EWS was not required to warn of the impending problem. It was clear early on that relief assistance would be necessary. The alerts which were issued from July 1990 were certainly timely. What was lacking was a more refined and detailed analysis of who was most at risk, to give more than just an overall picture of total needs. During 1991 the lack of this kind of detail became most apparent. In Darfur, it was not clear what impact the slow relief response was having, to what extent and how assets were being depleted, and whether a health crisis was developing. This kind of information could have been used to target the limited relief resources available, and to ensure that decision-makers in Khartoum were kept regularly informed about the changing situation.

Some of the reasons why EW capabilities were so undeveloped in Sudan have been described above. The EWS has developed in a piecemeal fashion, without clear strategic planning, symptomatic of dependence on donor resources. While a sub-national EWS was established and strengthened in Darfur after 1985, directly linked to new aid-funded projects, there was no parallel activity in Kordofan region. And the national EWS became increasingly centralized, losing touch with its regional contacts as it lost its internationally funded resource base.

There are strong arguments for a more decentralized EWS in Sudan, because of the size and diversity of the country, and because of its extremely poor communications. It is very difficult to monitor local food economies centrally when they are thousands of miles from the capital. The arguments hold strongest for Darfur. Yet, there has never been a well-planned approach to linking national and sub-national EWS since the very first project to support EW within the RRC in 1986–7, when decentralization to regional and local institutions was proposed (Eldredge and Rydjeski, 1988). Since then resources have been inadequate to promote a decentralized approach; sub-national EW data have been used at national level in an *ad hoc* way.

As a consequence of the weak formal EWS, NGOs rapidly set up their own rudimentary monitoring systems in 1991, in both Kordofan and Darfur. The classic problems of starting from scratch were encountered in both cases: the field monitors posted to run the relief operation collected large amounts of raw data which were beyond the analytical capacity of the limited resources available. A 'learning process' had to be repeated by the new teams and it took about nine months to establish an appropriate framework for data collection and analysis, which was also acceptable to the authorities.

The lack of systematic, detailed and reliable EW data in-country was reflected in reporting by the international community, which is usually only as good as the national or sub-national EW data available to it. Although the FAO and WFP end-of-year assessments were critical in gathering and analysing available data in order to come up with an overall picture of the food deficit and an estimate of relief needs, the respective missions have limited opportunity to carry out primary data collection. They mostly rely on government data, backed up with short field trips. Primary data collection is also beyond the remit of FEWS. And most of the information bulletins issued by other agencies in Khartoum, such as UNICEF, were similarly dependent on secondary data.

In the absence of adequate and regular food-security monitoring, donor agencies become dependent on one-off field trips to carry out rapid assessments. A number of such missions visited Darfur during 1991. Had good information and data been available in El Fasher, these missions could have been an important means of disseminating that information and conveying messages back to Khartoum. But the information was patchy or non-existent. The missions made their own best guesses on the basis of what they saw and heard. The danger was that these could become very subjective snapshots. Inevitably only a limited number of places could be visited and generalizations had to be made. Different people put different interpretations on the same indicators; for example, in July 1991 a USAID mission to Darfur brought back alarming reports of 'a serious famine, with local resources having been totally exhausted'. Famine deaths were reported, the abandonment of some villages, and that coping strategies had run out (USAID/Sudan Food Security Reporting Cable, July 1991). Less than a month later, an EU mission to South Darfur returned with a different impression, and reported that conditions were satisfactory.

If there is no baseline information or continuous monitoring, it is impossible to verify these widely differing impressions and to assess the severity of the situation. Yet, this kind of 'disaster tourism' by high-level agency officials can be highly influential for the agency concerned.

The EWS fulfilled its most fundamental function in Sudan in 1990–91: it provided timely warning of a major food crisis. The delays encountered in launching the relief operation cannot be blamed on lack of EW. The failing of the EWS was the lack of continuous monitoring in sufficient detail to demonstrate the impact of the severely delayed relief operation. In this information vacuum, uninformed conclusions were drawn, which conveniently underestimated the impact of the shortfall in relief. The experience in Sudan in 1991 confirms the importance of a well-established formal EWS, even if it is no guarantee that a timely response will be launched. At least it provides continuous information, with some objectivity, and is an important counterbalance to the alternative — superficial 'disaster tourism'-type assessments, which are inevitably *ad hoc* and subjective.

Use of EW information

Figures 5.2 and 5.3 show clearly that EW information was not used to maximum advantage to launch a timely response in Sudan. This section investigates why.

Politics of relief in 1990–91

Political obstacles were the main hindrance. In none of the other case-studies in this book was EW information quite so politicized. In 1990, the government's position with respect to the emerging food crisis was very similar to 1984, when President Nimeiri refused to admit any danger of famine for fear of undermining the government's credibility. In 1990 the government did not totally deny the problem, but preferred to talk about it in terms of a 'food gap'. The government of President al-Bashir, which was barely a year old, was actively pursuing a policy of food self-sufficiency; among other things, this would give it greater independence from Western food aid donors. To acknowledge the possibility of famine would seriously undermine its position. Hence, although the national EWS within the RRC was repeating some of the alarming indicators from Darfur, including the results of the APU 'Rapid Assessment', government officials in decision-making positions took no heed. The government's own EWS was marginalized from the whole decision-making process.

On the donor side, Western governments were not well-disposed towards the Sudanese Government, which was viewed as a fundamentalist Islamic regime supportive of Iraq in the Gulf crisis. Donors were therefore determined to get involved in a relief operation only if guaranteed control. Stalemate resulted. The government was desperately trying to tone down the early warnings and predictions being made in 1991. Meanwhile, as noted earlier, the donors were stipulating a number of very specific and quite contrary conditions which the government had to meet before the relief operation could move forward.

In negotiations both sides were intransigent. On the government side, the head of the donor group was repeatedly denied access to a high-ranking member of the Revolutionary Command Council for many weeks; an audience was not granted with the President until 8 December 1990. On the donor side, one of the conditions given great prominence was that the government should admit that there was a 'humanitarian emergency' and issue a formal request for assistance — a condition not usually required, and which was not stipulated in Ethiopia, Chad or Kenya during the same period, where relief pledges were often made some time before an official appeal had been launched. Yet this condition and others relating to the modalities of the relief operation were stringently adhered to by the donor community until the end of 1990. Unofficial approaches to donors by members of the government were given no consideration.

EW information became caught up in the political wrangling, especially during the last four months of 1990, when the language used became highly sensitive. While donors talked of impending famine, the government stuck to its description of a 'food gap'. Public debate only intensified the antagonism. These sensitivities had most repercussions on the EWS within the country; government officers were expected to toe the official line, but at the same time the international community's condition of government admission of the existence of an emergency was common knowledge. No EW statement was free of political innuendo.

The international components of the EWS enjoyed more freedom; they were run by expatriates less restricted than their Sudanese counterparts in reporting what they saw. Nevertheless, they were not immune; two high-level expatriate relief officials were declared *personae non grata* by the government and asked to leave the country during the most hostile exchanges between the government and donors.[8] If information in the hands of the international agencies was to have any influence with the government then it had to recognize the unacceptability of certain terminology. For example, the FAO crop assessment never used the word 'famine', and was subsequently adopted by the government as the official food-balance estimate. The international components of the EWS thus played a particularly important role in Sudan in presenting and analysing information which might otherwise not have been freely available.

The political sensitivities of the relief operation meant that the UN ought to have played the central co-ordinating role, providing a strategic framework for Western NGOs and donor agencies. The reality was rather different. Responsibilities had not been clearly defined between different arms of the UN and individual agencies continued to follow their own agendas. In particular, there was inter-agency tension between WFP and the UN Emergency Unit in Khartoum, where a lack of clarity over role definition was exacerbated by personality clashes. It was usually WFP which took the leading role.

Meanwhile, there was antagonism between the donor community and WFP's field representative, especially during the most difficult period at the end of 1990. Both donors and NGOs were unhappy with WFP's position on how the relief operation should be run. Specifically, they did not want to see WFP handling resources on behalf of the government, and therefore lost confidence in its co-ordinating capacity.

These tensions hindered the UN from taking an authoritative lead based on a broad overview of humanitarian needs. Ultimately, it was the weekly donor group meeting, chaired in turn by one of the bilateral donor representatives, which was most influential in co-ordinating the donor position *vis-à-vis* the government, and which set the overall political and diplomatic context within which the UN agencies operated. Any potential benefits to be gained from a more 'objective' multilateral organization like the UN playing the key co-ordinating role were simply lost.

Like the Ethiopian famine, the Sudan famine in 1984–5 had a high media profile internationally, which prompted public debate about the adequacy of the West's response. However in 1990, during the critical months from August to the end of the year, when the relief operation should have started, the Western media were dominated by the Gulf crisis. When media coverage was stepped up after the end of the Gulf War, Sudan was given most coverage of all African countries because of the controversy surrounding its relief operation. For example, in April 1991 the BBC screened *Anatomy of a Famine*, which focused on the politics of the food emergency in Sudan, and finished with a panel discussion between ODA, USAID, the UN and the Sudanese Government. In both the British and the European

---

[8] The relief officer for Oxfam was asked to leave Sudan in October 1990, and the relief officer for the EU Delegation in Khartoum in January 1991.

Parliaments, questions were asked about the response to the Sudanese famine. It is reasonable to conclude that the media and international public opinion did have some influence on the response process, although the total commitments of food aid still fell far short of estimated need.

The most influential indicators

Eventually, as in Ethiopia and Chad, the FAO harvest assessment was the main trigger in getting the response process off the ground. But it was particularly significant in the Sudan case because it finally broke through the deadlock in negotiations between government and donors. The government endorsed the FAO results and recognized a 'food gap' in the order of one million tonnes, most of which would have to be provided through international assistance. On the donor side, the FAO and WFP assessments were seen as definitive evidence confirming earlier NGO reports about the need for relief. Serious planning at agency headquarters got under way only at this point.

Information available earlier, such as the results of the APU's rapid assessment in Darfur, seems to have had little impact on relief planning. It was only when it was incorporated into one of the high-profile UN assessments that it was really taken seriously by donors. The FAO and WFP assessments enjoy a credibility which information provided in-country does not. But decisions taken so late in the day are usually too late to ensure that assistance is provided before the hungry season starts.

In many African countries, evidence of acute food insecurity or famine is necessary to provoke an international relief response. This was exaggerated in the case of Sudan where, for political reasons, the donor community was reluctant to respond. Only sensational indicators would provoke action and maintain some momentum in the relief operation during 1991. In the words of one agency representative, the indicators had to be 'catastrophic' to be taken seriously and treated with urgency.

These were easily provided. Frustration about the slow response led to the use of evocative language in a desperate attempt to try and provoke action. In the BBC TV programme referred to earlier, the word 'megadeaths' was coined by one agency official to sum up the seriousness of the Sudan situation. Warnings of impending famine became ever-more dramatic and sensational. For example, FAO and WFP reports of the numbers of people requiring relief were soon translated into numbers 'at risk of starvation and death', especially in media reports,[9] although these terms had not been used in the original documents. It was widely bandied about that between seven and eight million people in Sudan were on the brink of death. This was a horrifying scenario which ensured that the crisis in Sudan was given a higher profile than might otherwise have been the case, and increased its political importance to many Western governments keen to show they were responding.

---

[9] For example, in *The Financial Times* of 11 December and *The Independent* of 15 December 1990.

By the end of 1991, however, these same terms had become counter-productive. They pandered to the notion of famine as mass starvation. Donor representatives were looking for evidence of 'megadeaths'; if this could not be proved the accuracy of the early warnings was immediately questioned. As argued above, this was an inappropriate reference point and diverted attention away from the less obvious yet insidious slide into extreme poverty and destitution during 1991, which was certainly associated with excess mortality.

It also became clear that the threshold between what is regarded as 'normal' and what is a 'crisis' seems to be rising in Sudan. As food-security conditions have deteriorated since the mid-1980s, the numbers of vulnerable people have risen. One agency representative has commented that, in parallel with this trend, the level of malnutrition which provokes alarm rose from around 15 per cent in 1984–5 to 25 or 30 per cent in 1990–91. This is particularly worrying in a country where development aid to tackle the underlying problems of marginal communities has been withdrawn, and because of the long-term costs of high levels of malnutrition.

Institutional aspects

As noted earlier, despite the facade of a formal meeting structure for the consideration of information, in practice informal channels of communication and negotiation tended to be more important in decision-making than formal ones. This was a direct reflection of the political sensitivities of the crisis. Information could not be freely circulated. Formal EW bulletins were often restricted in what or how they could report. Donors therefore came to rely on informal briefings by NGOs, usually NGOs from their own country, who had first-hand experience of what was happening on the ground. The disadvantage of this was that coverage could be very uneven. It was no coincidence that Kordofan state, where CARE had a long-standing presence and close relations with the local government, received the first pledges of food aid. It was initially regarded as being worse-off than Darfur where the demise of the aid-funded APU meant reduced exposure of the state's problems to the international donor community during the last few months of 1990. The uneven treatment of the two states was exacerbated by the different attitudes of the respective state governments: Kordofan state government was outspoken about its food-security problems, while Darfur state government was much more reticent.

The results of one-off agency missions also tended to have a disproportionate influence on decision-making in Khartoum compared with formal EW reports. Where these were carried out by senior officials, with immediate access to the heads of agency missions or to headquarters, they carried credibility and could prompt swift action. So it was that the decision was taken to launch an airlift to Darfur in July 1991, after a donor representative had visited the state.

Informal channels for negotiation between government and donors were also important. During the last few months of 1990 both donor and government positions were entrenched and there was little room for manœuvre. When agreement was finally reached on the role that NGOs should play in the relief operation, this was done informally on a one-to-one basis to avoid public confrontation and any public loss of face; an 'operational' agency representative came to an agreement with the RRC that NGOs should handle relief. This implied that there was room for negotiation and agreement *if* the will was there to start the relief operation. Unfortunately this will was lacking until late in the day, when pragmatism finally replaced staunchly defended points of principle, by which time it was too late to ensure a timely relief response.

During each relief operation to Darfur in the 1980s, food aid was delivered too little and too late. The experience in 1990–91 provides little evidence that lessons from previous operations have been learned or internalized by governments or the agencies involved. Of course, the circumstances in which an operation is launched are never the same. In 1990–91 the distinguishing characteristic was the hostile political environment. Nevertheless, some of the mistakes from previous operations were repeated, especially the timing of pledges, which took no account of how long it takes to deliver food to beneficiaries in Darfur and ignored *early* warning. In donor agency headquarters there seemed to be a lack of awareness that food pledged at the beginning of the calendar year had little chance of being delivered in time, and there was no provision for speeding up transport to ensure that the relief arrived before the next harvest. The railway which had failed the previous two relief operations, in the mid-1980s and in the Western Relief Operation, was re-introduced into the transport plan in 1991, only to fail for a third time. At the last minute, a costly airlift had to be mounted to carry food into Darfur during the rainy season when ground transport could not possibly meet the need.

One of the main reasons for this lack of 'institutional memory' is the rapid turnover of staff. On the government side, this has been very marked since the Bashir government came to power. On the donor side, it reflects the short-term nature of expatriates' contracts, and the fact that most do only one tour of duty. In some agencies, contracts for field officers during the relief operation were only three months, impossibly short for becoming familiar with local conditions. Recruitment for emergency relief work rarely makes allowance for adequate briefing before the high-pressure job starts on the ground, when there is no time to peruse past evaluations.

Implications for the final response

The reasons for the slow and inadequate relief operation in Sudan during 1991 were partly political and partly to do with the mechanics of the international food aid delivery system which is geared to the end-of-year harvest assessment. Three of the case-studies in this book — Sudan, Ethiopia and Chad — highlight the inappropriate timing of donor pledges at the beginning of the calendar year in view of the time it takes to mobilize international food aid. Reaching Darfur in the remote interior of Sudan simply emphasizes this point.

An obvious solution is the pre-positioning of resources and the advance preparation of programmed response options for a scenario like 1990–91.

In Darfur this has been planned and carried out once before (APU, 1988; Swift and Gray, 1989). After the delays in the Western Relief Operation, a strategic food reserve was set up in El Fasher and Nyala. Its size was initially limited by managerial and logistical capacity, but the objective was to have some resources available locally to bridge the time gap if food aid has to be transported from central Sudan or overseas. The reserve reached approximately 2 000t, funded by the EU. This was a promising start but ran into the common problem of lack of long-term planning and commitment. When the reserve was used up in 1990 there was no contingency plan or provision to replace it. The initiative collapsed and there was nothing available when it was most needed in 1991.

The current environment in Sudan for pre-positioning food stocks or other resources as contingency for an emergency is not encouraging. It will probably be dependent on donor funding, in which case it is only likely to happen where there is a genuine spirit of co-operation between donors and government. Even though USAID was holding about 30 000t of food stocks in central Sudan at the end of 1990, its negative experience in trying to retain control over those reserves was such that it has abandoned the policy.

The most feasible option would be some kind of food pool, established by donors, in Port Sudan or elsewhere in the region. If the pool was to be jointly owned by a number of donors and run by an independent management company, this could increase flexibility and speed up the response process considerably. However, the government may object to a food pool established in-country over which it has no control.

Insecurity and the EW/response process

Civil insecurity has worsened in Darfur during the last 10 to 15 years, although it is in no way comparable in scale or intensity to the war in southern Sudan. It has a direct effect on food insecurity, and the EW/ response system has so far proved inadequate to deal with this.

The causes of civil insecurity in Darfur are complex. The underlying fault lines generally follow ethnic divisions. 'Traditional' tribal conflicts over resources, especially between agriculturalists and pastoralists in South Darfur, have intensified. This has been fuelled by government policy to establish and support certain tribal militia for covert political ends, while the state's own military force has remained weak. Added to this, the availability of weapons among the population has greatly increased as a consequence of wars being fought in neighbouring countries. In South Darfur, especially towards the end of 1991, fighting from south Sudan was spilling over the border from Bahr el Ghazal. Ever since 1988 there have been large numbers of displaced southerners living in South Darfur, many in camps or shanty towns.

The link between civil and food insecurity in Darfur is direct. Assets are lost or destroyed, including livestock, grain stores and people's homes. Livelihood systems are disrupted. And displacement causes concentrations of people in camps and makeshift dwellings around towns with associated

106

health and hygiene risks. In September 1991, it was reported that there were at least 86 000 displaced people in Darfur, although many go unrecorded. The breakdown was as follows: 17 000 displaced from south Sudan; 30 000 displaced in South Darfur because of tribal conflict; 21 000 displaced in South Darfur by famine; and 18 000 displaced in North Darfur, mainly because of famine (SEPHA, 10–25 September 1991).

Information systems in Darfur have managed to cover the effects of insecurity only in a very general way, principally by monitoring the numbers, location and needs of the displaced who are easily identifiable if they are living in concentrated groups. Many are not, however, and are missed by normal monitoring procedures. During 1991 large parts of South Darfur and areas in the north were simply out of bounds for monitors because of the danger of travelling. Even in apparently 'safe' locations, such as along the Nyala–El Fasher road, an NGO vehicle was fired on and some of its passengers killed during the 1991 rainy season. The insecure environment during 1990–91 severely affected the mobility of those involved in data collection both for EW and for monitoring the relief distribution in areas which contained some of the most food-insecure people in the state.

Not only information collection but also relief distribution is affected by insecurity. Private transport contractors were reluctant to deliver to Area Councils which were reputed to be unsafe. This contributed to their preference to deliver relief within Kordofan in 1991 rather than make forays into dangerous territory in parts of Darfur.

Insecurity in Darfur is not on a scale, nor does it have the same impact, as in some other regions and countries in the Sahel and Horn of Africa. Nevertheless it illustrates a fundamental contradiction. Local people in insecure areas who are most in need of assistance tend to be least well served, both by information-monitoring systems and by relief operations. This is especially the case where only some parts are affected by insecurity; the EW/response system is not designed to cope with this, but instead is geared to the drought-affected, but politically and militarily stable, who are easier to monitor and have different needs.

Conclusions

The relief operation in north Sudan, particularly in Darfur, cannot be judged a success. By December 1991 less than one-fifth of Darfur's estimated relief needs had been delivered (and only about one-third actually pledged). This could not be blamed on a lack of EW. Indeed, it did not take a sophisticated EWS to spot the warning signs early in the 1990 agricultural season. After a poor harvest in 1989 it was obvious that there would be a large food deficit and few reserves to fall back on. Clear messages were relayed from July 1990 onwards, with relief needs quantified as early as September.

The four principal reasons for the failure of the relief operation, in roughly descending order of importance, were the following. First and foremost was the political environment; the relief operation became the focal point for antagonistic relations between the government and Western donors. This puts the role and importance of EW information in perspective. The potential benefits, in terms of timely response, of warnings signalled early in 1990 were negated by deadlocked negotiations between the government and donors about the kind and scale of relief response to be launched, especially during the last few months of 1990 when relief planning should have started. Even when the relief operation finally got off the ground, difficult relations continued to obstruct its smooth running.

The politics surrounding the relief operation were complex. In the international arena, the government and Western donors were in different camps. The former was distrusted as a fundamentalist Islamic government by the latter. More immediately, the donors were ill-disposed to assisting a government supporting Iraq in the Gulf War. A list of stringent measures was compiled on which the provision of international relief was conditional. In the domestic political arena, the Bashir government adopted an ideological stand on food self-sufficiency and independence from Western food aid donors, with memories of a highly interventionist style of relief management in the mid-1980s. There was little evidence of the will on either side to set aside political differences in the interests of humanitarian relief, until the beginning of 1991 when informal, behind-the-scenes negotiations to get things done replaced the inflammatory public statements of the last few months of 1990. By then, valuable planning time had been lost.

Second, the Sudanese operation fell foul of some of the most common 'institutional' constraints encountered in mobilizing international relief. Publication of the results of the FAO harvest assessment coincided with the breaking of the political deadlock in negotiations between government and donors. Until then, officials in donor agency headquarters were not unduly concerned about the delays which were inevitable if relief was not mobilized earlier than the beginning of the calendar year. This is 'normal' timing for decision-making about relief for the Sahel and Horn, yet experience in 1984–5 and again in 1988 had shown this to be too late, particularly for Darfur if food aid is to arrive before the start of the next rainy season. On the ground it is well known that it takes at least two to three months to transport food aid from Port Sudan to Darfur, and at least four months from Europe or the US to Port Sudan. In donor agency headquarters, however, the timetabling of the relief operation simply does not take time-lags into account.

Third, major problems were encountered on the logistical side, in the transport operations to Darfur. This reflected the degraded state of the private sector transport fleet, and was a consequence of obstructive government policies. It was exacerbated by a lack of institutional memory, repeating mistakes from past relief operations, such as relying on the railways. Even the most common logistical constraints encountered in running a relief operation in north Sudan were not taken into account in planning the 1991 operation.

Finally, execution of the relief operation was hampered by the unclear and sometimes impractical division of logistical responsibility within the international aid community, especially for transport. This was related to inter-donor politics and the stand-off between WFP and other donors. Not until late into the relief operation did WFP take responsibility for primary transport, despite the fact that it was much better equipped to do so than foreign NGOs, especially in the charged political environment.

The reasons for the inadequate relief response in Sudan in 1991 are to do with political, and to a lesser extent institutional and logistical constraints, rather than a lack of EW. Nevertheless, EW capacity in the country was much less developed than in most other countries in the Sahel and Horn of Africa. The EWS was able to sound the alarm that a relief operation was needed, but it was unable to provide a more refined explanation of what was happening. EW capacity in Sudan has fluctuated according to the availability of international aid; oscillating between well-funded periods when donor resources were available, and lean periods when they were not. This demonstrates the fragility of an EWS which is heavily dependent on donor funding, when the politics of aid can abruptly cut off the flow. There is a knock-on effect on the international components of the EWS, which are mostly dependent on secondary data sources. The quality of their information will also suffer if the national EWS is weak. And in the vacuum of formal information systems, highly subjective one-off 'disaster tourism' assessments have an exaggerated influence.

The most serious consequence of the inadequate EW capacity was the inability to monitor in sufficient detail the impact of the limited relief operation, especially in Darfur. Even retrospectively, information about what happened is sparse. In this vacuum, uninformed assumptions were made about whether there really was a famine, and therefore whether the early warnings had been correct. The commonly held view among donor agency representatives in Khartoum at the end of 1991 was that somehow local people had 'coped' better than expected, and that delivering such small quantities of relief food to Darfur was not a failure. The danger is that this view may be used in future to justify donor inaction in situations where there is a reluctance to become involved in relief operations. In such circumstances, even more dramatic indicators of famine may be required to provoke an international response. Sensationalizing EW was a ploy used intermittently during 1991 to inject a sense of urgency into the relief operation. Sometimes it can backfire, when the evidence does not support the claims made, for example of 'megadeaths' in 1991 if relief deliveries were not stepped up. But there is some evidence to refute the donors' view. The data which do exist show that malnutrition was very high, from which it can be inferred that child-mortality rates did increase significantly. This is supported by the limited mortality data available.

Depletion of assets and impoverishment in 1991 have undoubtedly left more people in Darfur vulnerable to future periods of drought, and more chronically food-insecure than before. This draws attention to the artificial distinction made between emergency and development aid. Because almost all Western development aid to Sudan has ceased, there is little investment in rural areas like Darfur. The danger is that a vicious cycle is set in motion: chronic food insecurity intensifies, exacerbated by years when inadequate relief assistance fails to make much difference, and humanitarian needs become greater and more frequent as food crises recur. The result is an 'endemic crisis', similar to conditions in Ethiopia since the mid-1980s, where relief is required year after year, especially if this is the only available aid resource. Since 1991, relief operations to Darfur have continued on an almost annual basis.

Although international aid is very restricted in the current environment in Sudan, there is some room for manœuvre to improve the workings of the famine-prevention process. In some instances, it has to be created, by relaxing the most stringent constraints on how aid is spent. Four areas are identified for urgent attention.

First, EW capabilities need to be strengthened, and supported by donor resources over the long term. A coherent strategy for developing them right across the country is required, taking account of sub-national systems set up by NGOs. Socio-economic monitoring should be strengthened within the RRC's EWS, to balance the emphasis currently placed on monitoring production indicators. Although the political environment may have a negative effect in suppressing EW information in-country, there is still a pressing need for continuous monitoring to build up a baseline and understanding of food insecurity, and to act as a counterweight to one-off assessment missions.

Second, over the last few years, it has been argued that local response capabilities should be strengthened to reduce the dependence on mobilizing relief resources thousands of miles away. But little progress has been made. The experience of 1991 and the slow delivery rate by the international relief system reinforce the arguments for developing local response capabilities, by pre-positioning food relief. Donors may be unwilling to do this in Sudan, although the establishment of a food aid pool in Port Sudan, jointly owned by donors, has been discussed. Alternatively, food relief could be pre-positioned in the region. This would considerably speed up the response process.

Third, the relief–development dichotomy which governs international aid flows to Sudan is not productive. On the ground in Darfur the distinction is hard to make. There is a need for emergency food aid to be used more flexibly, not only for free food distributions but also in ways which help to 'drought-proof' the rural economy taking a longer-term perspective.

Finally, the Sudan case-study reveals limitations of the international relief system in dealing with a politically difficult relief operation in Africa. Responsibilities were unclear and sometimes inappropriately allocated, for example within the UN and between the UN and NGOs. The cracks between actors have since deepened as other complex emergencies have developed on the African continent. The experience in Sudan underlines the need for a re-thinking and a restructuring of the international relief system, especially for the conduct of humanitarian operations in hostile political environments.

CHAPTER 6

Chad

Introduction

Chad suffered severe famine in 1984–5, when the impact of several years of drought was compounded by the effects of civil war. Large amounts of relief finally arrived, but late and less than estimated requirements. This was blamed partly on lack of information and lack of EW. In the aftermath a national EWS — the *Système d'Alerte Précoce* (SAP) — was established in 1986. In 1990–91 the SAP was put to the test, in many ways for the first time. It had set up a monitoring system, but could it trigger an adequate and timely relief response, to avoid the delays and shortfalls experienced during the 1985 relief operation?

Conditions during the 1990–91 agricultural year were not parallel to 1984–5. This was only the second year of drought, and there was no full-scale war. Livelihoods rather than lives were under threat during the following 12 months, especially in the northern Sahelian zone of the country. Assets were run down and there was a rise in malnutrition. Chapter 1 argued that an EWS should also warn of this kind of scenario; relief assistance is justified to protect livelihoods and to prevent a slide towards acute food insecurity. The SAP fulfilled this role, drawing attention to deteriorating food security in the Sahelian zone, and quantifying relief requirements.

In October 1990, the SAP estimated relief needs to be 34000t. (The relief operation in 1985 provided over 170000t.) During 1991, no more than 15000t of food aid were distributed, less than half of estimated requirements. Does this signal a failure on the part of the EWS to influence the relief response? Or does it imply that there are other more serious blockages to the timely provision of relief than lack of information? What are the explanations for the large discrepancy between estimated relief needs and final relief deliveries in 1991? These are the questions this chapter sets out to answer.

This case-study is interesting for a number of reasons. First of all, because Chad has gone through the classic sequence of famine, a delayed relief operation being blamed on lack of information, investment in a formal EWS, yet continued problems in delivering adequate quantities of relief on time. But also because it reveals some of the contradictions between an international relief system which is geared to dealing with large-scale, high-profile famine emergencies, and the more-common scenario of a smaller-scale food crisis, often triggered by drought, where livelihoods rather than lives are under threat. Chad does not command the same amount of media and political interest in Western donor countries as either

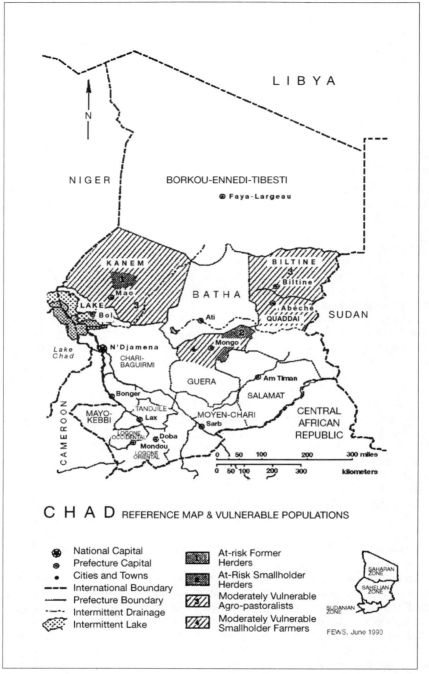

Figure 6.1 *Map of Chad showing vulnerable groups at the beginning of the 1990 agricultural season*
Source: FEWS, 1990a.

112

Ethiopia or Sudan. Its relief needs are much smaller, and they are easily overlooked in donor agency headquarters geared to the more-sensational and large-scale crises.

Food security

Chad is a large landlocked country with a relatively small population of only 5.4 million (see Figure 6.1).[1] It is one of the poorest countries in the world; GNP per capita was only $190 in 1989 (World Bank, 1991). Chad is divided into three zones; the very dry Saharan zone in the north inhabited by about 2 per cent of the population; the Sahelian zone with an estimated 55 per cent of the population; and the southern Sudanian zone of higher rainfall with about 43 per cent of the population. The economy is predominantly rural; the mainstays are livestock herding, small-scale rainfed agriculture, and fishing in Lake Chad and in the rivers which flow through the Sudanian zone.

A weak national economy, variable annual food production, and marketing constraints due to poor infrastructure, combine to create conditions of chronic food insecurity for many Chadian people. Parts of Chad have experienced periodic episodes of acute food insecurity and famine, usually triggered by drought, but worst of all when combined with conflict. The country's recent history has been overshadowed by conflict and war, which has caused immense human suffering and been a drain on economic resources. Since the end of the war in 1983, the country has enjoyed a period of relative peace although there is still instability. In December 1990 a military coup overthrew the government of Hassan Habré and brought to power the government of President Idriss Deby. The coup was accompanied by fierce fighting and displacement of the population in some parts of the country.

Food security

The level of national food self-sufficiency is a much-debated issue. Food balance sheets based on annual cereal harvest assessments indicate that the country has a structural deficit of about 100000t in so-called 'average' years (FAO, 1990). But it is widely believed that either production is underestimated, or population overestimated (the last official census was in 1964). Self-sufficiency is probably achieved when national cereals production reaches levels of 650000 to 700000t per year, which has occurred three times in the last eight years (see Table 6.1). This is supported by evidence of surpluses and falling prices in such conditions (FEWS, 1991:34). However, after a depressed harvest the deficit can be very substantial; in such years food aid has played a significant role in feeding the population (see Table 6.1).

These national figures mask large regional differences. The general flow of food is from the Sudanian zone, especially from the 'bread basket' of

---

[1] Population estimates are for 1990, from official statistics adjusted by the annual growth rate of 2.3 per cent.

Table 6.1 Chad: domestic cereals production, food-aid distributions and commercial imports (thousands of tonnes)

Year	Gross production	Commercial imports	Total food aid distribution	Emergency food aid distribution
1983–4	446	n/a	n/a	n/a
1984–5	346	n/a	127	127
1985–6	716	n/a	67	67
1986–7	646	n/a	32	15
1987–8	569	22	26	16
1988–9	769	37	12	3
1989–90	696	24	16	3
1990–91	605	n/a	n/a	14

Source: USAID.

Salamat *préfecture* in the south-east, to the deficit Sahelian zone, and within the Sahelian zone from south to north.

The Sahelian population is usually considered to be more vulnerable to food insecurity than people living in the Sudanian zone, mainly because crop production is more variable in the north. Within the Sahelian zone, the most vulnerable households are those dependent on rainfed cropping, without access to flood retreat agriculture, small-scale irrigated farming or fishing throughout the year, and with limited or no livestock holdings. Some of the most food-insecure are now concentrated in the north of the Sahelian zone, where transhumant pastoralism used to be the main source of livelihood and is most appropriate to the semi-arid conditions. During the drought and rinderpest epidemic of the early 1980s there were large livestock losses; many households have been unable to rebuild their herds since, and are now trying to eke out a precarious living depending on unreliable rainfed crop production.

Less is known about food insecurity in the Sudanian zone where agricultural yields and rainfall are higher. Chronic food insecurity is not regarded as a widespread problem. Drought is a rarer occurrence, but when it does occur there is concern that Sudanian households are actually less well-equipped to cope with it than their Sahelian neighbours. Their livelihood and income sources are not as diverse, and they may be particularly vulnerable to transitory food insecurity after only one drought year.

Figure 6.1 reproduces a FEWS map showing the location of groups which were considered particularly vulnerable at the beginning of the 1990 agricultural season.

Food policy

During the first half of the 1980s, food security was interpreted very narrowly as famine prevention. The *Ministère de la Sécurité Alimentaire et des Populations Sinistrées* (Ministry of Food Security and Vulnerable Populations, MSAPS) was established in 1983, geared to disasters and food-relief needs. During the second, more peaceful half of the 1980s food-policy objectives were defined more broadly as: increasing food production to self-sufficiency; stabilizing the availability of food mainly through better marketing; and improving access to food with more equitable distribution of income (FAO, 1990). With the assistance of FAO, the formulation of a National Food Security Programme (*Programme National de Sécurité Alimentaire*, PNSA) has been ongoing since 1989. During this period the state has committed itself to economic liberalization and development of the private sector as the way to improve food-security conditions (Arditi and Bouquin, 1990). This approach has been positively encouraged by the donor community.

Privatization and/or restructuring is being extended to almost all state-owned enterprises. The changing role of the *Office National des Céréales* (National Cereals Office, ONC) reflects this. Created as a parastatal in 1977, it was expected to play a major role in stabilizing market prices. In practice it was much less influential than cereals marketing boards in many other African countries. Dogged by a failure to remain financially viable, it has been criticized for poor management in recent evaluations (for example, Arditi and Bouquin, 1990). Reflecting the new climate of market liberalization, the ONC's role is now restricted to managing a national food security reserve. This proved to be an important resource for the relief operation in 1990–91.

Chad has experienced two major episodes of famine in the last two decades: in 1973–4 and again in the mid-1980s. Drought has been the trigger causing famine, but against the backdrop of war in the early 1980s. Cereals production can vary widely (see Table 6.1). The national coefficient of variation of production between 1983–4 and 1990–91 was 22 per cent.

Although the rural population is well adapted to fluctuating food production, a run of poor harvests will usually culminate in acute food insecurity or famine if there is no counteracting intervention. The famine of 1984 was the culmination of four years of drought and inadequate harvests, on top of several years of fighting and a scorched-earth policy in parts of the country. Large numbers of people had been displaced, their asset base destroyed, and there was widespread disruption to food production and the rural economy. Meanwhile, a rinderpest epidemic in the early 1980s had inflicted severe losses on cattle herds.

During 1984–5 a large-scale international relief operation was launched: 210000t of emergency food aid were pledged by the international community, and 178000t were delivered by October 1985. This operation was associated with numerous bilateral, multilateral, and non-governmental relief agencies moving into the country. No EWS was in place. Cries for assistance reached the international donor community very late. The first quantified needs assessment was carried out towards the end of 1984, by an FAO/WFP mission which estimated that about 1.5 million people were in need of food assistance, and a further 500000 were displaced. The relief finally arrived very late, attributed to the lack of *early* warning, the lack of contingency plans, and the paucity of organizations prepared to distribute the amount of food needed. When the rains failed — for the fourth year running — in 1984, the donors were criticized for waiting for the results of

115

the harvest assessment before declaring an emergency, thus exacerbating the delays. Although the provision of relief reduced the impact of famine, there was still a significant rise in mortality during 1984–5 (Brown *et al.*, 1987).

As the relief operation eventually got under way, monitoring systems were set up rapidly to direct the effort. Nutritional surveillance played a central role. This was the origin of the current EWS.

The EW/response system

Early warning

There are now five main EW components in Chad, three national and two international. The SAP, set up in 1986 on the basis of a temporary monitoring system run by *Médécins sans Frontières* of Belgium (MSF) during the 1984–5 emergency, is the cornerstone of the system.

The SAP was set up only to monitor the Sahelian zone, because it is regarded as more food-insecure than the Sudanian part of the country. It is essentially a famine-oriented system geared to identifying, recommending and justifying required distributions of food aid. It publishes a monthly bulletin summarizing information for each *préfecture*, and making recommendations for action. Additional EW reports are produced if the situation deteriorates. SAP's brief is restricted to the provision of information; it is not supposed to be involved in decision-making nor in the implementation of a response. It is run from N'djamena, and is located within the *Direction* (previously *Ministère*) *de la Promotion des Productions Agricoles et de la Sécurité Alimentaire* (DPASA). The SAP is funded by the EU, with technical assistance provided by the *Association Européenne pour le Développement et la Santé* (AEDES). Its network of monitors extends down to the level of the canton.

SAP's methodology is based on a three-phase approach. Phase One comprises qualitative monitoring of the agricultural production season in four stages: the beginning of the season at the end of July/early August; pre-harvest assessment in September; provisional food needs calculations in October; and definitive food needs calculations in December. Phase Two involves socio-economic monitoring throughout the year, for example of population movements and market prices, to identify zones at risk. Phase Three is launched only when Phase Two signals deteriorating food security and identifies 'at-risk' areas, to confirm and corroborate the results. Phase Three is carried out by a mobile team of the *Centre National de Nutrition et de Téchnologie Alimentaire* (CNNTA) of the *Ministère de la Santé Publique*, which carries out one-off anthropometric surveys and collects supplementary information on food conditions (SAP, 1990a).

The Chadian SAP is less developed than its Malian counterpart (see Chapter 7), but is the only part of the EWS in Chad which collects socio-economic data. It does not carry out harvest surveys or conventional cereals balance-sheet analysis. Food aid requirements are calculated from a range of indicators used to identify zones and numbers of people at risk and the minimum amount of food required to avoid nutritional crisis (SAP, 1990c).

116

The other four components making up the EWS in Chad are the following:

- *Bureau de la Statistique Agricole* (BSA) and *Organisation Nationale de Développement Rural* (ONDR). The BSA is the main source of EW information for the Sudanian zone, based on its agricultural surveys. The ONDR collects similar data for the Sahelian zone. These are written up in monthly agricultural bulletins during the production season from July to November. A food balance sheet is usually available by the end of March/ beginning of April the following year. The BSA provides data, but does not make recommendations.
- AGRHYMET. This project is run by the *Service Météorologique*, with support from CILSS. It monitors physical production indicators during the agricultural season, using satellite imagery and rainfall estimates, backed up by regular reports from field monitors. Monitoring is based on 10-day intervals, and reported in 10-day bulletins.
- FEWS. There has been a FEWS field representative in N'djamena since 1985. FEWS primary objective is the provision of EW information for US government decision-makers, but more emphasis is now being placed on developing EW capability within the Government of Chad.
- FAO/CILSS. An annual harvest assessment is carried out, usually in October, by FAO and CILSS in association with AGRHYMET. The first estimates are available by the end of October/beginning of November, and are used to construct a national food balance sheet. FAO also reports regularly on the food situation in its GIEWS publications, with information supplied mainly through its country office in N'djamena.

There are relatively few individuals involved in EW in N'djamena. As a result, there is usually close co-operation and collaboration between the different EW components, although personalities can exert an exaggerated influence.

Only SAP is in the business of making recommendations to decision-makers. These are always geared to the provision of relief food. Of course, informal sources of EW information also feed into relief decision-making, for example from NGOs and local government authorities. But the formal system is run entirely from N'djamena. Unlike many other Sahelian countries, there are no examples of small-scale local or community-based EWS at sub-national level.

Figure 6.2 shows the five components of the EWS and how they link with decision-making.

Response system

The system for responding to EW information and for taking decisions about appropriate relief actions in Chad is long-standing. It centres upon the *Comité d'Action pour la Sécurité Alimentaire et l'Aide d'Urgence* (CASAAU), first set up by legal directive to administer food aid towards the end of the civil war in 1983. Its members include relevant government

117

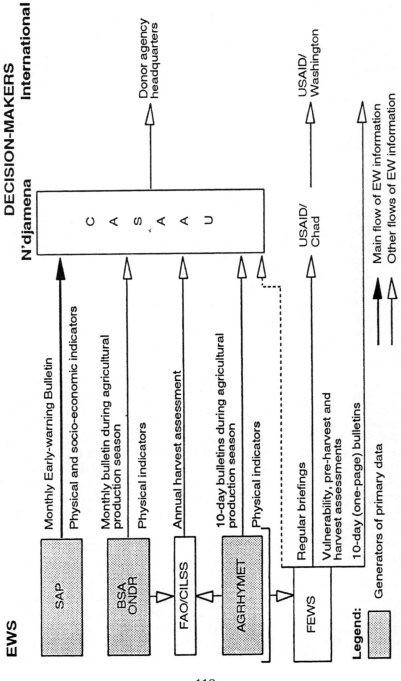

Figure 6.2 *Chad: diagram of components of EWS and links with decision-makers*

officials, SAP representatives, members of bilateral and multilateral aid agencies, and NGOs, chaired by the Secretary of State for Food Security. This committee structure has survived political upheaval and change and the establishment of a formal EWS, and remains the principal forum for debating information and taking decisions on a consensual basis. Unlike many other countries in the Sahel and Horn of Africa, there are no parallel donor or NGO committees to this joint governmental/donor/NGO structure.

Just as EW is centralized in N'djamena, so is decision-making to respond. Local-level committees like the *Comités Régionaux d'Action* (CRAs) at *préfecture* level have virtually no decision-making powers. They tend to be reactive, drawing up distribution plans for food aid which CASAAU has decided to allocate to their *préfecture*.

In practice, the international donor community usually funds all aspects of emergency relief operations, making donors particularly influential in relief planning. Decisions are taken at two levels: by donor agency representatives in N'djamena, and by their headquarters in Europe or the US, who are, strictly speaking, responsible for allocation decisions. In practice, it is the local representatives who recommend how much should be allocated and co-ordinate the various pledges. It is therefore the job of the EWS to persuade donor representatives in N'djamena of the need and magnitude of relief.

After a drought, relief is needed most in the 'hungry season' between June/July and September/October in the following year. Responsibility for distributing relief is usually split between government and NGOs.

The story of EW/response in 1990–91

EW signals and decisions to respond

The famine in 1984–5 is the benchmark against which conditions in subsequent years can be compared. The food crisis in 1990–91 was not of the same magnitude. It was the culmination of two rather than four successive drought years, without the context of a major civil war. Cereals production in 1984–5 was estimated at 346000t; in 1990 it was estimated at 605000t. Nevertheless, during 1991 many people in the Sahelian part of the country had inadequate food. It was not so much lives that were at risk but livelihoods, as assets had to be sold. Of course conditions varied, with some parts being much more severely affected than others. The rainy season was unusually short in 1990. Most rainfall stations in the Sahelian zone had recorded rainfall levels which were more than 30 per cent, and in some cases 60 per cent, below the 30-year average. From the end of August AGRHYMET's bulletin warned of drought and its impact on vegetation (*Direction des Ressources en Eau et de la Météorologie*, 1990). In September FEWS entitled the Chad chapter in its pre-harvest assessment of cereals production (FEWS, 1990b, published in October) 'Drought in Northern Sahel'. SAP, in its first special handout for CASAAU in September, reported on the deterioration signalled by these production indicators, and warned that cereal prices had already started to rise and the grain/livestock terms of trade to decline (SAP, September 1990).

119

Table 6.2 Chad: SAP's food-needs assessment for 1991

Préfecture	At-risk population	Number of months for which food aid required	Total food-aid required (tonnes)
Kanem	47 133	5	2 830
Batha	115 155	5	6 910
Biltine	66 396	5–7	4 273
Ouaddai	174 479	5–10	12 556
Guera	100 414	5–8	7 314
Total	503 577		33 883

Source: SAP (quoted in FEWS, 1991a).

There was also evidence of unusual population movements apparently provoked by food insecurity (SAP, October 1991).

These early warnings were translated into recommendations for action for the first time in mid-October. SAP presented details to CASAAU (SAP, 1990b) of food aid requirements per *préfecture* and per month between March and October 1991, revised a couple of weeks later in its final recommendations (SAP, 1990c). A rather crude methodology for calculating the number of vulnerable people was used: 40 per cent of cantons in the Sahelian zone, and 60 per cent of their populations, were identified as 'at risk', based on the reasoning that the Sahelian population does not depend entirely on rainfed agriculture, is well adapted to a structural food deficit, and has diversified sources of income. Therefore, not everyone in a drought-stricken area was in need. SAP estimated that about 34 000t of relief food aid were needed (see Table 6.2). The joint FAO/CILSS harvest assessment at the end of October forecast an estimated cereals deficit of 150 200t. FEWS likened the situation to 1987–8, when about 26 000t of food aid were distributed (FEWS, 1991a). But in parts of the Sahelian zone the 1990–91 harvest was expected to be less than 50 per cent of average, following a poor harvest the previous year.

The first warnings of drought were heeded by the government which raised the issue at high political levels in early October, including in the UN General Assembly. Local donor representatives also conveyed these early warnings to their agency headquarters from October onwards. But CASAAU refused to take a final decision on relief requirements until the results of the FAO/CILSS harvest assessment were available in November, despite the fact that SAP had issued its recommendations on relief needs a month earlier.

It took a further two months, during which the military coup caused upheavals and delays, before the government issued a formal appeal to the international community, on 3 January 1991, asking for 150 000t of food aid (with an extra 30 000t for refugees). In other words, the national estimated cereals deficit was translated directly into relief needs. The appeal dramatized the severity of the situation, and compared conditions in the Sahelian zone with those in 1984–5. The EU, USAID and

Coopération Française had all started mobilizing relief resources before the government's official appeal (although all encountered major delays). Only WFP was unable to respond before an official request had been lodged; this was finally accepted at WFP headquarters in mid-February, six weeks after it had been issued. In mid-December, the EU's Food Aid Committee had approved an allocation of 10000t of relief for Chad. The decision was not communicated to the government until the end of February 1991, and the government's approval came in early April 1991, three and a half months after the decision had been taken. The food eventually arrived in June.

The delays encountered in allocating relief within USAID's system were even more serious, especially as it was by far the largest donor. When the harvest results were available in November, the USAID mission in N'djamena recommended that 5000t of sorghum be mobilized; no decision was taken in Washington until the beginning of April. In mid-March 10000t of US food was allocated to Chad through WFP. None of this relief was shipped until June and finally arrived in October 1991, 12 months after the first recommendations had been made by the USAID mission. In the interim, mission staff had sent increasingly exasperated telexes to their headquarters urging action as the timetable for distribution became more and more hypothetical and the rainy season approached.

The mission of *Coopération Française* had alerted Paris to the impending food crisis in September and October 1990. Five million French francs were eventually released for local purchase in April 1991, again after a delay of some five to six months. The Swiss and German development aid programmes also made funds available for local purchase.

In one donor agency after another, it took months for the bureaucracy to take a decision and then to execute it. Yet this was an operation to relieve a short-term crisis. Time was of the essence, but bureaucracies failed to react with any sense of urgency.

Meanwhile, the SAP continued to warn of deteriorating food security in some *préfectures*: in the east abnormal population movements were compounded by an influx of returning refugees from Sudan (SAP, February and March 1991). Eventually the event which had greatest influence in triggering the relief operation was a large donor/government/NGO mission to five of the six *préfectures* in the Sahelian zone, in February 1991. N'djamena-based decision-makers were able to see the effects of the drought for themselves. This convinced some of the more doubtful; impressions were conveyed back to agency headquarters, and in the capital the crisis was treated with rather more urgency. Relief distribution plans were drawn up immediately by a CASAAU subcommittee for the *préfectures* visited. SAP data were referred to in the exercise, as the only information available to canton level, but the plan appeared to be more influenced by the itinerary of the February field trip than by regular monitoring of the whole zone.

Phase Three nutrition surveys were carried out by CNNTA in the locations most at risk. Initial results from the Sahelian zone showed relatively low rates of malnutrition, in February of less than 10 per cent.[2] Subsequent surveys showed pockets of much higher rates: from 16 to 19 per cent in

Table 6.3   Chad: results of anthropometric surveys carried out during 1990–91 (%)

Préfecture	Sous-préfecture	*Canton*	*Rate of malnutrition <80% weight for height, and month of survey*	
Guera	Mangalme	Dadjo II	13.9	April 1990
Ouaddai	Adre	Mabrone Traone	6.9	February 1991
	Adre	Kado	9.0	February 1991
	Adre	Marfa	3.6	February 1991
	Abeche	Bourtail	5.1	February 1991
Biltine	Biltine	Mimi	4.4	February 1991
	Lima	Guereda	2.0	February 1991
	Guereda	Guereda	3.5	February 1991
	Iriba	Tine	40.6	April 1991
Borkou–Ennedi–Tibesti	Ennedi	Kalait	20.7	April 1991
	Ennedi	Fada	23.4	April 1991
	Ennedi	5 cantons	25.0	April 1991
Kanem	Mao	Mondo	19.4	April 1991
	Moussoro	Kanembou	18.9	April 1991
	Nokou	Dogorda	16.7	April 1991

Source: CNNTA.

Kanem *préfecture*, with the highest rate of 40 per cent in Tine in Biltine *préfecture*, both in April (see Table 6.3). Periodic reports of the effects of the fighting and insecurity in the east of the country, associated with the coup, filtered through to CASAAU. Few reports were supported by hard data. One-off missions were dispatched to verify anecdotal information and requests for assistance.

The relief response
The relief plan drawn up in N'djamena by government and donors was entirely dependent on international donations. The US was expected to supply about 50 per cent of relief needs. The first tranche of food aid should have been distributed in March and April, but the earliest consignment arrived only in mid-June: 10000t of white sorghum from Thailand, provided by the EU. Approximately 4000t of this was distributed free. About 5000t was supposed to be sold, but in the end very little was traded because it was of poor quality and not popular, being quite different from the staple sorghum grown in Chad.

Most of the rest of the imported food aid, 5000t of US sorghum to be distributed by CARE and 10000t of US grain channelled through WFP, did not begin to arrive until October 1991, just as the country was on the brink of an exceptionally good harvest. This was far too late to be of any use to the relief operation. None was distributed during 1991.

---

[2]   In Chad there is a generally agreed threshold of a 10 per cent rate of malnutrition, above which a response should be signalled.

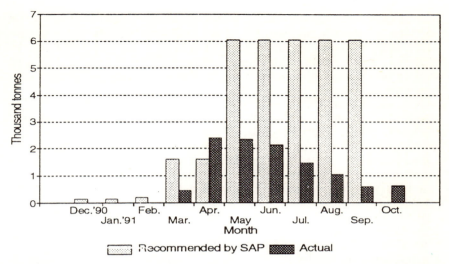

Figure 6.3 *Chad: distribution timetable for relief food aid – recommended compared with actual*
Source: SAP, USAID.

The second tranche of EU food aid, a further 12000t of sorghum, was never dispatched, despite being agreed in the Brussels Food Aid Committee in late May. Time had slipped and it would not have arrived until after it was required, so the allocation was cancelled. Had this food aid been sent in time, imported relief food would have surpassed SAP's recommendation of 34000t (although some would have been sold). As it was not sent, imported food aid fell well below the target level, and distributions were even further below target levels because of the late arrival of the relief.

As there was no sign of the donated aid by the beginning of March, a decision was taken to distribute grain from the national food security stock held by the ONC, to be replenished when the imported food aid finally arrived. The ONC stock stood at approximately 10000t at the beginning of 1991. About 3000t had been looted during the December coup. The ONC reserve provided more than half of the total amount of relief food distributed during 1991. It helped to compensate for the late arrival of US relief.

The final amount of relief distributed, all free, was between 12000 and 14000t of cereals, and 880t of non-cereals. Figure 6.3 shows the timetable and quantities distributed compared with what the SAP had recommended per month. Distribution fell far behind schedule and far short of the recommended amounts.

Attempts to buy food locally — using French, Swiss and German aid — failed. The assumption that there were adequate supplies in-country which could be redistributed proved wrong. In March 1991 the ONC tried to buy grain in the surplus-producing *préfecture* of Salamat. It found prices escalating beyond the levels at which it had been instructed to purchase, in the face of high local demand and from neighbouring Sudan. In order to try and stem the massive outflow of food, the local authorities began to impose restrictions. A similar situation was found in neighbouring countries like Nigeria and Cameroon in May; prices were rising rapidly and export bans were imposed on most cereals. A much smaller quantity was bought than originally intended.

Another alternative, *Opération Viande*, was proposed by FAO partly in response to the delayed relief efforts. This involved the purchase of local cattle which were slaughtered, the meat dried and distributed as relief. The aim was twofold: to support the purchasing power of herders, and to provide a source of food to the most needy. The reasoning was sound, but it failed in practice. *Opération Viande* was implemented on a small scale but stumbled over organizational and managerial obstacles, and was eventually abandoned.

As in other countries, donors wanted food distribution to be overseen by NGOs or WFP, and the government accepted this condition. CARE, the Chadian Red Cross and WFP were responsible for almost all food distributed during 1991. The discrepancy between relief plans and what was actually available created practical problems. For instance, the Red Cross found that distribution lists quickly became out of date; by the time the relief arrived more people had been identified as beneficiaries. CARE also experienced problems; because of the very limited amount available, there was pressure to implement a rigorous approach to targeting the most needy. This proved extremely difficult to put into practice, and met with resistance from some local authorities (CARE, 1991).

In the event, the Sudanian zone never received the quantities of food aid intended for it because of the late deliveries. Indeed, a second distribution plan was never put into action because of the delays. This sometimes caused tension when food was to be transported from ONC stocks in the south to the Sahelian zone, while parts of the south were also facing food insecurity; there was resentment that they were not to receive any benefit from food stored in their own locality.

Evaluating the EW information

Although some members of the government claimed that 1990–91 was going to bring a repeat of the famine of the mid-1980s, the various components of the EWS were giving more moderate warnings. In October the SAP qualified reports of harvest failure in parts of the Sahelian zone by reminding its readers that some *préfectures* were structurally food-deficit and most households were dependent on diverse sources of income, not on crop production alone (SAP, 1990c). It stated the main objective of the relief operation to be the avoidance of 'a deterioration in existing rates of malnutrition . . . to maintain the *status quo* and avert a nutritional crisis' (SAP, January 1991:31). Unlike Sudan, it was not forecasting widespread famine deaths which could only be averted if there was a relief operation. Similarly, FEWS was drawing comparisons with 1987:

when production declined dramatically in the Sahelian Zone, resulting in food aid distributions of approximately 26 000t . . . Rather, based on historical precedence, it would appear that 30 000 to 40 000t of carefully targeted food aid would be sufficient to forestall disaster and meet the most critical feeding needs (FEWS, 1991a:33, 37).

None of the EWS succumbed to the temptation of making dramatic predictions or using emotive language to provoke a response. In more measured tones, they portrayed a situation which is much harder to describe than full-scale famine, where livelihoods are under threat, but not necessarily lives. This is a language that the international relief system does not understand.

The failure of the relief effort to meet the agreed target of 34 000t did not result in loss of life on a large scale, although there were occasional reported incidents of famine-related death, in Guera *préfecture* caused by eating toxic plants (SAP, February 1991). But there was evidence that livelihoods were under stress during 1991; for example, seasonal migration increased from the worst-affected *préfectures*, although it could not be described as large-scale distress displacement. In parts of the Sahelian zone, malnutrition rates rose to levels which caused concern (see Table 6.3), but not in all *préfectures*.

It is very likely that the main consequence of failing to deliver the relief on time was the depletion of assets, and therefore increased vulnerability to drought in future years. Unfortunately this was not properly monitored during 1991. All components of the EWS in Chad are firmly rooted in N'djamena where data analysis and bulletin writing take place. One of the casualties of such a centralized approach is a lack of detailed understanding of local food economies, and particularly of local people's resilience to acute food insecurity and the strength of their coping strategies. Hence, little is known about what happened to assets during 1991.

Indicators tend to be highly aggregated. The SAP's methods for estimating relief needs are pragmatic but crude. Only through a more decentralized system for collecting and analysing data is it possible to address some of these constraints, to interpret agricultural and other indicators more accurately, and to be sensitive to localized differences. This would require more investment in resources at local, probably *préfecture*, level. The mobility of SAP field agents is often restricted by lack of transport, which has negative implications for the quality of EW information if they are unable to verify data they receive in *préfecture* headquarters. Nevertheless, the different components of the EWS appeared to co-ordinate well with each other, and their signals were consistent in 1990.

Judged on their own merits, the EW signals were timely and predictive. They first showed evidence of the drought in August, drew attention to its possible impact in September, and the SAP quantified relief needs in October. The problems arise when the cumbersome machinery of the international relief system is taken into account: warnings issued as early as October/November already seemed to be too late to ensure that the food would arrive by June, before the hungry season.

As in most of the other countries considered in this book, there is tension in Chad between the food-balance-sheet and needs-assessment methods of reaching an estimate of relief requirements. In 1990–91 the results of the harvest assessment carried out by FAO/CILSS were given precedence by decision-makers over SAP's earlier food-need calculations based on numbers of vulnerable people.

The harvest assessment and food-balance-sheet exercise is probably one of the least accurate parts of the EWS, because of the difficulty of measuring the parameters on which it is based. There has been no population census in Chad since the mid-1960s, since when there have been two famines and a civil war, all of which have caused population displacement and upheaval. There are also major logistical difficulties in quantifying cereals production. There are limited trained staff to carry out the survey, the list of producers on which the Sudanian sample is based is very out of date, and in the Sahelian zone the approach is much less scientific, based on general observation (pers. comm. from a BSA official).

Some donors are sceptical about the estimated structural deficit in Chad, believing that either production is underestimated or population overestimated. If they are right, this has serious implications for the food balance sheet, which would consistently overestimate relief needs. In 1990–91, USAID in Chad refused to attempt this exercise because of the lack of reliable data:

> A cereals balance table, which is supposed to finely tune needs and availabilities, does not yield satisfactory results for Chad. For 1989, the cereal balance for Chad showed a net deficit of 100000t, yet only 26000t food aid were imported and no crisis developed. The pattern is consistent throughout the past decade (FEWS, 1991a:34).

The food-balance-sheet exercise is most useful for identifying trends and for making annual comparisons because it uses the same methodology from one year to the next, even if this methodology relies on general observation.

SAP adopted an approach dependent on fewer variables to estimate relief needs. As noted earlier, it simply identified the cantons where relief was required, and assumed that 60 per cent of the population was in need of relief, on the basis that a minimum of 40 per cent was likely to engage in seasonal out-migration. According to the range of socio-economic indicators available, it then estimated the number of months for which relief was likely to be required. This approach was crude, but rather more pragmatic in the vacuum of reliable quantitative data.

There was a further difference between the two approaches. A consumption rate of 127kg per year was used in the food balance sheet, based on CILSS/DIAPER surveys of actual consumption rates in 1987–9. The food-balance-sheet exercise is supposed to indicate the surplus or deficit based on the *status quo*, assuming chronic malnutrition and food insecurity remain unchanged. SAP based its assessment of relief needs on the WHO standard minimum cereal consumption requirement of 400g per day, or 146kg/year. If this rate was applied to the food balance sheet, consumption requirements would increase by 15 per cent, and hence the estimated deficit would also increase substantially.

Under pressure, SAP tried to square its results with those of the harvest assessment (SAP, 1990d). By making various assumptions, estimating that at least 60000t of production were probably 'missed' by the harvest assessment, and using its consumption rate of 146kg/year, it ended up with a minimum relief requirement of 50000t based on the food-balance-sheet exercise. It is alarming to observe the significant effect of a small change in one of the parameters on which the harvest assessment is based, and the extent to which the results can be manipulated by making various assumptions. This indicates the flimsiness of the exercise in a country where any of the parameters can only be the roughest of figures because of lack of reliable data.

It could be argued that monitoring the impact of the relief operation is beyond the remit of the EWS, but the fact remains that this was overlooked during 1991. Decision-makers in N'djamena were preoccupied with planning and deciding on the geographical allocation of food aid. Only CARE produced a final report on distribution of the 5000t for which it was responsible (CARE, 1991).

A further weakness of the EWS in Chad is its coverage. There are two major gaps. Pastoralists represent the first of these. Pastoralism is an important part of the Sahelian economy, but the SAP monitors only a few pastoral indicators: a brief qualitative description of the state of the pasture, livestock prices and terms of trade with grain. Monitoring transhumant pastoralists is much more difficult than monitoring sedentary farmers. SAP recognizes the limitations of its approach and the difficulties of estimating relief needs by administrative unit for a population which is on the move (SAP, n.d.), but it has not yet addressed this issue. Problems can arise when food distribution takes place if pastoralists turn up when they have not been included in the initial food aid calculations.

The second gap is the exclusion of the Sudanian zone from any regular or systematic monitoring and reporting. Anecdotal evidence from local authorities, NGOs and others in the area can only be followed up by one-off assessment missions and this inevitably delays a response if one is required. There is a danger that initial warnings are dependent upon those who shout loudest. The one-off assessment missions are a poor second-best to a regular monitoring network. They typically provide a snapshot of a small part of the area, there is no baseline for comparison, and they therefore tend to be very subjective. In 1991 an assessment mission to the south of the country was continually postponed, precisely because there were inadequate relief resources to supply the region, and it was feared that expectations would be raised which could not be met. In contrast, some of the local authorities in the Sahel lodged alarmist reports with CASAAU about food conditions in their respective *préfectures* in 1990–91. The SAP was usually able to confirm or deny anecdotal evidence of food stress from its monitoring work.

Another argument for extending the EWS to the Sudanian zone is that parts of it, like Salamat *préfecture*, and also Lake Chad which is currently omitted from regular EW monitoring, are safety nets for the Sahelian population. Having an idea about the scale and nature of migration from the Sahel southwards can help in assessing the severity of drought in the Sahel and the effectiveness of this particular coping strategy.

Since it began, the SAP has been funded by the EU, but always on the basis of short project cycles. Eventually, it is supposed to be handed over to the government. Sustainability of the system is a key issue. Although the SAP is well integrated into government at all levels — relying on local government officials to carry out much of the data collection — it is unlikely that the government would be able to retain the same capacity without donor funding. For a resource-poor government, maintaining an extensive information network that is only used in drought years is unlikely to be a high priority. CNNTA has already suffered from the withdrawal of donor funds, and its capacity to carry out Phase Three nutrition surveys has deteriorated sharply.

The costs of running an EWS have to be compared with the expected benefits. It is not in the interests of the international donor community to stop funding the SAP if it means that they will not have reliable information on which to plan a relief operation, to decide whether it is necessary and how it can be targeted most effectively. The annual costs of running an EWS are very small relative to the costs of launching a food-relief operation; in Chad, the international donor community will have to foot the bill for emergency relief for many years to come. The question of who funds the EWS is also relevant to the credibility of the information, an issue discussed below.

There are limitations to the design and set-up of the EWS in Chad: it would benefit from a more decentralized approach, better able to detect localized pockets of food insecurity and to monitor coping strategies; its coverage should be extended to include pastoralist groups and the Sudanian zone; and the needs-assessment exercise carried out by SAP should be accorded the credibility it deserves over and above the problematic harvest assessment. But the shortcomings of the EWS cannot be blamed for the serious delays experienced in launching the relief operation in 1990–91. The different components of the system accurately forecast the nature of the food crisis affecting most of the Sahelian population. The warnings should have allowed enough time for something to be done before the next rainy season began. This time the obstacles were not on the side of EW. It is to the response system that we must now turn.

Use of EW information

Figure 6.4 compares the actual relief distribution during 1991, by *préfecture*, with the plans and recommendations. There is very little correlation between SAP's recommendations and the plan drawn up by CASAAU, or between either of these and the final outcome. There is not even a pattern in the way the SAP's recommendations were ignored. For example, in Ouaddai *préfecture* only 16 per cent of SAP's recommended relief requirements were met, compared with over 70 per cent in Batha *préfecture*.

128

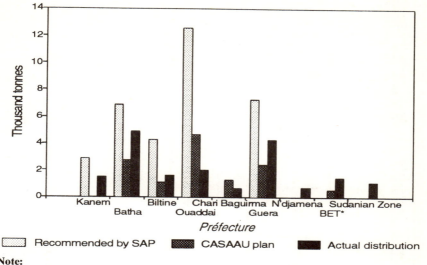

Figure 6.4   *Chad: relief food aid distribution by* préfecture –
recommended, planned and actual
Source: SAP, WFP.

Figure 6.3 showed a similar discrepancy between the SAP's recommended timetable for distributing relief and what actually happened. Figure 6.5 shows the dismal record for most donor agencies of recommendations being translated into decisions and finally action. In the worst case, a year elapsed between recommended action and relief food arriving in N'djamena. Most of the delays seemed to take place at headquarters level. Why did Chad's well-established EWS apparently have such little influence?

The most influential indicators
It was only after the results of the harvest assessment were available that donor agency representatives were prepared to make firm recommendations to their headquarters, thereby losing a month of valuable planning time. It is ironic that the harvest assessment was so influential in triggering response decisions, given such scepticism among donor representatives about production and consumption estimates and apparent levels of self-sufficiency in Chad. The importance attached to the annual harvest survey was almost certainly because these were the kind of data demanded by donor agency headquarters, as the officially recognized assessment of relief needs.

Meanwhile, the SAP suffered from a lack of credibility. Donors were unclear about how the system operated, and demanded to know exactly how its calculations were made, because it was not using the straightforward

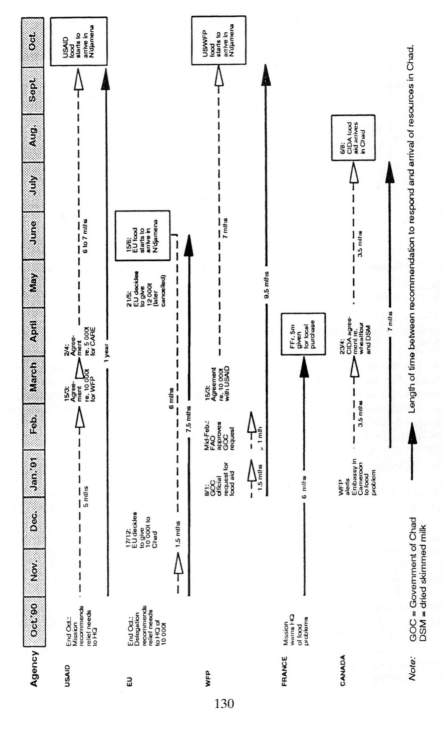

Figure 6.5 *Chad: decision-making and response time for the relief operation, by donor agency*

Agency | Oct.'90 | Nov. | Dec. | Jan.'91 | Feb. | March | April | May | June | July | Aug. | Sept. | Oct.

USAID
End Oct.: Mission recommends relief needs to HQ
5 mths
15/3: Agreement re. 10 000t for WFP
2/4: Agreement re. 5 000t for CARE
6 to 7 mths
1 year
USAID food starts to arrive in N'djamena

EU
End Oct.: Delegation recommends relief needs to HQ of 10 000t
17/12: EU decides to give 10 000t to Chad
1.5 mths
21/5: EU decides to give 12 000t (later cancelled)
6 mths
15/6: EU food starts to arrive in N'djamena

WFP
8/1: GOC official request for food aid
1.5 mths
Mid-Feb.: FAO approves GOC request
≈ 1 mth
15/3: Agreement re. 10 000t with USAID
7.5 mths
9.5 mths
7 mths
USWFP food starts to arrive in N'djamena

FRANCE
Mission warns HQ of food problems
6 mths
FFr. 5m given for local purchase

CANADA
WFP alerts Embassy in Cameroon to food problem
3.5 mths
23/4: CIDA agreement re. wheatflour and DSM
3.5 mths
6/8: CIDA food aid arrives in Chad
7 mths

Note: GOC = Government of Chad
DSM = dried skimmed milk

△ Length of time between recommendation to respond and arrival of resources in Chad.

130

and ubiquitous 'food-balance-sheet' approach. Only the EU Delegation which was funding the SAP was fully familiar with the system and methodology and had confidence in it. Of course, SAP's credibility was not enhanced by the need to revise its first calculation of relief needs in October, but the bias towards the harvest assessment at SAP's expense was deeply entrenched; it cannot be completely explained by this small error alone.

The attitude towards SAP improved during the year. It stuck to its estimate of relief needs of just over 30000t and this eventually became the figure on which pledges were based. With its large component of donor funding, and a combination of two expatriate advisers and a team of government staff, the SAP gradually earned a reputation for the objectivity and reliability of its assessments, and its resistance to political pressures. It was seen to be a reliable guarantee for informal reports of deteriorating food security (pers. comm., donor representative). However, these generous expressions of confidence, retrospectively, from both donor and government staff, were not borne out in the way they used the information for planning the relief operation, as illustrated in Figure 6.4.

Although most of the donors eventually accepted SAP's figure for total relief needs, many were doubtful about the urgency of the situation. As Sahelian people are well adapted to periodic drought, they questioned whether they could not 'cope' without external assistance.

The turning-point for the sceptics was the joint field trip in February 1991, of government, donors and NGOs, after which the first relief-distribution plan was drawn up. They had toured the Sahelian zone and seen signs of distress for themselves. Women digging up ant-hills and termite mounds in search of grain had a particularly powerful impact, and was regarded as a desperate stage in the sequence of coping strategies. It was often quoted by donor representatives as evidence of the severity of the crisis, both verbally and in telexes to agency headquarters. Firsthand experience of acute food insecurity proved to be the trigger where SAP's data had failed.

Even so, the planned distribution bore very little resemblance to the SAP's recommendations. Kanem *préfecture* was absent from the plan entirely, and only when the nutrition survey provided evidence of food crisis (malnutrition rates of over 15 per cent in April 1991) was it put back on the relief distribution map.

Institutional factors

One of the positive influences on the relief-planning process was the remarkable degree of openness in decision-making within the CASAAU forum (Lea and Reed, 1991). The small size of the aid community in N'djamena and good relations between donors and government during the period undoubtedly contributed. Even if requests for relief were received from high political levels, CASAAU usually took the decision to launch a field mission to verify the need, and sometimes amended the request in the light of its findings. But this was not enough to ensure that the recommendations were put into practice.

Two institutional reasons help to explain why it took so long for decisions to be made at headquarters level to release relief resources for Chad. First of all, due to 'normal' bureaucratic procedures, except in exceptional circumstances like the EU's Special Plan for Africa in 1991 (see Chapter 3). Second, a lack of awareness of the need to respond *early* to the food crisis, and to ensure that the food arrived before the rainy season. After the relief operation had ended, civil servants in some donor headquarters appeared to be surprisingly unaware that it had been so severely delayed in relation to the period of greatest need. Both these reasons have to be understood within the political context.

Political influences

Information can be used for political ends, and manipulated to suit the user's agenda. Relief food was a valuable commodity for the impoverished government and resource-poor country. It was in the government's interests to maximize Chad's allocation. Thus, its stated objective for the relief operation was not only to relieve famine, but to eradicate all malnutrition, to justify the request for a very large quantity of relief aid (*Direction de la Sécurité Alimentaire*, 1990). Meanwhile, donor representatives were trying to minimize the aid pledged, to cover only basic needs to avert famine, to keep costs to a minimum, and in the knowledge that they would have to justify their recommendations to headquarters, competing with food-aid demands from elsewhere.

This divergence of objectives explains why the government ignored the SAP's assessment and issued an appeal for 150000t of relief food. It was more politically expedient to translate the national cereals deficit calculated by FAO/CILSS into total relief needs. The international donor community, which had so insistently awaited the results of the harvest assessment, eventually fell back on the much lower estimate of 34000t provided by the SAP, which was more in line with their objective of minimizing relief needs and seemed to them reasonable based on previous experience of relief operations.

Although the decision-making process was informed by the EW information available, it was a process of negotiation between donors who owned the resources and the government which asked for them which determined relief levels. In this hierarchical relationship (see Chapter 2), the donors had greater bargaining power. The government's large appeal may have initially attracted attention in donor headquarters because it was so much greater than recommendations they had received from their own field offices, but ultimately it was a necessary formality to signal to agencies such as WFP to launch a response. It was not influential in determining how much aid was pledged or finally received. The figures favoured by the donors, who controlled the resources, became the accepted CASAAU figures for planning the relief distribution.

One of the reasons why the international response was so slow was because of the lower priority some donor agencies attached to Chad than the bigger and more politically sensitive operations in countries like Ethiopia and Sudan. Ironically, the fact that Chad needed a small fraction of the amount of relief destined for either of these countries did not work in favour of a timely and efficient response. Instead, Chad's needs were simply overlooked.

The military coup on 1 December 1990 put a halt to relief planning in N'djamena for at least a month. In the headquarters of some donor agencies, however, it had much less impact on relief planning: in the EU, for example, the first decision to provide relief was made on 17 December, barely two weeks after the coup. Discussions and decision-making about the relief operation resumed fairly early in January in N'djamena partly because of good relations between donors and the new government, which issued its appeal for food aid soon after it took power on 3 January. Some of the key government officers who participated in CASAAU meetings remained unchanged after the coup. Thus, its disruptive effect on relief planning was short-lived.

The new government ushered in an era of much greater freedom of speech and of the press than had been enjoyed for many years. Newspapers critical of government performance began to be published, such as the *N'djamena Hebdo*, which carried occasional stories of deteriorating food security and of the delayed relief response. This put pressure on those responsible for the relief operation, but the impact of a free press in its infancy was limited.

The overall picture is of EW information not being used to its full advantage, nor given the credibility it merited. This may improve now that donors are more convinced of the SAP's objectivity and accuracy, but serious obstacles to relief being provided on time remain. The main obstacles were encountered at donor headquarters level. Some local representatives became extremely frustrated by their own agency's slow performance and its consequences, reflected in a FEWS project report to Washington, where the USAID mission in N'djamena stated:

> So long as administrative and logistical road-blocks continue to impede the timely delivery of donor food aid, developing improved information systems, which is the stated purpose of FEWS, will remain, to a large extent, academic (USAID, 1991:3).

The fact that the government did not launch its official appeal until January does not explain the slow response. This was not a pre-condition for any of the donors, except WFP, and most had started the decision-making process before January. It is more to do with the low political priority accorded to the Chad operation by some of the principal Western food-aid donor agencies, and the cumbersome decision-making process within many donor bureaucracies.

Relief planning was *ad hoc*. Without knowing early on how much total aid was going to be available (because of the extreme delays in delivery), and with little attention paid to SAP's recommendations, decisions to allocate relief to particular areas or groups of people took place in CASAAU in a piecemeal fashion. Much less food aid was available than had been expected, so relief was often allocated according to evidence of immediate need: in Borkou-Ennedi-Tibesti (BET) when malnutrition of over 20 per cent was recorded; in Tine when malnutrition rates of 40 per cent were reported in April; and in the Sudanian zone in response to a Red Cross mission in July. These decisions were reactive. Little use was made of the predictive capacity of EW.

Implications for the final response

The need to deliver relief food before the rains was repeated again and again, at CASAAU and in communications between donor missions in N'djamena and their headquarters. Experience dictated that the food had to arrive by March/April so that it could be distributed before July; only the EU food aid came near this target, arriving in mid-June. Fortuitously for the logistics of the relief operation, the rains were late so this food reached beneficiaries in July. Most of the agencies now acknowledge a lead time for delivering food to Africa of four to six months (see Chapter 3). The timing of headquarters' decisions to release the relief was completely at odds with the delivery time.

At the last minute, local resources had to be relied upon. It is ironic that the national food-security stock, about which some donors had been ambivalent, came to the rescue in the event of their failure to deliver. The stock had been set up in 1989 as an FAO initiative. The recommended level of 20 000t was disputed by a WFP consultant as being too high and too costly. A financial fund for emergencies was proposed instead (Valère-Gille, 1990). WFP and other donors, apart from USAID, had refused to sign the *Accord-cadre* (agreement/contract) with the ONC, committing them to replenish the strategic reserve as it was drawn down, on the premise that this was incompatible with their usual budgetary procedures. But in the words of one donor representative referring to 1991: '[we] would be in a complete mess without the security stock'.

The experience of 1990–91 makes a strong case for pre-positioning relief reserves in-country. This could decentralize decision-making about allocating relief resources from donor headquarters, where Chad's needs are often likely to be overlooked, particularly within anglophone donor agencies, to donor representatives in-country. Pre-positioned reserves cut out lengthy delays encountered in importing food aid from Europe and the US. In short, they make it much more likely that relief will be provided *on time*, in response to early warnings. Indeed, there was a change in attitude among some donors after the 1991 relief operation. A USAID report concluded that, had 20 000t been held in the reserve, 'most of the hunger [in 1991] could have been avoided' (Lea and Reed, 1991:9). The proposal that a financial fund be set up instead of a stock proved infeasible in the conditions of 1991. The general shortage of food in the country, and in the Sahel as a whole, was reflected in inflated prices. Attempts to buy locally failed.

In 1994, the national food security stock once again played a key role in providing relief resources to the population in need. (Estimated relief needs for 1993–4 were about 18 000t.) Yet there is still no long-term commitment by donors to replenish the stock, and to integrate it into disaster preparedness plans in a coherent way with a *long-term* perspective. There is a danger that it will be empty next time a relief operation is needed. Although donors have paid lip-service to the value of a pre-positioned reserve, they are not prepared to support it, other than in an *ad hoc* fashion, arguing that there are more urgent feeding requirements elsewhere in Africa and Eastern Europe (pers. comm., donor representative). And it is unrealistic to expect the impoverished government to assume the costs of the reserve. Once again, Chad seems to be losing out to other countries and regions which are politically more important to the main food aid donor governments. Indeed, when USAID, the largest food aid donor to Chad, closes its mission in 1995, the likelihood that Chad's needs in the event of a food crisis are overlooked could increase considerably.

Insecurity and the EW/response process

Insecurity in Chad has been caused by fighting between rival ethnic groups. Its recent history has been punctuated by coups and attempted coups as different groups have tried to take power. In 1990 the main fighting was in some eastern parts of the country on the border with Sudan. For some weeks after the coup it was difficult to assess the needs of the people affected because of continued insecurity and restricted access. This is a problem for EW because it is precisely these cantons which face the biggest food problems when production and trade are disrupted by fighting. But the SAP has not been designed to detect such effects as the sudden destruction of assets and the effects of high male mortality by monitoring conflict zones; it is geared to warning of slow-onset disasters. Eventually a mission was sent to the east in March 1991; three months elapsed before anything was done. During the assessment, it proved extremely difficult to establish how many families and children were in need of assistance through interviewing. In this situation, the Phase Three nutrition survey which showed a very high malnutrition rate in part of Biltine *préfecture* was most influential in confirming the need for an urgent response. Given that a 40 per cent rate of malnutrition had already developed, the response was too late.

As long as political instability continues to be a threat to food security, how to monitor and provide assistance in this kind of situation will continue to be an enormous challenge to the EW/response process — a challenge which has not yet been taken up.

Conclusions

The tale of EW/response in Chad in 1990–91 is a disappointing one. Efforts to establish and strengthen a famine-prevention system after the deficiencies of the 1984–5 relief operation have met with only limited success. Some of the same mistakes from the mid-1980s were repeated in the early 1990s, leading to the same 'failure to have sufficient food in the right place at the right time' (Brown *et al.*, 1987:xi).

Although there are weaknesses in the EWS in Chad, the SAP and the other EW components performed satisfactorily during 1990 and 1991. They provided timely warnings of the impact of drought, they did not exaggerate food insecurity, they were consistent and painted a clear overall picture about conditions in the Sahelian zone. This should have been enough to trigger a prompt response. This time the delayed relief operation certainly cannot be blamed on lack of EW. A food crisis did develop across the Sahelian zone in 1991. It was not a full-blown famine, but people suffered from food shortages, malnutrition rates rose and livelihoods came under stress. A relatively small amount of food aid was all that was needed to protect the population from the worst effects of the drought — less than 5 per cent of the needs of Sudan or Ethiopia. To be effective, the relief had to be delivered to beneficiaries before the rains and the hungry season began. Less than one-third of total estimated needs met this target. Even by the end of 1991, less than half had been distributed.

Political events and the military coup in December cannot be blamed for much of the delay. The new government enjoyed the support of most of the donor community, and after only a month of disruption, meetings were resumed in N'djamena. The changed political climate allowed EW information to be circulated more freely. There was an undisputed view that the responsibility for providing resources lay with the international donor community, facilitated by the government.

Many factors should have conspired to facilitate a timely and straightforward relief operation in Chad. Predictions were early, relations were good between donors and government, only small amounts of relief were needed from international donors, and NGOs and WFP were prepared to carry out distribution on the ground with the government's seal of approval. On the face of it, there were no exceptional circumstances to block the relief operation. The international relief system clearly failed to meet the targets it had set itself. Relief was provided too little and too late. Local purchase of grain using aid money did not work. *Opération Viande*, which was scrambled together at the last minute as a contingency measure fell apart soon after it had begun. This case-study is revealing about what spurs the international relief system into action. The reasons why the operation should have been successful did not hold.

First of all, the same pattern was repeated in Chad as in other countries, namely, the annual harvest assessment and food balance sheet had a disproportionate influence on triggering response. Chad illustrates particularly well the flimsiness of this exercise. And as a result, weeks of valuable planning time were lost.

Second, hard evidence that people are already in the grip of a food crisis — in this case the decision-makers seeing it firsthand on a field trip — is much more influential than written or even verbal predictions provided by the EWS. There is a lesson here for how an EWS conducts its public relations: get the people you are trying to influence out into the field to see what is happening for themselves. But there is also a warning: the snapshots collected by influential representatives on a one-off mission can displace data collected by the EWS on a regular and systematic basis. Waiting for the harvest assessment, and planning the relief operation only when there was evidence of a crisis already under way, both seriously delayed the launching of the operation in Chad.

This case-study demonstrates how unresponsive the international relief system is to a low-profile, small-scale food crisis, which does not display the classic signs of famine in terms of population displacement and excess mortality, apparently necessary to convey a sense of urgency and to trigger the rapid release of resources in donor agency headquarters. The lack of responsiveness is made worse if there is no particular media or political interest within the principal food aid donor countries for the country concerned. It can be argued that the international relief system was overloaded in 1991, with the post-Gulf War crisis in northern Iraq, and large-scale emergencies developing in other African countries like Somalia, Ethiopia, Sudan and Mozambique; a less-severe problem like Chad's had to take lower priority. This was what happened, but it is not an acceptable excuse. The quantities of relief required for Chad were very small, and there were no unusual circumstances to make the operation a difficult one as negotiations resumed promptly after the coup. The delays encountered in donor agency headquarters, of up to five months before relief was even made available, were excessive.

Chad's experience makes a strong argument for pre-positioning relief resources. The fortuitous presence of the small ONC stock in 1991 saved the day. This was the main difference from 1984–5. It had enjoyed little support from most donors, but proved to be a vital resource to compensate for the delayed arrival of imported food aid. There is little reason to suppose that in the future the international relief system would respond much more efficiently to this kind of small-scale food crisis. In a drought which also affects the Horn of Africa, Chad is always likely to be a lower priority with the main food aid donors than other countries where food-security problems occur on a much larger scale and with greater international media coverage.

The most logical solution is to build up a national strategic reserve. In the most common scenario, when food problems are localized and a small-scale relief operation is all that is needed, a strategic reserve may be able to meet the total needs of the operation. In a larger-scale crisis where famine threatens, it could cover the critical bridging period while international aid is mobilized. It gives local donor representatives, who are more aware of the nature and seriousness of the problem, greater decision-making powers rather than having to rely on the cumbersome processes in their agency headquarters. More notice has been taken of the importance of Chad's strategic reserve since 1991 than before, but this has not been matched by donor commitment to longer-term support.

What about the government's use of EW information? Although the SAP was part of government, the politicians paid very little attention to its data. They manipulated the data from the harvest assessment to pursue their objective of maximizing food aid receipts, with the justification that all malnutrition should be eradicated. It is to the SAP's credit that it did not succumb to political pressure and alter its recommendations. This independence was probably only possible because it was jointly funded by the EU and the government, and because of the presence of expatriate technical advisers with greater autonomy than their government counterparts. This suggests that there are some major advantages to an EWS being funded jointly by donors and government. Not only do both have a stake in the system which makes it more likely that they will take its information seriously, but also this may be the best way of protecting an EWS from political interference.

In many ways the SAP has now proved itself. It is now at the centre of national EW and, despite poor infrastructure and a difficult operating environment, it has refined its approach and developed indicators for predicting food crisis. But there is still plenty of room for improvement. It is a highly centralized system firmly rooted in N'djamena. Its understanding of local food economies and the coping capacity and resilience of local populations is weak, especially in conditions like 1991 when there was not outright famine. And its coverage is inadequate. It could be strengthened by decentralizing its approach, with more analysis being carried out at *préfecture* level by monitors themselves. This would need greater resources at sub-national level to improve the mobility of the SAP agents. Coverage should be extended to the Sudanian zone, where transitory food insecurity is a recurrent problem, and to pastoralists who are an important component of the Sahelian population. There is also a need for better EW monitoring of the remote and sparsely populated BET area: the current system of one-off nutritional surveys is unlikely to provide *early* warnings of food stress.

The experience of 1990–91 indicates that priority should be given to improving response capacity. This is where the system is weakest. The most obvious improvement is the pre-positioning of resources in-country; this is the best way to ensure that the response is really timely and makes most use of EW. Chad should benefit from Mali's experience of the *Stock National de Sécurité*; better still would be a national strategic reserve built into contingency plans, with advance agreement by donors and government to replenish it. The reserve would not be big enough to meet the needs of every crisis. Its size should be determined by the frequency of food crises in Chad, the numbers of vulnerable people likely to require relief, and managerial capacity. However, the prospects for putting this in practice do not look good, as relief demands escalate in other countries and as some donors streamline their geographical focus.

If Chad must continue to rely on imported food aid in the event of a food crisis (which may still be necessary even if there is a small security stock), donor decisions to respond need to be taken earlier, in late September, to ensure that the relief operation is planned, launched, and delivers assistance in time, *before* the start of the hungry season in about June. If relief needs are still uncertain in September, the response should be phased. Small amounts can be pledged early on, to start the ball rolling. When a final assessment has been completed, a second phase of pledging can take place. This requires significant changes in the workings of the international relief system.

CHAPTER 7
Mali

Introduction

Despite localized food shortages, there was no threat of famine in Mali in 1991. Yet the Malian story is an interesting basis for comparison with the other countries in this study, because of the rare example it offers of a programmed response mechanism which is institutionally linked to the national EWS. A collaborative exercise between the government and donors, this mechanism is designed to ensure that EW information is used systematically to inform food aid distributions. It rests on a relatively well-developed national EW capacity and is backed up by a small national security stock, of which less than 20 per cent was needed to implement all recommendations made by the EWS in 1991.

There were important limitations to this system, which provide insights into the relevance of the model for other countries as well as to how it might be improved. The first drawback was the available response options, which in practice were limited to free food aid distributions. More serious was its failure to ensure — or even to monitor adequately — whether or not food aid reached the intended beneficiaries. Invariably much did not, thereby exposing a further missing link in the chain: it is not enough simply to take the decision to respond, nor even to back this up with resources, if the institutional arrangements to carry out these decisions are not in place. As the following discussion shows, it is by no means clear that this critical gap can be easily overcome.

This chapter explores the effectiveness of Mali's programmed response mechanism. Whether timely response was due to the relative sophistication of national EW capacity or to wider initiatives in donor/government collaboration and the long-standing national security stock is assessed. National EW capacity is not without contention: there are several systems operating in Mali, only one of which, the *Système d'Alerte Précoce* (SAP), is used in the mechanism, an information system with important shortcomings. There is disagreement as to how the EW/response system would operate in a real emergency: this has not yet been necessary. Nor is it clear how well it functions in areas affected by armed conflict. Finally, Mali is a country with a small population, threatened only intermittently with food crises and, until recently, not dogged by sustained armed conflict. It is important to bear this in mind when considering the replicability of the Malian model in countries facing endemic famine conditions and war affecting many millions more people, where the scope and cost of a similar exercise would be on an altogether different scale.

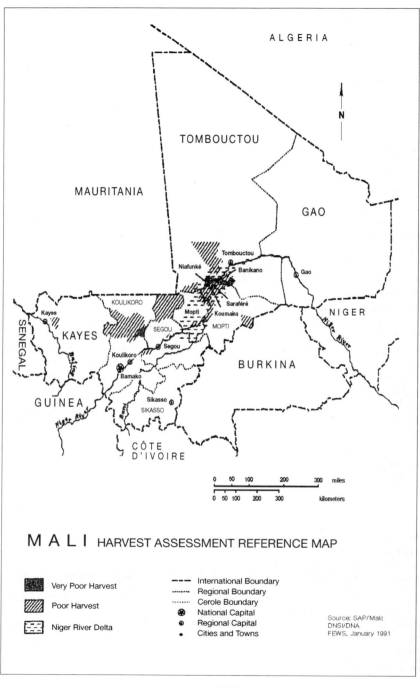

Figure 7.1 *Map of Mali, showing the harvest assessment for 1990–91*
Source: FEWS (1991a).

140

Food security[1]

The principal cause of Mali's food problems is poverty, exacerbated by climatic fluctuations, the long-term effects of successive dry years and macro-economic stagnation. Mali is one of the few Sahelian countries with a good potential for cereals production, 80 per cent of it millet and sorghum. The southern part of the country has historically been the bread basket of the western Sahel. Meanwhile in the Sahelian north where rainfed millet is the main crop, production is invariably in structural deficit. Figure 7.1 is a FEWS map of Mali, showing the 1990–91 harvest assessment.

Both inter-annual and inter-regional fluctuations in production are large (see Figure 7.2). Production in 1990–91 was 19 per cent above the average for the period 1971–2 to 1990–91 and average for the preceding decade. It was, however, well below the trend, as were other bad years of the 1970s and 1980s. In every year, aggregate figures disguise significant regional variations. At worst, Mali is hit periodically by successive years of drought. The most recent, in the early 1980s, culminated in a production deficit of over 500000t in 1984–5 — nearly a half of total needs.

Although a decline in per capita output is not in question, there is much debate as to whether Mali suffers from a structural food deficit, fuelled by unreliable (but improving) statistics for output and further complicated in recent years by controversy over the figure used to calculate consumption needs. Until 1990, the government and most food aid donors calculated total cereals consumption by multiplying the population by 167kg/year. In 1990, the government used the much higher figure of 212kg for the first time.[2] Problematic population estimates contribute further to the uncertainty. Until 1987, an annual growth of between 2.5 and 3.0 per cent was used to estimate population, from baselines of the 1976 census (6.4 million). The 1987 census revealed a population of only 7.6 million, indicating an average 1.7 per cent growth and a population of eight million in 1990 (rather than 8.3 million using the higher growth rate). Gross per capita production in 1990 was therefore either 200kg (160kg net) or 193kg (155kg net), depending on the population figure chosen.[3]

Widely fluctuating production and continuing uncertainty in estimates of both production levels and consumption requirements, not to mention little or no available data on household stocks[4] or other sources of food (e.g. livestock, fish, wild foods), make the calculation of a national food

---

[1] This section is based on Davies, 1995 (forthcoming).
[2] The figure of 167kg was derived from FAO standards for Mali set in 1975–7. The higher figure of 212kg was adopted following the DNSI/PADEM household consumption surveys carried out in 1988–9 (République du Mali, 1991b). The National Food Strategy (République du Mali, 1982) uses a higher estimate of 224kg/person/year (providing 2450kcal/person/day, which is quite high in a Sahelian climate).
[3] Net production is calculated using the FEWS figure of 19.6 per cent for 'non-food uses' (FEWS, 1991b). This is higher than the 15 per cent usually used to calculate losses, but takes into account rice production which has a higher coefficient for losses than millet and sorghum (0.51 compared to 0.85).
[4] Estimates of household stocks have recently been incorporated into DNSI surveys.

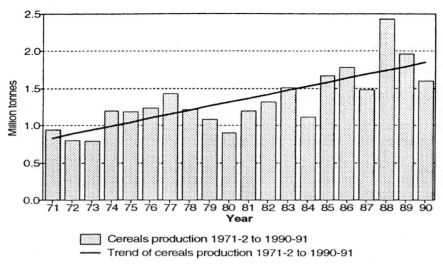

Cereals production 1971-2 to 1990-91
—— Trend of cereals production 1971-2 to 1990-91

Source: Davies, 1995 (forthcoming).

Figure 7.2 *Mali: cereals production, 1971–2 to 1990–91*
Source: Davies, 1995 (forthcoming).

balance for Mali more akin to art than science. Given that quite small variations can make the difference between a national food surplus and deficit, these data constraints are especially important.[5] Bearing these caveats in mind, Figure 7.3 summarizes the crude national food balance from 1971–2 to 1990–91. The pattern shows that in the 1970s Mali suffered a structural deficit in all but one year, and in the 1980s, in 60 per cent of years, implying some improvement in food security at the national level, particularly associated with better rainfall conditions towards the end of the period. When imports (including food aid) are taken into account, the 1980s show a clear improvement, with only one year marginally in deficit. The principal need of a national food-security policy, therefore, is not simply to produce more food, but to reduce inter-annual production fluctuations and to distribute domestically produced cereals more evenly.

Mali ceased to be an exporter of cereals in 1964, and in 1966 commercial imports of sorghum, maize and rice were required for the first time. By 1970 a programme of food aid had been introduced. Food aid as a proportion of total food imports averaged about half from 1970 to 1990, only rising significantly above this in drought years.

Emergency food aid was unknown in Mali until the 1973 drought. About 175 000t were delivered in 1973 and 1974, but its late arrival and chaotic distribution meant that the impact on the hungry was largely irrelevant. Counterpart funds from the sale of this aid were used in a variety of unprogrammed ways. Huge amounts of food aid again flowed in during the

---

5   The DNSI/PADEM Project (*Projet de la Mise en Place de Dispositifs Permanents d'Enquêtes auprès des Ménages*), financed by UNDP, aims to improve both the quality and availability of such data.

142

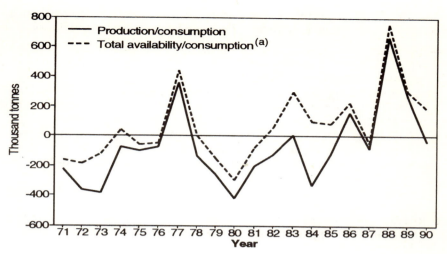

Note:
(a) Total availability = production plus imports including food aid.

Figure 7.3 *Mali: crude national food balance, 1971–2 to 1990–91*
Source: Davies, 1995 (forthcoming).

drought of the mid-1980s. Again, this influx was inappropriate (much of it was maize, unknown in the north), excessive and unmanageable: 86000t of aid arrived in 1985–6, a good year, half of which should have been delivered during the previous year and the balance of which was unneeded (Pirzio-Biroli, 1988).

Since 1980–81, when the *Programme de Réstructuration du Marché Céréalier* (Cereals Market Restructuring Programme, PRMC) was established, 72 per cent of food aid has been provided by a group of regular donors.[6] Part of the initiative behind the establishment of the PRMC and the use of food aid counterpart funds in cereals market restructuring was a desire to 'introduce some order in food aid management' (Pirzio-Biroli, 1988:11). The PRMC has significantly improved the management of food aid since the chaos of the mid-1980s, but the system has yet to be tested in an emergency year.

Mali has not been stricken by repeated episodes of widespread famine. Food shortages in late 1984 and 1985 gave rise to what the government and donor agencies called a 'food emergency', the extent and degree of which has since been questioned. Undoubtedly many people were hungry, but there is little evidence of what de Waal (1989) has called 'famine that kills', or indeed of emergency relief arriving soon enough in the right places to have prevented this. But chronic seasonal food insecurity, which becomes acute for some groups in deficit years, is endemic in much of the north of

---

6 WFP, Belgium, Canada, EU, France, Germany, the Netherlands and the United States. Of these, the EU, the United States and Canada are the most important.

the country. The problems now facing Mali are more complex than a permanent, structural food deficit. They can be summarized as follows:

- high annual variations in output, which can produce national surpluses at one extreme and acute food shortages (particularly in the northern zones) in drought years at the other;
- in the northern parts of the country, increasingly vulnerable livelihood systems which result in seasonal shortages of food in most years, during the lengthening hungry season from at least May to September;
- significant groups of rural people who, having lost their means of production and/or most of their capital in the last two periods of drought, are now too poor to be able to purchase sufficient quantities of food, at almost any price;
- growing urbanization as a consequence of the impoverishment of rural areas, and few opportunities for urban employment;
- logistical difficulties in distributing food from the productive south to the dry north, in a huge country with few roads, many of which are impassable during the wet season;
- until the progressive liberalization of the cereals market in the 1980s, a pricing policy which led to low producer prices, discouraging production and stimulating unofficial cross-border trade while at the same time failing to subsidize consumption for most of the population.

The reasons why Mali has avoided widespread famine are less to do with astute policies of famine prevention than with the nature of its food insecurity and the absence of contributory factors, which elsewhere have been closely identified with tipping the balance from serious food shortage to famine.

First among such factors is the fact that historically there has been little armed conflict. In 1990, however, conflict between Tuareg in the north and the Malian army erupted. In addition, the overthrow of President Moussa Traoré in March 1991 was preceded by outbreaks of unrest in urban areas. These events made 1990–91 unusual in recent Malian history in that conflict influenced food security for the first time in many years. Second, Mali has a relatively small population of around eight million and population growth is particularly low, averaging only 0.73 per cent in the northern regions most vulnerable to food insecurity. Third, the population is highly mobile, and has been able to migrate to the south of the country and further afield, where employment opportunities were sufficient to prevent migrants being a drain on low household food stocks. Fourth, producers have been able to cope in the short term with seasonal fluctuations in food availability and develop an array of coping strategies to raise food entitlements. Complementing this ability to cope is the capacity to adapt, by diversifying productive activities and increasing market dependence, in line with changing agro-ecological and economic conditions.

The EW/response system

Lack of information was widely believed to have hindered effective response in 1984–5, giving rise to a boom industry in famine EWS in

Table 7.1   Mali: stages of SAP early warning and response

Stages of early warning and response	J	A	S	O	N	D	J	F	M	A	M	J
1. Monitoring												
Monthly:												
Basic physical and socio-economic indicators[a]	■	■	■	■	■	■	■	■	■	■	■	■
Cyclical:												
Agricultural campaign[b]	■	■										
Livestock					■							
Population movements					■	■	■	■	■	■	■	■
Periodic:												
Socio-medico-nutritional surveys[c]	▨	▨							▨	▨	▨	▨
2. Reporting												
Monthly:												
SAP Bulletins	■	■	■	■	■	■	■	■	■	■	■	■
Cyclical:												
SAP Diagnostic Report					■							
SAP Provisional Balance Sheet						■						
SAP Definitive Prognostic Report									■			
Periodic:												
Socio-medico-nutritional surveys	▨	▨							▨	▨	▨	▨
3. Decision-making												
Cyclical:												
Recommendations in Bulletins					■				■			
COC Meetings						■			■			
4. Response triggered												
PRMC/CNAUR/OPAM						▨			■			

Key: ■   = regular monitoring;

▨   = monitoring and response undertaken on an 'as-needed' basis.

Notes:
(a) Depending on the season, these include: rainfall, insect infestation, the agricultural campaign, pasture conditions, fishing conditions, migration, market prices (millet and goats), food stocks and health and nutritional status.
(b) For flooded rice the period of monitoring is extended to January. For irrigated crops monitoring takes place from February to June, and for counter-season crops the harvest is estimated in February.
(c) This is variable, but the maximum period of monitoring is from January to August.

1986. Already part of the FAO's GIEWS and the CILSS/DIAPER/ AGRHYMET system, Mali set up a national system — the SAP — in 1986.[7] FEWS also began a programme in Mali, funded by USAID, and three NGOs[8] formed the *Suivi Alimentaire Delta Seno* (SADS) in 1987, a sub-national EWS in the Fifth Region. By 1990 the establishment of the SAP in particular had fundamentally altered donor and government perceptions of the availability and reliability of information for planning relief needs. Table 7.1 summarizes the three critical stages in the SAP system:

7   This was funded initially by the EU and executed by AEDES/MSF.
8   SCF (UK) and Oxfam (UK), and IUCN. For details of all these systems see Buchanan-Smith *et al.*, 1991.

monitoring, reporting and decision-making, which lead to the fourth stage of response being triggered.

The SAP has succeeded in standardizing data-gathering methods and reporting requirements, and regular monthly publication of results in SAP Bulletins has made sub-national-level information widely available. Crucially, by basing the SAP on existing government structures and implementing a phased system of consensus building (from *cercle* or district, to regional, to national level) about the information reported at each stage, by the time the bulletin is published many of the contradictions inherent in EW reporting have been ironed out. Nevertheless, a number of drawbacks remained in 1990–91: insufficient regional and sectoral differentiation; lack of credibility in some quarters; lack of clarity about how SAP recommendations were arrived at and the ways in which vulnerable areas were classified; failure to cover the south of the country and hence dependence on the annual harvest assessment; a tendency to take monthly snapshots of the food situation rather than to predict what will happen in the future; and the limited response options the SAP could recommend.

Other sources of EW information need to be assessed in relation to the SAP. The national harvest assessment, carried out by the *Direction Nationale de l'Agriculture* (DNA) and the *Direction Nationale de la Statistique* (DNSI), and supported by FAO/CILSS, is the starting-point from which all subsequent SAP data are assessed. Disagreement over this assessment can lead to delays in response. FEWS, used by USAID in its food-aid planning, relies on other sources of EW information (principally the SAP) to produce its own reports. SADS information, while making some input into regional SAP information and FEWS reports as well as producing quarterly bulletins, is not systematically exploited in the EW/response process, partly because its principal objective is to identify longer-term interventions to improve household food security. The *Système d'Information sur le Marché des Céréales* (Cereals Market Information System, SIM) is a project to broadcast cereal prices to improve the transparency of newly liberalized markets, but its data can conflict with those of the SAP and are not generally used in EW.

The second major component of the EW/response system is the institutional context which the SAP is designed to inform. The PRMC is at the heart of this, a co-ordinated donor programme which has supported, through a variety of macro-economic measures, the government's liberalization of cereals markets since 1981. As a means of offsetting some of the adverse consequences of liberalization in the event of food deficits, the PRMC sought to develop a response strategy to minimize the possible disincentive effects of free food distributions on the private commercial sector. There were three elements to this strategy in 1990: the financing of the *Stock National de Sécurité* (SNS) via counterpart funds (amounting to around CFAfr37 000 million a year in 1990); support for the *Comité National d'Actions d'Urgence et de Réhabilitation* (CNAUR); and two information projects — the SAP, for which the PRMC assumed financial responsibility in 1990, and the SIM. The SNS can rise to a maximum of 58 000t of local millet and sorghum,[9] a level established by CILSS in 1981. Such a stock would last approximately three months in the event of famine conditions.

In 1989–90 (the year prior to the case-study period), donors showed concern about the chaotic response process, despite substantial investments in EW. They undertook to agree to a concerted position and to stick to it throughout the following year. This strategy was vindicated in 1990–91: the 'fit' between SAP recommendations and distributions was very tight and repeated questions about the validity of SAP data were answered, in part at least, by improved methods.

Yet the story is less straightforward than this. As late as November 1990, an evaluation of the SAP (commenting on the misfit between SAP recommendations and actual distributions in 1989–90) concluded that:

> The impact of the project on decisions and free food aid distribution is weak. The divergence of interests between decision-makers results either in a reduction of recommended aid, or in long delays in distributing ... Although SAP recommendations are greatly anticipated, the direct impact of the project on food aid decisions is in reality weak and does not show any real progression (Egg and Teme, 1990:i, 26).

The principal criticisms of the EW/response system in 1991 were as follows:

- Donors' over-dependence on the harvest assessment, which reports its final balance in January, thereby negating much of the *early* warning of the SAP system.
- Over-institutionalization of the response process, leading to long bureaucratic delays.
- Over-dependence on donor resources and technical assistance, and consequent questions about the long-term sustainability of the SAP and its programmed response system.
- The necessity of continued donor co-ordination in the PRMC which, while a substantial achievement, can nevertheless come under serious pressure at times, almost inevitably to be accentuated in a bad year.
- An inability to overcome the endemic problems of conflicting interests, both between donors and government, and within these groups. PRMC donors were driven by the desire to prevent free food distributions disrupting markets, and to target only those with low incomes; while the government recognized food aid as an economic resource which could be used to meet a variety of political and social ends. The SAP found itself 'sandwiched' between its bureaucratic links to the *Ministère de l'Administration Territoriale et du Développement à la Base* (MATDB) and its financing by the PRMC (Egg and Teme, 1990).[10]

---

9   The US, Canada and France contribute food aid which is all sold and converted into counterpart funds; the EU donates the equivalent value of food aid in cash; and CIDA and the Dutch also contribute money. This all goes into a common fund. GTZ also provides technical assistance to OPAM, via the *Projet de Sécurité Alimentaire*.
10   This can also be seen as a strength of the SAP in that 'the project is situated between the two principal centres of decision-making about food aid' (Egg and Teme, 1990:40).

- Continued delays between the demand for food aid and its arrival in country (9 to 12 months). In 1990, for example, 10000t of rice supplied by USAID in response to the rice deficit arrived in 1991 when the next rice harvest was already under way (CCE, 1992:46).
- Insufficient targeting (the smallest unit being about 5000 people) and inadequate monitoring on the ground of what actually happens to the aid distributed.
- Failure of the EW/response system to deal adequately with conflict zones which, in 1991, were also those most vulnerable to food insecurity.

Despite these problems, Mali's EW/response system at the beginning of 1990–91 season was more developed and better co-ordinated than at any other time. The failure of the preceding year to exploit existing EW information fully in decision-making had been recognized by donors as a key weakness, into which they had invested resources via the PRMC. On the government side, the change of regime in March 1991, as well as armed conflict in the north of the country, gave rise to intense uncertainty, and a high political price was attached to getting the response right. Despite these upheavals, the programmed system worked remarkably well. This should not detract from the fact that, although many of the food-security problems facing local people in Mali are of a chronic, livelihood-undermining rather than a transitory, famine-threatening kind, the response process addresses only the latter. Unexploited SAP data, and information provided by the SADS (also largely unused in the response process), could be used to identify more flexible response options.

The story of EW in 1990–91

There was no consensus regarding the extent or intensity of food insecurity in Mali in 1991. Certainly initial harvest estimates were too high, confirmed by sharp increases in millet prices in February/March. Overall it was an average year for the decade, but one that was below the trend as Figure 7.2 above shows. The previous year had been only satisfactory, hence many producers had no carry-over stocks. Nationally, production in 1990/91 was higher than in 1987/88, the worst year since the drought of 1984. Overall there were pockets of severe food insecurity, but no indication of a threat of famine. Conflict in the north led to the disruption of traditional transhumance and commercial routes, which added to food-insecurity problems resulting from especially poor harvests in the Sahel. The existing programmed response mechanism continued to operate despite the change of regime in March, indicating the robustness of the system. What EW information was available in 1990–91?

The 1990–91 DNSI/DNA harvest assessment was dogged with controversy. A promising start in July indicated a very good harvest, but this was followed by an exceptional drought in August and limited grasshopper attacks in September,[11] not detected by the assessment. A provisional

---

[11] Losses from pest attacks in the Fifth Region were estimated to be 30 per cent of the millet crop and 60 per cent of the rice crop, by the *Direction Régionale de l'Agriculture*.

estimate of 2.1 million tonnes was made in October,[12] 4.5 per cent less than the previous year, revised downwards to a final figure of 1.6 million tonnes in April,[13] due largely to a deficit in rice production (see Figure 7.1 above). Failure to arrive at an agreed harvest assessment was exacerbated by disagreement over national demand, notably the government's decision to use a higher figure to estimate consumption requirements for the first time. Table 7.2 summarizes the various estimates of the national food balance in 1990–91, depending on the different harvest estimates and maximum (212kg) and minimum (167kg) per capita consumption requirements. The first sign of a deficit was in January using the high consumption requirement figure (disputed by donors), and agreement on a deficit was only reached in February. In fact, the final PADEM harvest survey results show a small surplus if the minimum per capita consumption requirement is used. With quite small adjustments, particularly on the demand side, the food situation moves from surplus to deficit, indicating that relatively imprecise information about the *national* food balance can give a misleading picture. The pre-eminence of the annual harvest assessment undermines the potential for the well-developed *sub-national* EW capacity to inform in a timely and accurate manner.

Critical times for SAP reporting are October/November (provisional outlook and recommendations); February (definitive harvest results); and March (definitive recommendations for food aid distributions).[14] In May 1990, the FEWS Vulnerability Assessment (FEWS, 1990) had indicated that most categories of producers in the Sahel would be moderately vulnerable during the coming year, with only cultivators singled out as being extremely vulnerable. SAP reports of the October harvest reflected the early optimistic results of the harvest assessment, subsequently revised downwards to indicate average harvests in the north and good ones in the south of the country. FEWS was the only EWS to arrive at the finally agreed harvest assessment (1.6 million tonnes gross) by the end of 1990, a figure indicating that the country was narrowly in deficit overall. The government's claim in December of a deficit of 400 000t (based on a harvest estimate of 1.7 million tonnes and per capita consumption of 212 kg/year) was greeted with scepticism by donors in early January. There were, however, pockets of harvest failure, especially in the Sixth, Seventh and parts of the Fifth Regions. Prices remained stable, or fell only slightly, after the harvest, reflecting this patchy story. The rice harvest was good in irrigated areas, but mediocre in flooded ones. Both pasture and fishing conditions were average to good according to the SAP, but SADS judged fishing conditions to be poor or satisfactory for the fourth year in succession.

This pattern of a year that was generally satisfactory, with isolated incidences of food stress, was not fundamentally challenged either by the SAP or other EW data. SADS bulletins showed that people in the Fifth Region

---

[12] This estimate was broken down as follows: millet 737 007t; sorghum 531 433t; *fonio* 21768t; maize 196 579t; paddy 112 294t (FAO, 1990).
[13] FEWS arrived at the same figure of 1.6 million tonnes as early as August 1990, but this was not officially recognized until the following February.
[14] Recommendations are made from October onwards and continue after July, but March is when the major decisions about response are taken.

Table 7.2   Mali: comparison of national food deficit/surplus in 1990–91 according to different harvest and consumption estimates (million tonnes)

	Net availability estimate[a]	Consumption estimate[b]		Size of national food deficit/surplus	
		167kg	212kg	low pcc[c]	high pcc
October	1.94[d]	1.37	1.74	+0.6	+0.2
January	1.45[e]	1.37	1.74	+0.1	−0.3
February	1.30[f]	1.37	1.74	−0.1	−0.4
July	1.45[g]	1.37	1.74	+0.1	−0.3

Notes:
(a) Includes carry-over stocks at both national and producer level.
(b) Based on a population of 8 186 000 (CILSS, 1990). A consumption level of 167kg/capita/year results in total requirements of 1.37 million tonnes; and a level of 212kg/capita/year, in 1.74 million tonnes.
(c) Per capita consumption.
(d) CILSS figures for provisional food balance sheet, assuming carry-over stocks of 302 230t and the following coefficients for transforming gross production into net production: rice 0.55; millet and sorghum 0.85 (CILSS, 1990).
(e) Based on government's revision of harvest to gross production of 1.79 million tonnes. The net figure has been calculated using an overall coefficient for losses of 0.795 and the same stock levels as identified by CILSS.
(f) Based on USAID's figure for gross production of 1.6 million tonnes. The net figure has been calculated using an overall coefficient for losses of 0.795 and the same stock levels as identified by CILSS.
(g) Based on final PADEM harvest survey results, and includes rice, millet, sorghum, maize and *fonio* production (République du Mali, 1991d). These last two account for only 0.2 million tonnes. This estimate is the same as that issued by the government in January.

were relying on a range of coping strategies by March, the returns to which were low and uncertain; millet prices were around 50 per cent higher than the previous year, but there was no indication that people were facing destitution. Private traders confirmed this view, with market demand peaking in June and July 1991, then falling sharply as wild foods became widely available. It is interesting that both the SAP and FEWS attribute significant improvements in the situation during the hungry season to the distributions of free food aid, although, as subsequent evaluations showed, very little of this reached those apparently at risk.

In the 11 nutrition surveys carried out by the SAP in 1991, as a means of verifying qualitative indicators of food stress, the highest incidence of children measuring less than 80 per cent weight for height was 13.8 per cent, and in half the surveys undertaken the prevalence was under 11 per cent.

The exception to this general pattern was those parts of the Sixth and Seventh Regions rendered inaccessible by armed conflict both to the SAP and to traders. FEWS claimed in January 1991 that 238 000 people in the north were moderately vulnerable to food insecurity as a direct result of civil unrest, rising to 343 500 by June. CARE Mali argued as early as August 1990 that the harvests would fail in two *cercles* in the Sixth Region, a situation greatly exacerbated by civil conflict leading to the breakdown of law and order and reciprocal ties. The SAP did not monitor this area and CARE left in May 1991. Conditions during the dry season of 1991 were akin to those of 1985, as adequate stocks of food had not been mobilized in time.

Evaluating the EW information

With the exception of these regions, lack of information was not a constraint in 1990–91. Although information provided by the SAP system was widely regarded as having improved substantially, particularly since 1988 when an evaluation identified validation and quality control as key weaknesses of the system (Lalau-Keraly and Winter, 1988), problems persisted in 1991.

First, the story in the SAP Bulletins was difficult to follow because reporting was limited to standard indicators with little analysis, and issues raised were not always followed up in subsequent months. Users at regional level criticized the SAP's inability to distinguish between the overall food situation of a *cercle* and pockets of food insecurity within it.

Second, SAP information tended to take a static snapshot of the current situation, making no attempt to *predict* what this might entail in subsequent months (except implicitly in recommending food aid distributions). SADS, in contrast, was more dynamic in its analysis, and attempted to predict how the situation would evolve and how food-insecure groups might cope. The SADS Bulletin, however, is limited to only three *cercles* within the Fifth Region plus the regional capital. For it to be used as a regional planning tool, full coverage of the region would be necessary.

Third, dependence on local administrative structures is both the greatest strength of the SAP system (in terms of institutional sustainability) and its greatest weakness in terms of objectivity. The tendency to overestimate needs is strong and this is especially important in years when there is confusion over the harvest assessment and hence whether the country is in surplus or deficit.

Although the lack of quantification in both SAP and SADS Bulletins did not appear to be a constraint to the credibility of the information, the fact that the harvest assessment is the sole source of quantified EW information goes a long way towards explaining its pre-eminence. The ability to quantify the numbers of people affected in each production system in each *cercle* covered would make the SADS interpretation more precise, particularly for users unfamiliar with the zone, and might improve the exploitation of SADS qualitative data overall.

The story of response in 1990–91

Programmed response

Decisions based on SAP information are taken at national level; in 1991, regional government officers perceived their relationship to the SAP as providers rather than users of information. By centralizing decision-making, opportunities may be lost for identifying more sensitive and flexible local response options.

During the year, SAP recommended a total of 11310t of free food aid distributions. Table 7.3 summarizes authorized distributions from SNS stocks

Table 7.3 Mali: authorized free food aid distributions from SNS stocks in 1991 (tonnes)

Region	Feb./April	May/August	August/Sept.	Total
1st Kayes			80	80
2nd Koulikoro		850	370	1220
4th Ségou			500	500
5th Mopti		1810	430	2240
6th Tombouctou	2774	2050		4824
7th Gao	500	2840		3340
TOTALS	3274	7550	1380	12204

Source: République du Mali, 1991c.

in 1991, slightly above SAP recommended levels. These figures do not represent food being received by beneficiaries,[15] which was considerably less as subsequent evaluations would show.

The PRMC agreed to SAP's March recommendations a week before the coup which ended the Traoré government. Some have argued that the SAP system was on the verge of collapse just before the coup, not least because regional governors were receiving conflicting reports from *commandants de cercle*: SAP questionnaires on the one hand, and regular monthly political reports on the other. Despite the uncertainty the change in government entailed, the *Comité d'Orientation et de Coordination* (COC) went ahead with

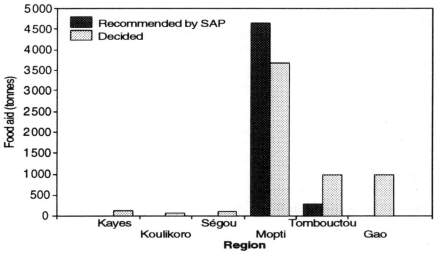

Figure 7.4 *Mali: SAP recommendations vs decisions to distribute food aid by region, 1989–90*

---

[15] This does not include an additional 4000t (in fact 3 600t were made available of the 4000 initially requested) distributed by USAID outside the programmed response mechanism, of which 3 192t had been distributed by December.

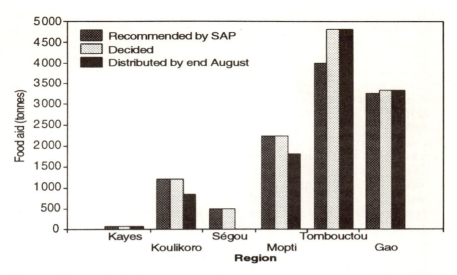

Figure 7.5 *Mali: SAP recommendations vs decisions vs actual distribution of food aid by region, 1990–91*

the authorization of distributions (i.e. endorsing the PRMC's recommendation) in April and May, which were completed by July/August. Distributions
were undertaken by NGOs via the local government administration. This
speed of decision-making and distribution is in sharp contrast to the previous
year, when distributions were not made until the following harvest.

Figures 7.4 and 7.5 compare SAP recommendations and distribution
decisions in 1989–90 and 1990–91. Figure 7.5 also shows a third variable:
the actual distribution of food aid. In 1989–90 the SAP recommended food
aid for only two regions, whereas distributions took place in all six covered
by the SAP. A total of 4946t were recommended for distribution, but 6000t
were allocated; the Fifth Region received 21 per cent less than was recommended, whereas the Sixth Region received 240 per cent more.

The correlation between recommendations and response is much tighter
in 1990–91: 11310t were recommended, 12204t were decided upon and
10904t actually distributed (Figure 7.5). This correlation remained close
even at *cercle* level, for two reasons: first, a commitment to exploit SAP
data in 1990–91 by adhering strictly to recommendations by PRMC donors;
and second, reduced pressure after March 1991 from the single political
party (the *Union Démocratique du Peuple Malien*, UDPM) to honour its
parallel lists of *cercles* requiring food aid. These lists explain, in part at
least, the distributions in excess of recommendations in 1989–90 and their
very loose distributional fit with SAP targeted areas.

Unprogrammed response
In addition to recommendations made by the SAP, the government made
a number of bilateral requests for food aid to donors: for 10000t in December

153

1990; for 190000t in January and for 100000t in February 1991, in response to rising prices in February/March 1991. The latter two requests, based on a calculated food deficit of 400000t (and consumption requirements of 212kg/person/year), were seen by donors as a means of trying to maximize food aid receipts by the crumbling Traoré government. The response of the *Coopération Française* raised reservations about the government estimates: the official deficit was to a large extent explained by a shortfall in rice production of 229000t; the revised consumption estimates of 212kg/person/year included a doubling of per capita rice consumption and took no account of how people had survived in previous years, when estimates of cereal needs were 167kg/person/year. It concluded that 1991 was a mediocre, but not a famine, year. Furthermore, commercial imports were underestimated in the calculations of the deficit, especially significant given that rice imports were fully liberalized in January 1991 for the first time, with taxes on them suspended during the 1991 rainy season. Total legal rice imports were about 50000t in 1991, with significant additional quantities (about the same amount again) being illegally imported from Guinea and Mauritania.

Unprogrammed distributions of food aid in 1991 were politically motivated, in response to both the insecurity in the Sixth and Seventh Regions and the changing political scene. In the last days of Traoré's presidency, 1000t of SNS food aid were divided equally between the Sixth and Seventh Regions, authorized by the PRMC, in response to a request from the president to coincide with a visit he was making to those areas. There was disagreement within the PRMC as to the required response in these regions; USAID's decision in February to act independently and allocate a further 4000t of emergency food aid to these regions was not widely endorsed by the PRMC. It was not until late April that USAID's 4000t of aid became available for distribution, half of it to be distributed by a number of American NGOs[16] and the balance by the government. The actual food distributed was 'borrowed' from the SNS stock, and subsequently repaid in kind with American sorghum.[17] There was a five-month delay in CARE taking over delivery for the Sixth Region, shortly after which it was forced to evacuate the area. By September, just before the harvest, NGOs actually handling the food were forced to reduce their proposed zone of intervention owing to insecurity; 3600t of free food aid were eventually distributed to all areas except Sikasso Region, on the basis that even if intended beneficiaries could not be reached, it should be distributed to someone.

Explanations for these delays are principally administrative: USAID's slowness in getting approvals for funding and government delays in requesting and administering food aid. The security situation made these delays all the more costly: much of the food was not distributed where it was needed, and that which was arrived too late. NGOs maintain that, in such situations, informal information networks are more effective than

---

16 CARE (1100t for the Sixth Region), World Vision, Africare.
17 USAID is legally not allowed to purchase food for free distribution locally. By borrowing from the SNS and replenishing the loan with American cereals, it was possible to overcome this constraint.

formal SAP channels, but they need to be believed by the authorities if they are to trigger timely response. The fact that any decision to draw on SNS stocks had effectively to go via the PRMC could act as a serious delaying mechanism for timely response in unusual circumstances.

Use of EW information

The fit between SAP recommendations and decisions to distribute food aid confirms the use of the EW/response mechanism, which certainly functioned much more efficiently in 1991 than in any previous year. There were, however, a number of issues directly arising out of EW information which inhibited the functioning of the response mechanism.

The first problem arose because of disagreement over the initial DNSI/DNA harvest assessment. This is potentially a serious obstacle to timely response, the final balance not being confirmed until the June or July following the harvest, too late to be of use in an EW exercise if additional food aid for the SNS is required. Disputes over consumption requirements further blurred the picture. The importance of the initial harvest assessment is such that the SAP does not really come into play until it has been agreed. Further development of the SAP system does not seem warranted until this imbalance is redressed and the disagreements on fixed variables in the harvest assessment (i.e. consumption requirements) have been ironed out.

Second, the SAP system itself was principally criticized for its patchy coverage of the Sixth and Seventh Regions in 1990–91 and its failure to tap other available sources of information. This, coupled with the determination of donors to hold on to the programmed response mechanism of the PRMC (i.e. responding only to SAP recommendations), led some agencies to criticize the PRMC for clinging too slavishly to the programmed response pattern.

Third, the October recommendations of the SAP were very limited, effectively putting most areas under surveillance and deferring any clarification of the situation until March. The system therefore seemed to have a scant capacity to trigger genuinely early response, although, if the deficit is less than the capacity of the SNS (58000t), donors argued that the present timing is adequate. In the event of a large deficit, SAP claims that October/November recommendations would be treated as definitive for the acquisition of additional stocks. While the timing may be adequate from the point of view of food aid reaching beneficiaries during the hungry season, the delay in food distributions inhibits the ability of food-insecure people to incorporate food aid into their own annual 'food balances' when they are planning how to cope until the following harvest.

Finally, there was very little commentary in SAP Bulletins on the impact of food aid distributions, except to assume implicitly that food aid had been responsible for improved conditions. This contradicts the views of private traders, who argued that the quantities were too small to make any impact on cereal purchases for longer than a week or so. Even more significant, SAP reports of distributions in fact referred to stocks leaving the SNS and not to the receipt of the food by villagers.

The use of other sources of EW information in 1990–91 is harder to discern. Certainly, FEWS' reports were instrumental in informing USAID's decisions, but as these synthesized other EW sources USAID effectively relied on the SAP and the SADS. The use of SADS information was evaluated in 1990, the conclusion of which was that the bulletin: 'is read on a regular basis, used directly by some, and has a reputation for accurate information . . . but it is not being substantially exploited by those organizations involved in decision-making' (SADS, n.d.:3). Reasons for this include: the assumption that the SAP had incorporated SADS data into its regional report; the status of SADS as an unofficial EWS compared with the official SAP; the failure of SADS to make recommendations regarding food aid requirements (the only response option considered by the programmed response mechanism), or indeed other recommendations which might have triggered alternative responses from individual donors. SADS was thus caught in a bind: the response mechanism was geared to take decisions about food aid distributions on which SADS explicitly did not pronounce because it did not want to duplicate SAP activities; and no alternative programmed response options existed. But equally SADS did not systematically encourage such alternatives by making recommendations for other non-food aid responses. Given the depth of SADS monitoring of the food situation in the area it covers, it could easily have done so.

Whether or not the remarkably tight fit between SAP EW information and decisions taken by the programmed response mechanism resulted in a more effective impact on food-insecure groups has received surprisingly little attention and it is to this issue we now turn.

Implications for the final response

The greatest weakness of the EW/response mechanism was the failure to target distributions adequately. Food was sent to *cercle* level initially, but distribution plans at the *arrondissement* level were rarely followed. Although the PRMC agreed to cover transport costs, sales of food aid at *cercle* level were sometimes needed to finance transportation to villages, especially in areas where access is difficult. By the time the food aid was distributed in the dry season, the places in greatest deficit were often those which were initially the most secure. This was because of significant transfers of cereals to those *arrondissements* deemed to require food aid, via traditional reciprocal links. Alternatively, people may have already migrated to more secure areas. To prevent this movement of people and cereals, distributions would have to take place much earlier. But it is by no means clear that such prevention is desirable: traditional coping strategies have always included transfers of labour and resources from deficit to surplus zones. Related to this is the fact that, although a proportion of distributions are calculated for strangers to a particular *cercle* or *arrondissement*,[18]

18 Normally, requirements are calculated on the basis of the resident population (at the time of the census).

they rarely receive aid. If distributions were to be made during the dry season, it would be logical to make them in places where people are, rather than in those they have already left.

The CNAUR carried out a number of evaluations of SNS food aid distributions, which was the only attempt made to assess the impact of the response. For example, a joint CNAUR/USAID mission visited Kayes in February 1992, where 800t of food aid had been distributed by CNAUR as part of USAID's 4000t of bilateral aid. Local distribution committees were set up and identified recipient areas according to the degree of stress; the number of people; and the isolation of the area. Although problems were encountered in transporting cereals from the *cercle* to *arrondissement* level, this was the most positive of the CNAUR evaluations and distributions were generally seen to have been carried out in a transparent manner.

The evaluation for the Koulikoro Region was carried out in December 1992 and covered three *cercles*. NGOs distributed 1058t and the government 370t. The regional government argued that it was marginalized in the distribution process. Targeting bore little relation to the SAP recommendations. Nevertheless, the food was seen to have been beneficial.

The Mopti Region evaluation identified a number of problems including difficulties in locating people when distributions were made, owing to the extreme mobility of the population; and problems with transporting food from the Mopti SNS to Tombouctou (including delayed payments to private-sector transporters in Bamako and hence their refusal to take subsequent loads). Distributions to all but one *arrondissement* were, however, completed by September.

Examples abound of the local administration taking cuts for themselves. In the *arrondissements* of Koro and Dinangourou, for example, the distribution committee took three cuts out of the food aid, amounting to 7t in all: one sack per member; one sack for each civil servant; and one for the security stock. In Youvarou, the *arrondissement* of Dogo argued that they received no food aid because they were the best taxpayers in the *cercle* and were being penalized for this; as a result they would not pay next time.[19] In Guido Sah, local people actually put their own padlock on the store to prevent the administration from helping itself. In Mopti, the displaced populations had not been targeted by SAP, which was seen to be a weakness of its recommendations. That they were not registered in the *arrondissement* led to fictitious lists and the distribution commission taking the part of the stock set aside for these people. As the report summed it up: '*pour la population, une distribution sans contrôle est un don à l'administration de base*' (République du Mali, 1991a:10). The Mopti evaluation also covered some of the distributions to Tombouctou which were supplied from the Mopti SNS. By July only 813t of the 2050t authorized had been distributed, due to a combination of insecurity and non-payment of transporters.

---

[19] In 1985, in contrast, in Youvarou free food distributions were withheld from people who had not paid their taxes.

The distributions in Niafunké, the *cercle* which received the lion's share of all food aid distributed in the Sixth Region, were evaluated in September 1991. Substantial quantities of the 710t from the Mopti SNS were sold to meet transport costs: only 394t of this were distributed, the balance being absorbed by a variety of malpractices, including sales for maintenance of government buildings, sales to traders and gifts to fictitious posts in the administration. As a result of food aid being stolen by the administration, often at the highest levels, actual distributions were small and in some cases purely 'symbolic'. Some recipients argued that they would have preferred financial support or investment in irrigated areas.

Criticisms focused on the fact that the regional authorities had encouraged local authorities to keep part of the stock for displaced people: this they indeed did, but omitted to distribute it. Second, local authorities were poorly informed as to how distributions should be carried out. Third, the MATDB was slow in paying transporters which led to unnecessary delays. Fourth, insecurity and displacement of people made distributions even more difficult. As in other regions, the local and regional authorities resented the fact that SAP recommendations alone were taken into account in allocating food aid and that they were not consulted about the allocations. Distribution worked best when it was carried out with maximum transparency, as in the *arrondissement* of Banikane, where it was done in front of all the *chefs de village*.

Recommendations from the evaluations stipulated: greater monitoring of distributions; inclusion of village chiefs in the membership of distribution committees and training for all members; exclusion from contracts of private traders who did not deliver; greater involvement of local authorities in the food aid system; restrictions on unauthorized distributions by NGOs which bypass existing structures; and better overall co-ordination by the MATDB. In addition to these institutional issues, recommendations were made to ensure adequate stocks of food in inaccessible areas and the need for a commitment on the part of the PRMC to distribute enough food to allow concentration on cultivating during the rainy season, rather than having to diversify household labour to search for food or work. Most contentious of all, perhaps, was the suggestion from the Mopti evaluation that attempts to target *within arrondissements* should be scrapped in favour of a blanket distribution at this level.

Taken together, the recommendations of these evaluations were a serious indictment of the impact of the programmed response mechanism on food-insecure groups. Without doubt, the system failed up to this point to follow through the implications of national-level planning for local impact. Given that the PRMC's principal motivation was to protect newly liberalized cereal markets, the impact on food insecurity of food aid distributions was not a primary concern. The CNAUR, theoretically responsible in the past for co-ordinating all parts of the EW/response/impact chain, had been institutionally marginalized by 1991.[20] The system

---

[20] The CNAUR has since ceased to exist as an independent structure and is now part of the *Cellule d'Appui au Développement à la Base*.

lacked any locus of institutional responsibility for overseeing what happens to food aid once it leaves the SNS and thus for preventing its failure to reach food-insecure groups.

Insecurity and the EW/response process

Armed conflict between Tuareg and the government began in June 1990 in the Seventh Region, and continued in the Sixth and Seventh Regions throughout the rest of 1990. After the Tamanrasset agreement of January 1991, which agreed in principle to the creation of an Eighth Region in the *cercle* of Kidal, three months of stability followed until the overthrow of the government in March, after which hostilities in the north resumed, including the Fifth Region for the first time.

The greatest problem from an EW point of view was the shortage of SAP information about the Sixth and Seventh Regions as unrest disrupted the local administration. Information available from other sources was not fully exploited. Even in years with no conflict, SAP coverage of the north is at best patchy. Furthermore, many of the people who were theoretically vulnerable in these regions had moved south, both in search of pasture and to avoid the conflict.

In response to this lack of information, the PRMC sent its own mission to Gao in January 1991, immediately prior to the last visit there by the outgoing president. Two sets of *arrondissements* were identified by the mission: those where the SAP should pay particular attention during the month of February; and those where free food distributions were required immediately. The subsequent SAP recommendations included: immediate free distribution of food aid in zones at risk rather than food-for-work, to be carried out with NGO help; distribution of food to those who were actually in the zone, rather than simply to those who were recorded as being there; and the carrying out of a census of displaced people in the area. There is some disagreement as to the extent to which the SAP was forced to incorporate these recommendations under political pressure.

By July 1991, the PRMC was pressuring the new government to make food aid distributions in the north. Distributions were made, but most of these targeted the riverine Sonraï populations rather than the nomadic Tuareg. Access to Tuareg areas was impossible according to the government, although convoys to feed the army got through conflict zones. A 4000t stock was requested for Gao, but was opposed by the government on the grounds that it would be a target for rebel attacks. Between July and September, *Radio France* was reporting acute food insecurity in the north and that people were dying of starvation. These claims were backed by the Red Cross and the Government of Mauritania, although officially denied by the Malian Government. In August the National Conference was held, leading to a second conference in Mopti in December. It was this that calmed the situation, but throughout 1991 the area was in a state of armed conflict.

Whereas political factors have always played a significant role in famine EW in Mali, most evidently perhaps in the UDPM's lists of recommendations parallel to those of the SAP, 1990–91 was a particularly interesting year because of the change of government in the middle of the response calendar. To both Moussa Traoré and the government which replaced him, food aid was a highly important political weapon, particularly in the context of the conflict in the Sixth and Seventh Regions. As noted earlier, Traoré, immediately before his fall, ordered 1 000t to be distributed in these regions, entirely outside SAP recommendations, which illustrates how the system can be circumvented. Furthermore, delays in distributions in these regions have been linked to the government's refusal to agree to this before the peace accord was signed. Acord Mali (1991:23–4) argued that, given that 1990–91 was a deficit year in the north:

> If the weapon of a food aid blockade is used by the government, it will undoubtedly reduce the support of Tuareg communities for the insurrection. This would deprive MPA/FIAA of one of its principal justifications to legitimize its actions to the outside world: the general discontent of the nomads. Until now, only 4 000t are available for distribution (Essor, 8 July 1991) in the Regions of Kidal, Gao and Tombouctou. Moreover, their distribution in nomad areas is impeded by the climate of insecurity.

Conclusions

Considerable progress has been made since 1985 in respect of EW and programmed response in Mali. During the 1984–5 crisis, the only variable which was consistently and adequately monitored was rainfall (WFP, 1986:6) and no system for response existed. By 1990–91, despite uneven progress in the intervening years, one of the most effective EW/response systems in the Sahel and Horn of Africa had been established. There are a number of reasons for this:

- Unlike most of the other case-study countries, Mali is not often threatened by famine. EW and response, in most years, are limited to relatively small quantities of food aid.
- Both the SAP (initiated in 1986) and the PRMC/COC programmed response mechanism (introduced in 1988–9) took several years of trial and error to function as planned, stimulated in 1990–91 by the aim of improving on what was widely judged to be a failure to respond adequately the previous year. Furthermore, the PRMC took on the funding of the SAP for the first time in 1990 and so had a vested interest in using the information which the SAP provided. Prior to this, SAP information was used only sporadically and unsystematically in determining food aid requirements.
- The quality of SAP information had undoubtedly improved and, although still a slow and incomplete process, its credibility appeared to have been greater in 1990–91 than previously.
- The long-standing SNS provided the opportunity to develop a national response capacity in most years which was not dependent on recourse to the international relief system.
- The change of political regime in March 1991 helped to alleviate the conditions under which food aid distributions were governed by UDPM requirements, rather than those identified by the SAP.

The PRMC was central to the development of the EW/response capacity. It has proved successful in fulfilling this role not by directly executing

160

policies but by providing financial support to existing state organizations to do so. An evaluation of the PRMC thus argued that:

> the policy pursued by the state, with the support of donors, is one of structural adjustment of the cereal sector . . . [its success] is due not . . . to the promotion of a global but inoperable food strategy, nor to an agricultural development plan, but to a concentration on the reform of cereal markets (CCE, 1992:74).

The Malian case is interesting in that the success of EW and response is driven not by an initial objective of famine prevention, but rather by building on existing donor/government co-ordination established for the purposes of cereals market restructuring. The intimate link between EW/response and cereals market liberalization has meant that the former is implicitly assessed in terms of its impact on marketing policy. And by linking funding of the SNS to SAP recommendations, the PRMC has indeed succeeded in keeping free food aid distributions to a minimum: only 5.4 per cent of the population received food aid in 1991 (Cekan, 1991:25), thereby meeting the objective of the PRMC to prevent large and untimely quantities of free food aid from disrupting the private cereals market.

At the end of 1991, there remained, however, a number of unresolved problems. First, use of non-SAP information both by the SAP itself and by bilateral donors for additional distributions was inadequate, especially given the reservations about some SAP data. Information from NGOs was perhaps the greatest casualty in this respect, although there is a danger that this can lead to in-built bias towards areas of NGO operations. USAID was noted as being the greatest exploiter of NGO information and frequently questioned SAP information as a result. A further untapped source of information was the cereals private trading sector and food-insecure people themselves, both of which have highly developed intelligence networks about local food security. The SADS goes some way towards exploiting these sources, but its information was only partially incorporated into the SAP format, which had little room for additional information on local conditions.

Second, the question of the timeliness of recommendations remained a thorny issue. The SAP argued that, in a bad year, October/November recommendations would be regarded as definitive, rather than waiting until the final harvest assessments have been confirmed. Nevertheless, without an attempt to use SAP indicators to predict rather than simply give a snapshot of the current situation, it is hard to see how timeliness can be improved.

Related to this is a third question of how the system would cope with a real crisis. Opinions were divided on this. The most important factor is the existence of an in-country reserve stock (the SNS), which can buy time while additional food aid is imported. This is especially critical given the time negotiations and decision-making can take, as the other case-studies graphically illustrate. The pre-positioning of the SNS at regional level further removes some of the potential pressure on the programmed response mechanism in a full-blown food crisis. Some argued that the co-ordination which existed for normal PRMC programmed response could be expanded to cover a much wider remit. In contrast, others asserted that food aid negotiations would revert to bilateral discussions, with the possibility of the revival of the CNAUR/donors committee which was set up to deal with the 1984–5 emergency. This second view was based on the assumption that the PRMC should not become involved in emergency food aid, given that its principal concern with food aid stems from the desire to protect recently liberalized markets. As such, this position seemed more consistent with PRMC objectives and practice than envisaging an expansion of the PRMC to cover a large-scale emergency operation. Another suggestion was to increase the flexibility with which the PRMC could respond. Thus it was argued that the use of *actions de substitution* (i.e. donors providing the equivalent in cash to a pre-set level of food aid: currently 150000t for the PRMC) should be informed by the year in question: in a good year the transfer should be in cash, but in a bad year in kind (CCE, 1992:77).[21]

Fourth was the persistent problem of time-lags within the decision-making process itself. The COC was considering asking the government to give SAP recommendations the authority to release SNS stocks once the PRMC had agreed to finance them, rather than having to wait for MATDB approval. Delays at the level of the MATDB were seen to be one of the major bottle-necks in the programmed response process. The government is unlikely to agree to this, however, as it would effectively remove government control over food aid distributions and could, conceivably, be seen to compromise its sovereignty.

Fifth, although the greatest strength of the SAP system is its integration into existing national structures down to local level, there is an in-built bias in that local government agents will almost inevitably overestimate the degree of food insecurity in order to maximize the likelihood of receiving food aid. This is not simply a question of receiving free food but, in a climate where the local administration is as starved of resources as in Mali, any structure which permits resources to be channelled to local level will be exploited by local administration. One outcome is that the information received from below is often not believed by the top: a decentralization of information collection does not amount to a decentralization of resources or of power. The SAP/programmed response mechanism remains firmly in central hands in terms of both resource allocation and decision-making. Accountability within the SAP/PRMC system is only to the top: neither the local administrators who provide the information nor the potential beneficiaries of food aid have any way of holding organizations accountable for the failure of the system to respond in time or in an adequate and appropriate manner.

Sixth, by far the greatest problem is what happened to food aid once it left the programmed response mechanism. The story of EW/response in Mali in 1990–91 is of a successful forging of the link between the provision and use of EW information by decision-makers, to the point of

---

[21] Some PRMC donors (e.g. Canada, the Netherlands) always pay in kind, as they are unable to provide cash under the terms of their own food aid programmes.

rigid adherence by the PRMC to SAP recommendations. But the system failed almost completely to follow this through to the point of ensuring that decisions about distributions were reflected in who actually received the food. Recommendations made by WFP in 1986 are still valid in this respect: improved information to beneficiaries so that they can plan and monitor distributions; closer co-ordination of NGOs with other donors; food to be distributed prior to the harvest and carefully targeted; and distributions to be planned and monitored to ensure that intended beneficiaries receive what is due to them (WFP, 1986). At national level in 1991, government attention was still focused only on the overall tonnage of food aid rather than on distributional issues, implying a low commitment to improved targeting. Thus, the only people responsible for the food aid between the time it left the SNS and the control of OPAM and the time it arrived in households was the local administration or the NGO responsible for its distribution. As CNAUR's own evaluations indicate, this was fraught with loopholes.

Seventh, the political context within which EW/response operated in Mali changed fundamentally in 1990–91. Most significant was the fact that the UDPM ceased to draw up parallel lists of food aid requirements to those of the SAP. But increasing democratization has other implications for EW, including the freeing of the press which, it is sometimes argued, renders the need for EWS obsolete. Four points indicate that this is not relevant to Mali. First, a free press does not mean a national press, and in a large, sparsely populated country with the press highly centralized in Bamako, resources do not yet exist for regular flows of information from rural areas to the centre. Second, urban interest groups (the primary constituency of the press) are not automatically interested in advertising the need for famine relief in rural areas, particularly if this will divert food resources from cities. Third, whereas the press can report on actual conditions, it is much less well equipped to *predict* famine. Fourth, the nature of press freedom has to be explicit: any government, particularly a newly elected and fragile one, will seek to control a press which reports against its interests. EW has never been about an absolute *lack* of information, but rather about access to it and its credibility: a free press is a vehicle which can go some way towards meeting these needs, but cannot do so in isolation from the political context in which it operates.

Finally, the impact of programmed response on food security remains very narrowly defined and largely divorced from overall food-security planning over and above market liberalization. Response options are limited to food aid. Little use was made of the potential for SAP data to indicate the chronically food-insecure who, while not threatened by famine in most years, are nevertheless hungry for part of most years, or to identify more flexible and appropriate response options. SAP information could be used to identify more appropriate uses of food aid in areas periodically at risk (e.g. seasonally targeted food-for-work projects), as well as to address the underlying causes of food insecurity and to identify longer-term interventions to improve resilience to drought and food insecurity sustainably. Other sources of EW information, notably the SADS, similarly did not feed systematically into a policy framework which seeks to address the underlying problems of food security. While early warning of *famine* has been the mandate of the SAP so far, the nature of food insecurity in Mali implies that the EW/response process needs to reorient itself away from famine towards wider food-security planning issues. This is not to argue that famine EW/response should be abandoned — the system can be geared up to respond to famine when it does pose a threat — but in most years it is not famine but chronic, structural food insecurity which threatens livelihoods. This is the challenge facing food-security planning, which free food aid distributions cannot address. Success in famine EW/response has the potential to form the basis on which this issue could be tackled.

In conclusion, the following broad recommendations for improving the EW/response capacity of the Malian system and for building on its considerable achievements need to be considered:

- While the quality of SAP data continues to improve, a more dynamic analysis of those data and the inclusion of other available sources of information could greatly strengthen the predictive capacity of the system. This, in turn, would help speed up the response mechanism, to enable food aid to be distributed early enough to allow recipients to plan their own hungry-season strategies on the basis of these supplementary resources.

- The EW/response process certainly worked well in 1990–91, but only 10 000t or so of food aid were distributed. Contingency planning for a full-blown crisis could be worked out relatively simply, given the institutional framework now in place.

- The greatest gap in the system is what happens to the food aid once it leaves the SNS. As CNAUR evaluations clearly show, closer monitoring and more systematic controls over distributions are a matter of urgency, if food aid is to reach intended beneficiaries.

- Linked to this is the issue of developing more flexible response options, over and above free food distributions. This includes both short-term responses to immediate food shortages and longer-term interventions to increase the resilience of food-insecure populations.

- The EW/response process is intimately linked to cereals market restructuring. While a necessary precondition for wider food security planning, the opportunity now exists to build on the success of the EW/programmed response mechanism to address the more fundamental problems of food security.

- The range of information about food insecurity in Mali is only very partially exploited by the existing EW/response process. Ways of systematically exploiting all available information, not just for informing about free food distributions but also for wider food-security planning issues, need to be explored.

- Some aspects of the Malian EW/response system are already more decentralized than in most other countries, providing scope for the development of regionally specific contingency plans and longer-term food security planning. Given the diversity of local conditions, this is essential for more sensitive response options.

CHAPTER 8

Turkana District, Kenya

Introduction

Turkana District in Kenya has its own EWS, set up to serve the specific needs of this drought-prone and semi-arid region, and to a large extent independent of any national EW strategy. This case-study differs from the others, first, in that it assesses the performance of a sub-national system, operating within a much more decentralized government structure. The experience of Turkana's EW/response system offers some important lessons about the successes and potential pitfalls of a decentralized approach.

A second distinguishing feature of the Turkana system is that it represents a rare attempt to link information to response in a structured way, principally through a district-level contingency plan which is drawn up in advance and is designed to be triggered 'automatically' by EW signals. Third, the EWS monitors a population consisting mainly of pastoralists, a group frequently overlooked by EW/response systems in other parts of Africa. Monitoring pastoralists poses special challenges because of their mobility, the particular sequence of coping strategies employed and the processes which lead to famine. This is very different from a sedentary farming population for which EW experience in Africa is much stronger.

The Turkana system has sometimes been hailed as a success story, with lessons transferable to other drought-prone countries in Africa. Within Kenya, it is being used as a model for replication in other arid and semi-arid land (ASAL) districts in the north of the country. It has been called a 'pioneer in drought management in Kenya' (EC *et al.*, 1992:ii). Despite the innovative design of the system, and an impressive EWS, forging the link between information and response in practice has not always proceeded as smoothly as planned. Progress has sometimes been hindered by institutional and political obstacles external to the system, while internally its development is part of a learning process.

Common to many other EWS in Africa, the Turkana system is relatively new. It was set up in 1987, in an effort to strengthen preparedness and management after a devastating drought in the late 1970s and early 1980s, which culminated in famine. A new unit, the Turkana Drought Contingency Planning Unit (TDCPU), was created within the district government, charged with responsibility for EW/response planning.

During 1990 and 1991, the system was put to the test for the first time. Localized drought and livestock raiding created pockets of acute food insecurity in parts of the district, although not of famine proportions. It is often such small-scale localized problems which are overlooked by

Table 8.1 Turkana District: EW/response interventions between 1990 and 1992

Date	Early warning	Response intervention
March 1990	Normal[a]	
June 1990	Alert	
August 1990		Decision to launch ELP.
September 1990	Alert	
mid-October 1990		ELP auctions take place.
December 1990	Alert	
March 1991	TDCPU carries out survey of displaced people in Kakuma and Lokichoggio Divisions. Reports submitted to TRP project manager.	
March 1991	Alert	
April 1991		Decisions to step up FFW, and provide supplementary feeding in Kakuma Division. These decisions are executed before the end of the month.
June 1991	Alert (acknowledges that interventions in Kakuma and Lokichoggio have relieved food insecurity).	
August 1991		TDCPU recommend scaling down FFW in Kakuma, as crisis has passed. This is carried out.
September 1991	Alert	
December 1991	Alert	
March 1992	Alert	
June 1992	Alarm	
August 1992	Emergency	
September 1992	TDCPU identifies 50000 in need of relief.	First small-scale distribution of relief food by government. UNICEF commences supplementary feeding.
October 1992	Emergency	
November 1992	TDCPU identifies 270000 in need of relief.	NGOs commence large-scale, district-wide food-relief distribution.
December 1992	Emergency	

Note:
(a) Denotes warning stage for the district, accorded on a quarterly basis by TDCPU's EWS.

centralized national EW/response systems, especially if they are dependent on the international relief system. In Turkana, the system was relatively successful in triggering a timely response. From April 1990 to the end of 1991, the EWS signalled an 'alert' stage of warning for the first time, one above normal in its four-stage warning sequence (see below). There were two specific response interventions: an Emergency Livestock Purchase scheme (ELP) in selected parts of the district in 1990 and intensified food-for-work (FFW) activities in Kakuma division in 1991 (see Table 8.1). The time-lag between warning and action for both these interventions was very short, especially when compared with the relief operations launched in the other countries in this book. Nevertheless, the interventions in Turkana did encounter some problems, principally the lack of decentralized access to resources to match the decentralized information and decision-making processes.

The system performed much less successfully in 1992, by which time the drought had persisted and intensified, accompanied by a marked increase in livestock raiding. By the middle of 1992, the first signs of famine were evident, the final warning stage of 'emergency' was signalled by the EWS, but no relief response was under way. Eventually, a large-scale relief operation was launched, but too late to prevent a food crisis. This chapter reviews briefly the performance of the EW/response system in 1992. This was another important test for the system, as it was the first time it had to respond to a *district-wide* drought when widespread famine was imminent, and the political environment was not conducive to timely response. Also, drought alone is rarely the problem in Turkana. In the 1990s, livestock raiding has occurred on an unprecedented scale. The EW/response system was not specifically designed to deal with this, but it has been a major cause of food insecurity in parts of the district.

Food security

Turkana District is located in the Rift Valley Province in the north-west of Kenya. It borders Uganda, Sudan and Ethiopia (see Figure 8.1). It is one of 22 ASAL districts in Kenya, but is one of the driest and least productive. It is also the most remote. With a small population and low productivity, it has tended to be marginalized from the national economy and from processes of economic growth. Formal market systems are poorly developed, reflecting its lack of integration into the national economy.

The population of Turkana is in the region of 350 000 to 400 000 people.[1] The economy is based on nomadic pastoralism. For a very high proportion of the population — an estimated 70 per cent in 1985 — this is their principal source of livelihood. A feature of Turkana pastoralism is the herding of a number of different species: camels, cattle, goats, sheep and donkeys, to make best use of different types of rangeland. Milk, meat and

---

[1] A TDCPU aerial survey carried out in mid-1993 estimated the pastoralist population (excluding the settled population) to be 227 000. Registration during the relief operation in 1992–3 indicated that the total population is in the region of 350 000 to 400 000.

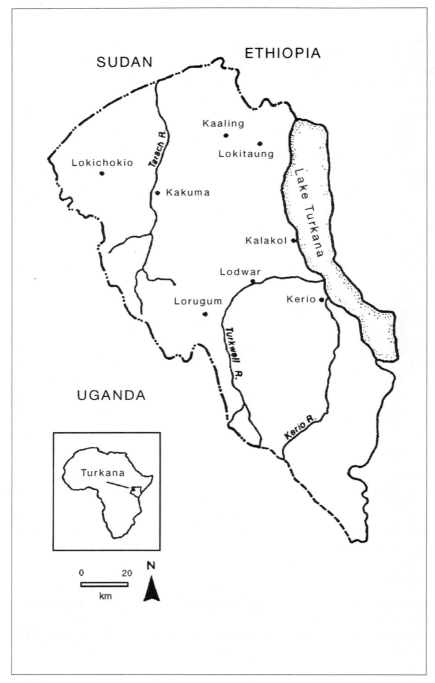

Figure 8.1 *Map of Turkana District, Kenya*
Source: McCabe, 1990.

168

blood are major components of the diet, supplemented by wild fruits, some hunted game, and fish from Lake Turkana. Sorghum is grown in the district, for example along river courses, but on a small-scale and in an opportunistic way to take advantage of periods of favourable rainfall.

Development policy towards Turkana and other northern pastoral areas in Kenya was for many years based on a misunderstanding of how pastoralist systems function. In the 1950s and 1960s agricultural programmes were favoured, especially irrigation schemes. Most of these failed, or registered only limited success. In 1979, recurrent famine and persistent poverty in the ASAL districts drew attention to these neglected areas and gave rise to a government policy paper on ASAL development. Initially the focus was on food self-sufficiency. In Turkana there was a strategy to settle pastoralists on agricultural schemes or in fishing villages. This was not successful. The Turkana were unable to achieve levels of subsistence based on fishing or agriculture alone. This highlights the importance of multi-resource exploitation patterns, which are more appropriate to the environment (Bush, 1991). What is remarkable about so many of these earlier development programmes and projects is their attempt to develop alternatives to pastoralism, despite the fact that it has been the mainstay of the economy for centuries, and is a well-developed livelihood system fine-tuned to respond to the vagaries of the climate and natural resource base.

Meanwhile, a growing body of evidence showed that nomadic pastoralism does not result in environmental degradation, that pastoralists have well-developed methods of range management and conservation, that programmes in fishing and agriculture cannot yet demonstrate that they are a viable alternative, and that pastoralism is a resilient system of production well adapted to conditions of sparse and erratic rainfall. This is precisely because of the mobility of pastoralists, who are *not* tied to fixed settlements, and who have complex, risk-diverse livestock-management systems. The approach to drought preparedness and drought management in Turkana since the mid-1980s has attempted to take these features into account.

The system of government in the country as a whole has also been changing. In 1982 the government embarked on a 'District Focus Strategy for Rural Development', promoting a decentralized approach unusual in Africa, at least in the 1980s. While responsibility for general policy and planning of multi-district and national programmes remained with central government departments, the operational aspects of district rural development projects were delegated to district government. District Development Committees were set up, and the District Commissioner became the Chief Executive Officer for rural development activities. Hence, Turkana's EW and drought-management system was set up to be largely independent of Nairobi, and has remained so.

The climate for international aid in Kenya in general, and in Turkana in particular, has also been changing. In the 1980s, after a well-publicized famine, Turkana was the recipient of large quantities of Western aid, mainly channelled through two projects: the Turkana Rehabilitation Project (TRP), set up in 1980 under a tripartite agreement between the Kenyan and Netherlands governments and the EU, with large quantities of food aid provided by WFP; and the NORAD-funded Turkana Rural Development Programme (TRDP), which at its peak absorbed $8 million. The fortunes of the TRP are described in the following section. NORAD's support to the TRDP terminated abruptly in 1990 following a rupture in diplomatic relations between the Kenyan and Norwegian governments. Because of the scale and size of the project, this had a dramatic impact on development activities in Turkana. By the beginning of the 1990s, the district was littered with remnants of former project activities and flows of international aid were reduced to a trickle. At the same time, resources provided by central government to Turkana were declining, with a negative effect on the capacity of district-level line ministries.

Average annual rainfall in Turkana is 300 to 400mm, but in the driest part, the centre of the district, it is only 150mm. Rainfall tends to be highest in the west, gradually decreasing eastwards towards Lake Turkana. There are two rainy seasons: the main one from April to July, the second from October to November. Rainfall peaks between April and May.

Rainfall is highly variable, and recurrent drought is a fact of life. When it is prolonged, and especially if it coincides with livestock disease or raiding, famine has often ensued. There is a strong positive correlation between the occurrence of drought and the incidence of raiding when competition for resources intensifies. A major and extended drought is expected by Turkana pastoralists approximately every 10 years, although its effects are unlikely to be uniform across the district. Table 8.2. summarizes some of the major droughts and famines this century.

The Turkana have well-developed strategies to cope with prolonged drought and to stave off famine and destitution. These include migration, splitting herds, gathering wild fruits for food, and circulating livestock through mutual support networks. Turkana pastoralists have been better able to rebuild their herds after recent droughts than many pastoralists in the Sahel. For example, after the famine of the early 1980s, the number of Tropical Livestock Units (TLU)[2] per person in Turkana more than doubled between 1984 and 1990. But at the same time, some of their coping strategies are under increasing pressure as the amount of available grazing land decreases, partly because of the encroachment of cultivated agricultural land, but particularly because of insecurity and threats of livestock raiding. In the 1990s the intensity and severity of raiding have occurred on an unprecedented scale, and become associated with increased violence and loss of human life. Raiding has mostly occurred along the border areas of Turkana, including the southern border with Pokot District. These are the best areas for grazing, especially during drought. The threat of raiding has rendered some of the best pasture inaccessible and under-utilized.

Relief has been provided to pastoralists in Turkana in times of severe drought or food crisis since the colonial period. The first large-scale relief

---

[2]   TLU is equivalent to 250kg of live-weight cow, and is used to compare different livestock species in terms of their forage requirements and production. The rates used in Turkana are: 1 sheep/goat = 0.095 TLU; 1 camel = 1.2 TLU; 1 cow = 0.66 TLU; 1 donkey = 0.56 TLU.

Table 8.2 Turkana District: major periods of drought and food crisis

Year	Local name	Comments
1925	Ekwakoit	Prolonged drought, coupled with disease. Human and livestock deaths.
Early 1930s	Abrikae	Drought and bad hunger.
1942	Lolewo	Animal disease.
1943	Ekuwam-Lonyang	Prolonged drought. Famine and livestock deaths.
1947	Ataa Nachoke	Animal disease and famine.
1952	Lotira	Prolonged drought and famine, associated with animal disease.
1953–4	Lokulit	Bad years, famine continued.
1960	Namotor	Severe drought for only one year. Widespread deaths of humans, livestock (reduced by over 80%) and wild animals. Dislocation of drought victims from traditional subsistence economy, and a number of large settlement sites established.
1966	Etop	Serious but short drought.
1970	Kimududu	Severe but extended drought with large loss of livestock. Shift into irrigated agriculture by some as a rehabilitation strategy. Livestock raiding by Karamajong.
1978–81	Lopiar	Extended drought combined with animal disease, and insecurity along Turkana's borders. Widespread loss of livestock and famine mortality. Relief food supplied through TRP.
1984	Kilejok	Poor rains which forced pastoralists across the border into Uganda where they experienced raiding and were turned back by the Government of Uganda. No loss of livestock nor human lives: interventions provided, e.g. FFW, vaccination campaigns.
1992–3	Kiyoto-Tang'aa	Extended drought, with severe livestock raiding and associated loss of human life along the border areas of Turkana, including the southern border with Pokot District. Large-scale food–relief operation launched in 1992 by Oxfam and other NGOs.

Sources: TDCPUa, 1992:8–10; Swift, 1985; Buchanan-Smith, 1993.

operation followed the drought of 1960–61. During the last 15 years there have been three periods of acute food insecurity — 1979–81, 1984 and 1992–3. *Lopiar*,[3] in the early 1980s, was the most serious famine in recent years, especially in the north of the district; it has sometimes been erroneously associated only with drought, although recent studies have emphasized the impact of livestock disease in precipitating the crisis, again particularly in the north (Cullis and Pacey, 1992). This has been linked to raiding. Turkana warriors, well armed as a result of conflict in Uganda following the collapse of Idi Amin's regime, had carried out large-scale raids in southern Sudan and north-east Uganda. The livestock brought back in the raids carried infectious diseases with them across areas which would normally have acted as a buffer, separating the herds belonging to different ethnic groups.

The immediate response of the pastoralists to this crisis, as their herds were wiped out, was to move to permanent settlements like Khaleng and Lokitaung. Very limited relief assistance was available, which only served to accelerate the drift towards main settlements. Eventually the crisis was brought to international attention and an emergency declared. But because of transport and infrastructure problems as well as shortages of staff, relief continued to be distributed only in towns and settlements. A classic 'camp crisis' developed: the limited number of distribution centres acted as a magnet to distressed pastoralist families; service facilities became overwhelmed, especially the water supplies; there was a rapid deterioration in health and hygiene and eventually cholera broke out, claiming many lives.

In late 1980/early 1981, the relief effort evolved into the large-scale Turkana Rehabilitation Project (TRP), funded by the EU, with the objectives of providing relief food to destitute people and starting rehabilitation activities mainly through FFW. The TRP has had a chequered history. It was praised for the logistical handling of the relief operation, for example transport and storage, and it certainly saved hundreds of lives. However, its emergency relief operation continued to work with the destitutes' camps, which it to some extent 'institutionalized', storing up future problems. An evaluation in 1985 (ODI, 1985) noted that the camps prolonged dependence on food aid because of limited employment- and income-generating activities for such large numbers of people.

In 1985 it was agreed that the TRP, originally intended as a temporary organization, should be established permanently to provide development support and promote disaster preparedness. The TDCPU grew out of this initiative, as the focal point for EW and drought contingency planning.

However, an EU review of the TRP in 1989 revealed mismanagement and suspected fraud. As supplies of relief food had dried up, there had been a shift to FFW, but there was often little to show for the food which had been distributed because the programme was poorly administered. There were major problems of accountability within TRP, and reports of

---

[3] Roughly translated, *lopiar* means 'wipe-out' or 'finishing everything' in the Turkana language.

172

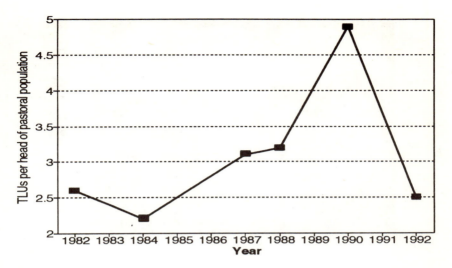

Figure 8.2 *Turkana District: TLU/person ratio*
Source: TDCPU.

relief and rehabilitation programmes being 'increasingly manipulated for personal gain' (Cullis and Pacey, 1992:12). EU funding was suspended, although the TDCPU continued to be supported under separate arrangements by the Netherlands Government.[4] The TRP has since been a shadow of its former self, with very limited resources.

By 1990–91, the TDCPU was well established. Some of the lessons from the early 1980s about how not to run a relief operation had been learned, and the unit already had a strong information system and a valuable data base on the pastoralist economy. This was put to good use in launching the ELP and expanded FFW programmes, in response to localized pockets of food stress.

With hindsight, it is possible to see the first years of the 1990s as the beginning of another extended period of drought in Turkana which continued through to 1993. In the second half of 1992, as the drought intensified, food-security conditions deteriorated rapidly, typical of how famine can develop in a pastoralist economy. The final slide can occur very suddenly. Human nutritional status may be protected early on because of the availability of meat from dead and dying animals. As herds are depleted and milk, blood and meat are no longer available, famine conditions develop rapidly. Figure 8.2. shows the dramatic fall in the TLU per person ratio during the first two years of the 1990s. Figure 8.3. shows how household food-consumption patterns changed at the same time. Milk consumption declined as yields fell; meat was consumed at higher than the seasonal rate due to the increased number of dying livestock; the consumption of blood declined in order to preserve animals during this period of stress; and

---

4   The TDCPU had initially been funded by a consortium of the EU, Oxfam and the Netherlands Government.

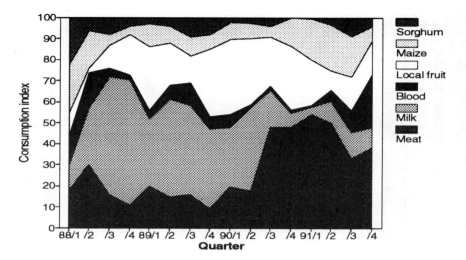

Figure 8.3 *Turkana District: household food consumption pattern, 1988–91*
Source: TDCPU

maize consumption increased. During this early period of drought, pastoralists were able to maintain a reasonably balanced diet, high in protein, and therefore there was only a small increase in malnutrition rates among children. But as the drought continued, meat sources ran out and malnutrition increased abruptly, from a district average of 16 per cent to 36 per cent in just three months in mid-1992 (based on middle upper-arm circumference (MUAC) measurements of less than 13.5cm among children under five).[5] Eventually, a large-scale relief operation was launched throughout the district in October 1992, managed by NGOs, and has continued into 1994.

To summarize, an effective EWS for a pastoralist area like Turkana must be: sensitive to local conditions and coping strategies; able to incorporate change in the economy as these strategies become less effective with the intensification of external pressures, for example livestock raiding; and able to detect the signs of deteriorating food insecurity *before* famine threatens. Above all, it must be able to trigger a preventive response before the slide into famine. In 1990–91 the system was reasonably successful in triggering small-scale interventions well before famine threatened. In 1992, the relief operation started a few months too late; the EWS did not trigger a timely response, although it had monitored and warned of deterioration in food-security conditions.

---

[5] MUAC measurements are generally considered to be less reliable than weight-for-height measurements. But MUAC surveys are easier and quicker to conduct. The TDCPU uses the MUAC approach, and this is the best time series data on malnutrition in Turkana. A UNICEF survey at about the same time, in August 1992, showed a similarly high rate of malnutrition of 35 per cent for the whole district, using weight-for-height measurements.

The EW/response system

The TDCPU plays the key role in drought management in Turkana. Its twin objectives have been to set up and run an EWS for the district, and to draw up a drought-contingency action plan. The unit has made most progress in achieving the first objective. It has adopted a broad interpretation of EW and drought management, stressing drought recovery as well as famine prevention.

Early warning

The TDCPU has over 30 field monitors and a number of divisional co-ordinators responsible for information collection. It relies on four main sources of EW data: regular household and community surveys carried out on a quarterly basis by TDCPU staff; aerial surveys every one or two years to monitor livestock numbers and distribution, and settlement; satellite imagery for monitoring rainfall and the NDVI; and secondary data provided by other technical departments in district government. The data are analysed in Lodwar, the district headquarters, where the TDCPU is based and the quarterly bulletins produced.

Three categories of indicators are monitored: environmental; rural economy, mainly livestock, although some agricultural indicators are included; and human welfare. The number and range of indicators monitored is larger than for most EWS. As well as the standard indicators such as rainfall, crop conditions and market prices, less-conventional indicators specific to the pastoralist population are measured: livestock indicators include milk yields, bleeding rates and slaughter rates; indicators of human welfare include school attendance and the breaking up of households (see Table 8.3).

An innovative feature is that each quarter the situation is defined according to one of four predetermined 'warning stages', to facilitate interpretation of the information (TDCPU, 1992a:28):

- 'Normal': environmental, livestock and pastoralist welfare indicators show no unusual fluctuation but remain within the expected seasonal ranges.
- 'Alert': environmental and livestock stress indicators start to fluctuate outside the expected seasonal ranges within certain localized areas. An alert stage can also be signalled when unusually low asset status is reached within the district.
- 'Alarm': environmental and livestock stress indicators continue to fluctuate outside the expected seasonal ranges and this situation extends to most parts of the district. Pastoralist welfare indicators begin to fluctuate outside expected ranges. Reports of displaced population groups (due to the collapse of the pastoralist system) become more frequent.
- 'Emergency': the environment and the pastoralist population are in a state of emergency. Displacement of herders and their families continues due to large-scale mortality of livestock and the further collapse of the pastoralist system. All indicator values including those of pastoralist welfare fall to very low or minimum levels.

Table 8.3 Turkana District: indicators used by EWS

Category	Indicators monitored	Method of monitoring
A. Environment	1. Rainfall	Rain gauges/satellite images
	2. Water sources	Aerial surveys/community surveys
	3. Vegetation cover and quality	Community surveys/aerial surveys/satellite images
B. Rural economy	**Livestock:**	
	4. Livestock numbers and distribution	Aerial survey
	5. Livestock production (milk yields, bleeding rates, slaughter rates, birth rates)	Household surveys/community surveys
	6. Livestock pathology and mortality	Household surveys/community surveys
	7. Livestock nutritional conditions	Household surveys/community surveys
	8. Livestock sales and prices	Household surveys/community surveys
	Agriculture:	
	9. Crop conditions	Household surveys/community surveys
	10. Crop harvest	Household surveys/community surveys
	11. Sorghum storage and sales	Household surveys/community surveys
	12. Cereal prices	Household surveys/community surveys
	Other:	
	13. Income-generating activities	Household surveys/community surveys
C. Human welfare	14. Diet	Household surveys/community surveys
	15. Nutritional condition of children <5 years	Household surveys/community surveys
	16. School attendance	Household surveys/community surveys
	17. Breaking up of households	Household surveys/community surveys
	18. Numbers of displaced people	Household surveys/community surveys/chief's reports

Based on TDCPU, 1992a:30.

Response

Responsibility for responding to EW of crisis lies with the District Drought Management Committee (DMC), which was set up in 1989 as a sub-committee of the District Development Committee, and is chaired by the District Commissioner. Its members comprise representatives from all the main district departments concerned with the impact of drought, plus representatives from NGOs and donor agencies. The TDCPU acts as the secretariat, and the DMC meets quarterly to consider the unit's bulletins and more frequently in times of crisis. It makes recommendations for appropriate action which have to be approved by the District Development Committee, and is responsible for their implementation.

The key to linking information to action is supposed to be the District Drought Contingency Plan, the aim of which is:

> to plan interventions in advance, and then to implement them as soon as a particular warning level is declared without need for major new decisions, so that natural bureaucratic inertia operates in favour of pre-planned actions rather than against action of any sort (TDCPU, 1992a:74).

It has taken some years to draw up this plan. It provides background on drought and famine in Turkana, explains in depth how the EWS functions, and provides guidelines for seven types of targeted action in the event of drought or food crisis, drawing on past experience: emergency veterinary campaigns; drought-related livestock marketing; maintenance of cereal availability; employment guarantee through FFW; relief feeding; restocking; and health and nutrition support.

In 1990 and 1991, the focus of this case-study, the EWS was not yet linked to a drought-contingency action plan. The system moved to 'alert' for the first time, and interventions were triggered by the EWS. Although the *type* of intervention had been agreed upon by the district government beforehand, for example destocking through livestock auctions, *how* this should be implemented had not been pre-planned. This proved to be one of the stumbling blocks in the implementation of the ELP. Even during the 1992 drought, when a draft plan existed, it was not yet integrated into district-level planning and was therefore not used. The basic design of the EW/response system makes an explicit link between information and action; the foundations have been laid for putting this in place, but in the early years of the 1990s it was not yet functioning.

The national context

In Kenya responsibility for drought has been decentralized to the District Development Committees. There are many positive aspects to this approach; the decision-makers are closer to what is happening, and are likely to have a better understanding of the impact of the drought and a greater sense of urgency in doing something about it. However, for a number of years it was only in Turkana that a concerted effort had been made to put in place a system and structure for promoting disaster preparedness and drought management at this level. It did not happen in other ASAL districts until much later. The Turkana system developed in isolation, independent even of an overall national strategy which did not exist. There was no formal EWS in Nairobi nor pre-planned national response mechanisms to support recommendations made by district-level EWS. The initiative to develop a system in Turkana was initially donor-driven.

A number of different ministries in Nairobi collect data and information which play an EW role. The Meteorological Department collects rainfall data and issues short- and long-term weather forecasts; the Department of Resource Surveys and Remote Sensing conducts aerial surveys of vegetation, crops and livestock; the Ministry of Agriculture monitors crop performance. What has been missing has been a co-ordinating body to collate these disparate sources of data, as well as district-level information, into a single EW source at national level.

In the mid-1980s, Kenya was praised for launching a swift and effective response to a major drought (Cohen and Lewis, 1987:285). This relative success in preventing famine was attributed to a prompt initial response by the government, large-scale availability of Western food aid, a well-developed infrastructure, and a large number of NGOs in the affected areas (RDI, 1985:66). During 1992, the next episode of widespread drought in the country, this pattern was not repeated. One of the principal reasons was political upheaval as the country moved from a one-party state towards multi-partyism and prepared for elections. This was a distracting influence, delaying the launch of relief operations. The lack of coherent and co-ordinated EW signals at national level meant that it was difficult to build an understanding of the extent of and reasons for food insecurity across the country. Decision-makers had to depend on external sources such as FAO's GIEWS for an overall assessment of the situation. Eventually, a national drought management committee was set up within the Office of the President, charged with co-ordinating and directing the relief operation. But the delays encountered in launching a relief operation in Turkana during the severe 1992 drought underline the importance of a decentralized EW/response system being linked into a national-level strategy through which more resources can be mobilized if necessary.

The Emergency Livestock Purchase Scheme: 1990

Early warning

The EWS signalled the 'alert' stage of warning for the first time in June 1990. Only the environmental indicators had fluctuated outside their normal seasonal range because of poor rainfall, but the TDCPU was concerned about the impact on the livestock sector. Livestock numbers had increased in previous years, and the livestock population could exceed carrying capacity in this first year of drought. These concerns were borne out: by September 1990 livestock indicators had also fluctuated outside their normal seasonal range. Livestock mortality and disease were increasing, and production indicators like milk yield and the animals' nutritional condition were deteriorating. Pastoralist welfare

178

indicators, however, remained stable: there was not yet evidence of human stress.

In August 1990 the DMC responded to the TDCPU's early warnings, just over a month after they had been given, by taking the decision to launch the ELP. Its objectives were, first, to prevent a deterioration of pastoralists' purchasing power as a result of a collapse in animal prices and barter values, by intervening to buy at reasonable prices at least some of the animals offered for sale by the herders, thereby protecting their food security status; and, second, to reduce pressure on scarce and diminishing grazing resources, thus maintaining some kind of ecological balance (DMC minutes, 11 September 1990).

Cost recovery was implicit in the plans, as the animals bought at auction were to be resold. This was a condition stated in the WFP Plan of Operations for Turkana, which made funding available for destocking and restocking activities (Government of Kenya and WFP, 1990). The NORAD-funded TRDP was also to provide funding in the region of 2.5 million Kenyan Shillings (KSh) (US$110000). Five auction sites were selected along the lake shore and in north-eastern Turkana in the areas most affected by drought. Responsibility for implementing the project lay with the Livestock Marketing Department. A mobile extension team had the job of publicizing the auctions, which were to take place in the second half of September. They were delayed by a month, mainly because of funding problems. The principal source of funding from WFP was to come from the monetization of a consignment of food aid. The funds had to be channelled through the NCPB to the Ministry of Regional Development in Nairobi, and eventually transferred to Lodwar. They did not arrive until after the ELP had taken place, when KSh2000000 ($87260) was finally made available. In the meantime, an advance had to be made from the Livestock Department to WFP using TRDP funds.

Eventually the auctions were carried out between 12 and 27 October in five sites as planned, a time-lag of about three months after the TDCPU warning about the threat to the livestock economy — very much shorter than for any of the relief operations in the other four case-studies in this book. A total of 2768 sheep and goats were bought at auction, with the aim of eventually selling them down-country in Nairobi.

A survey of the impact of the ELP was carried out a year later (Wekesa and Bush, n.d.), which shows that its impact was small but significant (Bush, 1992). It probably did have a short-lived effect on pastoralists' food security. But where the proceeds of the sale were spent on food, it usually lasted less than a month, reflecting the small number of animals sold per household. The survey confirmed that the main motivation among the herders for selling their animals was drought-related stress, in line with the ELP's objectives:

> The greatest immediate impact of ELP is in improving the purchasing power of the sellers. The cash and food subsidy which was provided in the form of 'fair prices' represents an important income transfer to rural households (Bush, 1992:26).

179

Learning from the ELP

Organizing and running the ELP, which involved the handling and transport of live animals, was a much greater logistical challenge than free food-aid distribution. This kind of intervention was chosen because it was directly linked to the current problem: the imbalance between livestock and natural resources during drought, and the threat to pastoralists' purchasing power. In this sense, it was a much more appropriate choice of response than the usual free food distribution.

Implementing this more management-intensive exercise was not without problems. Its value was as a pilot exercise, experimenting on a small scale before the district was hit by widespread or severe drought.[6] Evaluations by a special Destocking Co-ordination Committee and by WFP (Bush, 1992) identified a number of problems. On the planning side there were four. First, the DMC did not respond immediately to the TDCPU's warning in its bulletin issued at the end of June. Just over a month elapsed before it agreed to launch the ELP, mainly because the District Commissioner was not present to chair the DMC meetings, and therefore they lacked the necessary authority for decision-making (pers. comm., TDCPU). Second, there were delays in gaining access to donor resources to start the ELP, especially WFP funds. Third, overall responsibility for the ELP was unclear. The Livestock Department was expected to be the implementing agency, but perceived the ELP as a 'donor-funded' project, and the responsibility of TRP/WFP. The Livestock Department had therefore earmarked no funds for the ELP. Fourth, the lack of a regular marketing system increased the recurrent costs of the ELP. The exercise was dependent on donor funding, and the withdrawal of NORAD in October 1990 exposed the weak financial position of the Livestock Department to cover recurrent costs such as veterinary products, overnight allowances and transport.

A separate range of problems was encountered during implementation of the ELP. First of all, sick and dying animals were purchased in the auctions, mainly because of local political pressure, despite the fact that the (rather unrealistic) guidelines stressed that only healthy animals should be bought. Second, there was no guarantee that the most needy pastoralists were being reached, because of buying on a 'first-come, first-served' basis, the excess supply of animals beyond the ELP's resources, and the participation of well-off pastoralists in the auctions. Third, the death rate (78 per cent) among the animals purchased was very high. More than a third died soon after the auctions, because they were already very weak, and because of inadequate trucking to the holding ground. Fourth, the plan to transport the animals to Lotongot holding ground before re-selling them did not work. There was a lack of appropriate facilities for transport and at the holding ground, where there was competition for pasture from migrating pastoralists and inadequate vaccination programmes because of a lack of funds.

---

6 It should be noted, however, that the experience was not capitalized on in the run-up to the 1992 drought and food crisis. There have been no further attempts at an ELP in Turkana since 1990.

The Destocking Co-ordination Committee concluded that the whole exercise had been hampered by financial problems. The ELP had run into high costs, not least because of the high death rate of the animals purchased which offered little chance for cost recovery.

Many lessons have been learned from the ELP. Its performance can be compared with a more successful project carried out in March 1988 in four settlements in north-eastern Turkana. During this operation, most of Turkana had received good rains. There was better pasture and less competition at the Lotongot holding ground, and the exercise was not as politicized. NORAD played a major role in funding the operation, including vaccinations, salaries and transport (EC *et al.*, 1992). The availability of funds was perhaps the most significant difference between the 1988 and 1990 operations. Also, this kind of scheme may only be feasible on a very small scale, and not when drought is widespread.

One of the main lessons concerns the feasibility of cost recovery. The 1990 experience highlights the difficulties of transporting animals to a holding ground for onward transport out of the district for resale. The evidence stacks up in favour of regarding this as a relief operation, with the primary aim of providing price and hence income support to vulnerable pastoralists forced into distress selling as a result of drought. It does not seem feasible to try and recover costs by selling the animals elsewhere in Kenya, but makes more sense to slaughter them and use the meat for relief distribution.

Food crisis and food-for-work in Kakuma Division: 1991

The food crisis in Kakuma Division developed during the first few months of 1991, triggered by livestock raiding on Turkana pastoralists along the border with Uganda, during drought. An estimated 1 000 households were displaced, almost two-thirds as a direct result of the raids. They had sustained very heavy livestock losses: more than 90 per cent of their sheep and cattle, and more than 80 per cent of their goats (TDCPU, 1991). The effects were quickly reflected in high malnutrition rates among children. This is an example of a rapid-onset disaster caused by livestock raiding, compared with the slower-onset disaster caused by drought alone. The abrupt deterioration in food security was a particular challenge for the launching of a rapid response.

The TDCPU's local monitors for Kakuma and Lokichoggio Divisions reported on the problems early. They submitted their first report warning of the crisis that was developing in Kakuma in mid-March 1991, specifying that just over 4 000 people were in need of relief assistance. This was reiterated in the EW bulletin for the first quarter of 1991. A baseline survey carried out by the TDCPU at the end of March showed 59 per cent of children malnourished. The TDCPU made recommendations for urgent action: stepping up FFW, supplementary feeding for malnourished children, intensifying security in potential grazing areas and the continued close monitoring of the situation. An interim EW report, circulated in May, reiterated the seriousness of the situation and reported population

181

movements to TRP sites where FFW was ongoing at a low level; 8000 displaced pastoralists were by then reported in Kakuma.

Meanwhile, some agencies in the area were issuing alarmist reports of famine deaths. Local chiefs were encouraging people to gather at the TRP centres in Kakuma to strengthen their case for relief food by presenting the worst possible scenario. The TDCPU was a valuable and moderating influence, with its procedures for systematic data collection and objective interpretation; it refuted the exaggerated claims made by some of the agencies. Ultimately, its views prevailed with decision-makers in district government.

A DMC meeting held on 3 April, shortly after the TDCPU's first warning reports were issued, approved the TDCPU's recommendations and announced that FFW and supplementary feeding would start immediately. More than 1000 bags of maize were delivered, more than 3000 adults took part in FFW, and over 2000 children were registered for supplementary feeding in April alone. TRP, Catholic Relief Services and the International Committee for Red Cross were all involved in providing food relief. The available evidence indicates that the response was effective. For example, there was a 60 per cent drop in the number of malnourished children by mid-June (Lokong and Etheri, 1991). Few other data are available but the EW bulletin for the second quarter of 1991 argued that the interventions had alleviated the crisis. The TDCPU called for the slackening off of the FFW and other emergency interventions as conditions improved.

Effectiveness of the response

The response was very swift. Barely a month elapsed between EW and implementation of an expanded FFW programme and supplementary feeding. The TDCPU addressed its first reports on the crisis to the TRP which took no action until the DMC was addressed. This delay may have caused people to congregate in larger concentrations in the centre than would otherwise have been the case if the interventions had been launched earlier (pers. comm., TDCPU). But this couple of weeks delay pales into insignificance when compared with those experienced in launching the relief interventions discussed in other chapters, especially where they have been dependent on the international relief system. The fact that a FFW programme was already going on in Turkana, and in particular in Kakuma Division, facilitated the rapid response. There would inevitably have been longer delays if the intervention had had to start from scratch.

There were nevertheless problems with transport. Although there was WFP food in store in Lodwar for the Kakuma programme, the TRP was unable to provide funds to transport it. In the end the Diocese of Lodwar stepped in to provide transport.

Response to the Kakuma food crisis was not subject to the same level of scrutiny as the ELP, although a small evaluation team was sent from Lodwar to Kakuma in June 1991 to review the situation (Lokong and Etheri, 1991). It confirmed that the interventions had been effective in tackling food insecurity, although the amount of food available for FFW was not enough to supply the eligible FFW participants numbering over 6000.

District-wide drought in 1992

1992 was the culmination of three years of drought in Turkana District, by which time livestock numbers had dropped dramatically. According to the TDCPU's surveys, the TLU per person ratio had decreased from 4.9 in 1990 to 2.5 in 1992 (see Figure 8.2). (The unit estimates that a ratio of 4.0 is the required level to ensure that pastoralists have sufficient means on which to survive.) The drought was most severe in the southern and central divisions of the district, where pastoralists claimed it was the worst in living memory, even worse than *lopiar* in the early 1980s. Some of the best grazing land along the southern boundary with Pokot District was out of bounds because of insecurity and the dangers of raiding. Further north, in Kakuma, Lokichoggio and Lokitaung Divisions, the effects of raiding were sometimes more serious than the drought and the principal cause of livestock losses and food insecurity. The drought in 1992 was not confined to Turkana alone. A nation-wide shortage of cereals exacerbated the district's food problems as maize prices soared.

Food-security conditions had gradually deteriorated from 1991 onwards, monitored by the TDCPU which had registered the 'alert' stage of warning throughout 1991 and for the first quarter of 1992 (see Table 8.1). When the rains failed in the main rainy season in 1992, the TDCPU notched up its warning to 'alarm'. For the first time in the existence of the TDCPU, pastoralist welfare indicators declined to abnormal levels in the most drought-affected parts of the district. In the middle of 1992, the economy showed signs of rapid collapse — the typical famine scenario described above. The terms of trade between meat and cereals suddenly deteriorated; for example, the price of a sack of *posho* (maize flour) rose from KSh600 to KSh1400 in Lodwar town in the space of one month — July 1992. And malnutrition among children shot up to an average of 36 per cent for the district, and as high as 48–50 per cent for the worst-affected areas (based on MUAC measurements). The EWS declared the 'emergency' warning stage, which was maintained until the end of 1992. The TDCPU's first estimate of numbers in need was approximately 50000, increasing to 280000 by November.

The impact of the drought in northern Kenya was brought to international attention in mid-1992. FAO carried out an assessment in August, declaring Turkana to be one of the 'starvation-belt' districts, with 51000 people in need of assistance (endorsing TDCPU data). UNICEF carried out a district-wide nutrition survey the same month, showing the very high malnutrition rate of 35 per cent (based on weight-for-height measurements).

The transition from information to action was much less successful in 1992 than in either of the two previous years. There was no relief response until there were already signs of famine and the EWS signalled 'emergency'. The first relief food distribution took place in August 1992, on a small scale; the government distributed approximately 400t of finger millet through the chiefs. Very little reached the most needy and hardly any reference was made to the TDCPU's information about worst-affected areas when allocating the food. The quantity provided was not nearly enough to address the scale of the problem. A District Famine Relief Committee was eventually formed in September, at which point the District Commissioner invited NGOs to manage a district-wide relief operation. But the NGOs' mandate was not finally ratified until November, at which point the first distribution of general relief rations took place on a scale large enough to begin to address the crisis.

This was regarded by pastoralists as several months too late. The hungriest months for them had been August and September (Buchanan-Smith, 1993). There were anecdotal reports of famine deaths. Although these are hard to verify, some pastoralists who tried to migrate out of the area, especially those heading towards Samburu, did not survive the journey. And the TDCPU's estimate of 50 000 in need of relief assistance quickly became outdated as the situation deteriorated without any preventive action being taken. Oxfam and World Vision registered 280 000 pastoralists as eligible for relief assistance by the end of 1992, a figure endorsed by the TDCPU. The agencies involved in the relief operation on the ground took the view that selective targeting was inappropriate, and that, instead, the operation should aim to support the pastoralist economy, as well as simply saving lives, by distributing to almost all pastoralists in the district.

There are a number of reasons why EW information was not translated into timely action in 1992. The TDCPU did not issue clear and specific recommendations for action until its interim EW report in November, by which time the first stages of famine were evident and plans for a large-scale relief operation were already under way. Nation-wide, there was a tendency for the government to play down the seriousness of the crisis. Many officials were preoccupied with political events. Turkana was no exception in the way key decision-makers ignored the problem. These and other explanations for the delayed response are discussed in the following two sections.

Oxfam was the leading NGO, together with the International Federation for Red Cross and Red Crescent Societies (IFRC), Kenya Freedom from Hunger and World Vision. In the first eight months, more than 12 000t of relief food were distributed to over 370 000 registered beneficiaries. The relief operation was designed very differently from those of the early 1980s. Pastoralist mobility was taken into account, with a network of dispersed distribution centres, and the camp syndrome was avoided. Women were registered as recipients in most areas, thus recognizing gender-differentiated roles for securing food within the household and the complexity of a polygamous society. Food was mostly allocated per person rather than per household, based on detailed registration, regarded as a fairer approach to distribution. Some of the management problems of the early 1980s were avoided with better-trained administrators and checks built into the system to minimize misappropriation of resources. In short, a number of principles normally applied to development projects were successfully incorporated into the design of this relief operation. The approach was endorsed by the TDCPU, which continued to provide valuable monitoring information on the operation's impact and on the process of recovery. The unit also played a co-ordinating role with the operational NGOs.

184

Nevertheless, some problems were encountered, the most serious being the shortfall in deliveries of relief food, which were erratic and consistently fell below target, at least in the first year of the operation. Initially this was due to a general lack of food aid as Kenya's needs competed with much larger relief demands in Somalia, southern Africa and the former Yugoslavia. Later on, this was exacerbated by a difference of opinion between the operational NGOs and the principal donor, WFP, about the objectives of the operation. While the NGOs adopted the broader interpretation of saving livelihoods, WFP defined the objectives as saving lives alone, which had implications for the amount of relief it was prepared to make available.

UNICEF also started a supplementary feeding programme towards the end of September 1992, initially targeting areas where malnutrition was highest. But as malnutrition rates continued to rise, the programme was extended to the whole district.

Evaluating the EW information

An evaluation of the TDCPU in 1992 concluded that:

> The TDCPU is the first of its kind in Kenya and in Africa, in terms of district focus. Its success in creating an EW capacity must be regarded as an important achievement since there were no other models to use as examples and it is succeeding in providing the service for which it was created. The TDCPU is successfully, reliably and accurately providing an EW system in the district (TDCPU, 1992b).

This section aims to point out some of the key features of the EWS which have contributed to its success, some of the challenges it faces and hence to provide the context for assessing how the information is used. What emerges is a contrasting picture of the effectiveness of the EWS in 1990 and 1991, compared with 1992.

There seem to be three key reasons for the TDCPU's success in setting up a working system specifically designed to monitor a pastoralist economy. First, it relies on a decentralized and extensive network of monitors, geared to collecting information from mobile households, and supported by divisional co-ordinators equipped with motor cycles. Second, considerable knowledge exists about pastoralist livelihoods and the impact of drought and famine in Turkana. The TDCPU has used this in building and expanding a strong data base, which has enabled it to identify deviations from 'normal' seasonal patterns for most of its indicators. Third, a wide range of indicators is monitored, with a good understanding of how they interact. The EWS has been able to monitor the process of deteriorating food security, facilitated by the concept and definition of four warning stages. For a slow-onset drought disaster, the sequence is usually deterioration in environmental indicators, followed by a deterioration in livestock production indicators, finally impacting on human welfare. (Monitoring the impact of raiding, a man-made rapid-onset disaster, requires a very different set of skills, as discussed below.)

Turkana's experience has much to offer other EWS in Africa trying to grapple with the special challenges of monitoring a pastoralist economy. A Drought Monitoring Programme was set up to expand this kind of EWS across other northern pastoralist districts in Kenya, as far as possible based on the design of the Turkana system. But there are certain reasons why it may be easier in Turkana District than in parts of the Sahel. There is only one dominant production system in Turkana: nomadic pastoralism (although complemented by other activities like fishing), while there are often several distinct systems covered by a single EWS in the Sahel, such as rainfed and irrigated agriculture, transhumant pastoralism, and fishing. And the population of Turkana is not very large. Also, the EWS is set up to monitor only one administrative unit. In a larger more diverse area where communications are more difficult, it is unlikely that all aspects of the Turkana EWS could be easily replicated.

Timeliness and predictive capabilities

The monitors report back to Lodwar on a monthly basis. Although the bulletins are produced only quarterly, the TDCPU keeps its finger on the pulse in the intervening months. If necessary, an interim report will be produced; during the drought of 1992–3, the EWS produced monthly bulletins from January 1993. Monitors have sometimes taken the initiative to write their own field reports, independent of TDCPU headquarters, if they are particularly concerned about the situation. This happened in Kakuma in March 1991 as the numbers of displaced increased (Prigan and Chirchir, 1991).

The design of the EWS, geared to monitoring the sequential deterioration of different categories of indicators, offers the potential for strong predictive capabilities, and was effectively used in 1990 and 1991. It indicated 'alert' when only the environmental indicators had fluctuated abnormally in the second quarter of 1990; decision-makers' attention was drawn to the very early stages of stress and the ELP was launched. Similarly, towards the end of 1991, it signalled 'alert' when livestock numbers had dropped dramatically even though none of the regular indicators was abnormal. It warned in general terms of the likely outcome and need for intervention if the 1992 rains were poor because of depleted assets (TDCPU, first quarter, 1992).

The TDCPU was aware of the deteriorating situation, although, as the crisis developed during 1992, it seemed to lose its edge in terms of predictive capacity. With hindsight, it is easy to spot the start of the rapid slide towards famine in July/August 1992. On the ground, it was harder to predict the precise timing. But the signals emerging from the EWS in its bulletins did not convey an adequate sense of the seriousness of the food crisis developing, nor of the likely sequence of events leading to famine.

Interpretation, presentation and communication of EW information

In 1990 and 1991 the TDCPU was pro-active in the way it interpreted and communicated its information, despite the fact that there was not a full-blown crisis. The EWS made clear recommendations and lobbied for action, for the ELP in 1990 and for a relief operation in Kakuma in 1991. In

1992 it seems to have been rather less effective. For example, the bulletins for the second and even the third quarter of 1992, when the last stage of 'emergency' had been reached and there were already signs of famine, expressed the need for food assistance in very general terms without clear and compelling messages or detailed recommendations on which plans could be based.

Defining the warning stage each quarter is a useful tool to summarize conditions in the district, especially for busy decision-makers who do not have time to wade through all the data presented. But it was not used to its full potential during 1992 when the need for a response was greatest. In terms of presentation, there was no eye-catching or compelling summary of conditions and recommendations at the front of the bulletin. The declaration of the warning stage was reserved for the last pages. The language used conveyed no real sense of urgency.

This might not have mattered had the political environment been more conducive to a timely response. Unfortunately it was not, and there was therefore much greater pressure on the information gatherers to generate concern. This can be done both in the way bulletins are presented, and by using other influential channels, such as the media (although a government EWS may be constrained in the extent to which it can do this). Since this experience, there has been a marked improvement in the layout of the EW bulletins. Indeed, in November 1992, as the pressure for action intensified, the TDCPU issued a much more hard-hitting interim report, underlining the most important messages.

The stated objectives of the EW/response system in Turkana have gone beyond preventing famine, to emphasizing post-drought recovery as well. Once a relief operation is running, the challenge of shutting it down when the need has passed can be as great as trying to launch it in the first place. The operation has gathered momentum, and there may be vested interests in maintaining the flow of relief.

In the case of the Kakuma food crisis in 1991, the EWS was able to signal when the relief programme was no longer required, because good rains had relieved the situation in the division and the relief operation had achieved some of its objectives. The TDCPU recommended gradually scaling down the FFW activities and other relief interventions. For the ELP the situation was not so clear-cut. The project started late and fell short of achieving its aims mainly because of a lack of resources. There was therefore never a need for the TDCPU to indicate when it should be terminated. This happened prematurely for lack of funds.

During the large-scale relief operation in 1992–4, the TDCPU's information system has enabled the recovery process to be monitored, and has guided the phasing out of the relief operation as ration rates are cut back by donor agencies insisting that the relief operation be scaled down. In this respect, TDCPU has played a valuable role.

Sustainability of the EWS
Sustainability is one of the greatest challenges for the EWS, indeed for the whole TDCPU. There are three relevant issues: first, funding for the

TDCPU if or when donor support is withdrawn; second, the institutional location of the unit and the use to which the information is put; and third, the feasibility of continuous and detailed monitoring of the local population.

Since its inception, many of the unit's costs have been funded by the Netherlands Government: for example, the motor cycles and their running costs; field-work allowances; and much of the data-processing equipment. It is unlikely that the Kenyan Government could afford to maintain the unit's current capacity, especially in the prevailing stringent economic climate. In terms of national government priorities, Turkana represents a very small percentage of the total population of the country. Yet, if the motor cycles were not maintained properly, the TDCPU would lose one of its greatest comparative advantages over other government departments: the mobility of its staff.

There is a strong case for donor funding to continue, albeit at a lower level than when the unit was set up and there were high establishment costs. It is likely that for some years to come donor resources will be required to fund any relief interventions. Without timely and reliable information the response is sure to be late and the costs of launching an emergency operation at the last minute much higher. Without good information it is almost impossible to attempt cost-effective targeting. Maintaining a strong information system is a small price to pay to prevent the waste of resources in relief operations which are not directed and planned on the basis of reliable data. Continued donor support on a small scale is therefore likely to be a good investment. According to a budget proposal in 1989, Dutch funding for the TDCPU in 1991 would amount to approximately $60000 (KSh1680590). The government's contribution would amount to approximately $27000 (KSh738330). Considering the expense of most relief operations, $60000 seems a small amount to pay each year to ensure that the information is sound. If external funding were restricted to travel-related costs alone, this would have amounted to an estimated $13000 (KSh364276) in 1991.

The TDCPU has moved physically to the office of the District Development Officer in Lodwar. Its information has been used not only for EW but for development planning as well. This is not surprising as it holds by far the best data-base and documentation centre on Turkana's pastoralist economy. Its role in long-term food security and development planning is very important to ensure its sustainability, so that the unit is useful not only for drought and crisis years, but for intervening periods as well. There will be vested interests in maintaining the EWS if departments come to rely on it in their regular work programmes. The TDCPU's institutional location close to the centre of district-level planning is therefore crucial.

Finally, how long is it possible to continue intruding upon people's lives with questionnaires and detailed interviews month by month to collect the kind of data the EWS depends on? Some of the monitors already have to deal with reluctant respondents (pers. comm., TDCPU). And the TDCPU has been criticized for not feeding back its information to the people who are its source (Engomo, 1992). The answer lies in the critical issue of whether the information is seen to be used and linked to a response or not.

If local people have confidence in the EWS as a conduit for useful information from themselves to government, their co-operation is more likely to be forthcoming. Regular feedback will strengthen this. The relief operation since 1992, which (although launched late) has served the Turkana people well during a severe drought should encourage their co-operation with the EWS. But they must be convinced of the benefits of the information system during non-drought years as well — a more difficult issue.

Use of EW information

Until 1992, the TDCPU's EW information was used almost exclusively by district-level decision-makers, including local NGO and aid agency staff. The decisions to launch the ELP and the relief interventions in Kakuma were taken in Lodwar. This is when the system seemed to work best. Indeed, it was not geared to a wider sphere of influence as it had no means of rapid communication with Nairobi, nor was it well connected to national-level decision-making. This was a problem in 1992 when the scale of the drought and the food crisis extended far beyond district-level capabilities, and support and resources had to be mobilized nationally and internationally. Since then the unit has been equipped with a fax machine, and more attention has been paid to strengthening national EW capabilities.

The most influential indicators

In 1990, it was remarkable that EW information showing abnormal fluctuations in environmental indicators alone was sufficient to trigger a response — the launching of the ELP. This is quite a different story from how EW information was used in Chad and Sudan, where evidence of human stress was the most influential trigger when other indicators had failed. In both these countries, key decision-makers witnessing human stress firsthand, and high malnutrition rates, played important advocacy roles in speeding up a sluggish response. In Turkana, an EW bulletin in mid-1990 which warned of an imbalance between natural resources and livestock numbers was regarded as sufficient evidence for the ELP to be launched, even though no deterioration in livestock indicators was shown until September. Nor was there evidence of deteriorating nutritional status among people throughout this period: indeed in mid-1990 it was reported that malnutrition rates were declining. This is an example of a genuine, yet rare attempt to protect livelihoods *before* lives are under threat.

There are two principal reasons to explain why the decision to respond was taken so promptly, thus ensuring a more effective preventive intervention. One is that district-level decision-makers are close to the situation to which they are being asked to respond. They are more in touch with the problem, and in the absence of other obstacles it takes less to convince them of the need to take action, compared with officials hundreds or thousands of miles away who have to take decisions about an area with which they are less familiar or in touch — a situation typical of national and international EW and decision-making systems.

189

The second is that the ELP was not dependent on the international relief system in the conventional sense. Although WFP resources were used, they were not emergency relief resources, and had been earmarked for an ELP type of programme in Turkana *in advance*. The international relief system has shown itself to be crisis-oriented, which is why evidence of an advanced stage of food crisis is often required to trigger a response, and it tends to be geared to the simplified use of EW indicators — for example, depending upon the 'single indicator' of the harvest assessment. The TDCPU did not have to enter this decision-making arena in 1990. The Turkana system had defined its own parameters of EW/response which were better geared to recognizing a continuum of food security and insecurity and a range of different response options, rather than the simple and straightforward distribution of food aid once the crisis threshold has been crossed.

By 1992, however, the comparative advantage of Turkana's decentralized EW/response system no longer seemed to work in favour of *early* interventions geared to protecting livelihoods. The more common though less-effective pattern of a relief operation being launched when there was already a food crisis, and free food distribution was the last appropriate response, re-asserted itself. In 1992, the triggers were soaring malnutrition rates, an FAO assessment which labelled Turkana as part of 'the starvation belt' and brought the food crisis to international attention, local NGO staff alerting their offices in Nairobi, and eventually the Kenyan media. The reasons why earlier and less-dramatic signals had been ignored have to do with less-assertive translation of information into recommendations by the TDCPU, dependence on the international relief system which was tuned into a nation-wide relief operation, and a political environment which was not conducive to early response. These reasons are discussed below. A well-designed system is clearly no guarantee of a timely response. The political context is a crucial determinant, and this can change from one year to another.

Institutional issues
A positive feature of the Turkana system is that the TDCPU's mandate extends beyond EW to making recommendations for action, playing a key role in decision-making processes, and often co-ordinating the relief response as well. Thus, the information gatherers who usually have the best understanding of food-security conditions from their direct contact with local people have responsibility for recommending the most appropriate form of assistance. And the information gatherers who have a vested interest in ensuring that their product is used to maintain their own credibility, are responsible for following through to implementation. This has usually worked well in Turkana. At least during 1990 and 1991 the time-lags between recommendations being made and decisions being taken were short. The TDCPU's responsibility for drawing up a drought contingency action plan reinforces its mandate on the response side as well as in EW.

The TDCPU, as the secretariat for the most important decision-making forum, the DMC, has taken the initiative in calling extraordinary DMC meetings when there are important messages and recommendations to be

190

conveyed. This happened throughout 1990 and 1991. The unit has established a reputation of high credibility, and is in command of data and information which are available nowhere else within district administration. This has facilitated its recommendations becoming decisions in times of stress. In 1991 the DMC immediately endorsed the TDCPU's assessment of the food crisis in Kakuma Division, including its estimate of the number of people in need of assistance, without any time-consuming cross-checking or duplication of effort. The unit has played a valuable role in promoting awareness and understanding of the complexity and causes of food-security problems in Turkana. It is well integrated into district government, and its active involvement in the planning and final evaluation stages of a relief intervention gives it a high profile.

But in 1992, the system did not perform so efficiently. Its full potential was not realized, despite the fact that this was the most serious drought since the TDCPU's inception. Although the information was accurate, it was not translated into recommendations for action, as explained above. The EWS seemed to have lost the edge in terms of being pro-active. Its second- and third-quarterly bulletins in 1992 reported on what had *not* been done, rather than providing clear messages for action. By this time the drought-contingency action plan for Turkana had been drawn up, but rather than guaranteeing a response, it was not yet integrated into district-level planning. To some extent the TDCPU was marginalized as NGOs, some of them new to the district, geared up to administering the relief operation according to their ideas and past experience, under pressure and with minimum consultation (TDCPU, 1993).

Early attempts to couple information generation with decision-making, by creating the DMC, were very positive. The DMC is a transparent decision-making forum combining government officials and NGO and aid agency representatives. Information is discussed, and decisions are usually debated openly and taken collectively. The DMC operated most effectively during 1990 and 1991 in the launching of the ELP and the response to food crisis in Kakuma.

The District Commissioner plays a critical role in chairing the DMC. In 1990 and 1991 his presence was very important in ensuring the rapid and efficient endorsement of recommendations into decisions. His absence from some of the early planning meetings for the ELP was one of the reasons why it was delayed by a few weeks. But during the much more serious 1992 drought, when the government was reluctant to acknowledge impending famine, the District Commissioner was party to this line and did not heed the early warnings until late into the crisis, in effect immobilizing the decision-making role of the DMC.

In 1990 and 1991 each stage of the EW, decision-making and implementation process was carried out at district level. The TDCPU provided information, the DMC took decisions and identified resources which had already been allocated to the district, and district government departments implemented the relief programmes. The role of the national government was limited to channelling WFP funds from the monetization of food aid to Turkana. This was badly delayed, but because of the small scale of the

191

project the shortfall could be made up by a temporary virement of funds from elsewhere in the district budget. The launching of both the ELP and the expanded FFW programme were thus in many respects self-contained district-level affairs, made possible by aid resources committed in advance (although inadequate resources and delays did hamper some aspects of each intervention).

In 1992, however, the process was very different. There was very little donor aid available for Turkana, and the scale of the crisis meant that a relief response was beyond the district's capabilities. At this juncture, the fact that the TDCPU was not linked into a broader national strategy of EW/response was a major disadvantage. On the one hand, there was no obvious body at national level to receive and act upon TDCPU warnings, nor established lines of communication to Nairobi. On the other hand, the TDCPU was not in receipt of information about conditions in the rest of the country which had a bearing on the food situation in the district, such as the nation-wide shortage of cereals which had an impact on cereal availability in Turkana. There was a problem of information flow in both directions, and an unclear division of responsibility for acting upon EW information at national level. Although the TDCPU had signalled 'emergency' on its warning scale, the District Commissioner could not have declared an emergency in Turkana without the authorization of a presidential declaration.

Political factors
Changes in the Kenyan political context between 1990 and 1992 are probably the single most important factor explaining why the EW/response system worked well in the first two cases, and much less so in the third. In 1990 and 1991 when the EW/response process was 'district-based', the local political environment was relevant. This was conducive to a timely response. The resources were available, good relations existed between aid agency representatives in Turkana and the district government, and the latter was willing to act swiftly.

In 1992, the political context was very different. The drought coincided with the run-up to the December 1992 multi-party elections. At both national and district level, government officials and politicians were reluctant to admit that there was an impending famine for fear that it would reflect badly on the performance of the ruling KANU party. Early warnings were played down. Thus, high-level district officials in Turkana paid little attention to the TDCPU's EW information and, as part of government, the unit was constrained in the extent to which it could raise the alarm and use other channels of communication. It was not until June 1992 that the President made an international appeal for assistance. This delay hindered the response of UN agencies, such as WFP, which needed government approval before an appeal could be made to international donors for relief.

A second important factor is the politics of international aid. In 1990 and 1991 Kenya was coming to the end of a particularly well-funded period of aid programmes and projects. The ELP benefited from this, funded by

WFP and by the last of the NORAD funding. WFP funds were still available for an ongoing FFW programme, which could be scaled up to respond to the food crisis in Kakuma. But these resources were beginning to tail off. In November 1990 many aid programmes were suspended by Western governments pressing the Kenyan Government to move to multi-partyism, to hold a general election and to improve its human-rights record. By the time of the 1992 drought, Kenya's relationship with Western donors had deteriorated. They were slow to respond to appeals for emergency food aid, and were short of resources for Kenya's food crisis when their attention was diverted to other parts of the world.

International agencies receiving the TDCPU's bulletins in Nairobi were not well-disposed to taking action on its warnings. Unlike the late 1980s and beginning of the 1990s, there were few agency representatives in the district, and no aid funds to launch a district-level response before food aid was made available nationally. WFP had prematurely ended its involvement in the TRP's FFW programme in 1991.

Moreover, when relief was being allocated between districts, the fact that Turkana was the only district with an established EWS ironically became counterproductive. The TDCPU's objective and scientific approach to data collection and analysis led to its initial assessment of numbers in need, of 50000, being moderate and realistic. Elsewhere, EW and estimates of those in need were politicized; numbers tended to be inflated and based on little real data in a bid to maximize food aid receipts. At one point in Wajir District it was claimed that the affected population was greater than its actual population (TDCPU, 1993). It therefore appeared that Turkana was better-off than other northern districts, and it was accorded less priority when the relief started. As a result, conditions continued to deteriorate before adequate amounts of relief were provided for Turkana and it was accorded equal priority.

The national media played a very significant role in speeding up the relief response for Turkana in 1992. During the second half of September, there was almost daily coverage of famine in Turkana in national newspapers such as *The Nation* and *The Standard*. With sensationalized stories of Turkana selling their children for food, the media raised the alarm nationally about conditions in the district where earlier warnings from the formal EWS had failed to have any impact. The fact that electioneering had distracted attention from impending famine was openly reported. It is of note that the media, so recently freed from tight censorship, was able to play this role and to report upon officials and politicians who desperately tried to cover up the crisis. Nevertheless, by the time the stories hit the press, it was already very late. In no way were they a form of *early* warning.

Implications for the final response in 1990 and 1991

In the two examples of response interventions in 1990 and 1991, EW information was influential in decision-making, and the TDCPU played a central role. The weakest part of the system was the execution of those decisions. This can be attributed to two factors: principally the lack of resources to fund the interventions, but also the underdeveloped state of the drought-contingency action plan. Capacity to respond was not yet properly developed or thought through.

The message emerging from both interventions is that the ability to respond (in terms of funding, staff and other resources) must also be decentralized if a decentralized EWS and decision-making system are to realize the potential benefits of a timely and appropriate choice of response. At least this should be the case for localized and small-scale outbreaks of acute food insecurity. In a large-scale crisis, such as occurred in 1992, it is unrealistic to expect a district system to have adequate capacity to respond; the key is linking it into a more powerful national EW/response system.

Resource constraints

Funding was the major constraint for the smooth implementation of both the ELP and the Kakuma relief operation. The withdrawal of donor funds from Turkana, particularly by NORAD, had weakened the system. The ELP's performance in 1990, compared with the more successful destocking exercise in 1988, is testimony to this. Both the ELP and the FFW programme in Kakuma stumbled over lack of transport which was the district government's responsibility. In the ELP there was also confusion over responsibility for running the scheme and payment of field and overnight allowances for staff, with the Kenyan Government proving to be a reluctant funding partner wherever there was the possibility of international aid being made available. Yet the problems in mobilizing and releasing WFP funds in Nairobi for the ELP in Turkana revealed flaws in the system, even when international aid had, in theory, been allocated for drought contingency purposes to the district. Recognizing some of these financial constraints, in 1991 the DMC unanimously resolved to establish a Turkana District emergency fund:

> to be used in times of drought stress and famine and other related emergencies to support resources of Departments and/or organizations with limited resources (which are) called upon to intervene during such emergencies' (DMC meeting minutes, 6 August 1991:4).

The Provincial Administration, Veterinary Department, Agricultural Department, TRP, and Ministry of Health each pledged a contribution. But this did not work. For budgetary reasons, it was not possible to reallocate funds, already committed to other votes, to a contingency fund. Thus, this important initiative was never implemented. As the Kenyan Government faces increasing budgetary constraints, the likelihood of funds being set aside as a contingency reserve is increasingly remote. The pressing needs of day-to-day administration and of ongoing development work are likely to take precedence over the 'luxury' of an emergency fund which may remain unused for a number of years.

Yet, establishing a local-level contingency fund should be a key part of the decentralized EW and decision-making system to ensure that it actually has some power to act, and that decisions are rapidly executed. As most

194

relief assistance to Kenya is currently provided by international aid, and in view of the impoverished state of the government, donor support for an emergency fund is probably necessary for it to work. This is now being considered as part of a longer-term donor-funded drought-management project at the regional level.

Institutional preparedness

Building up institutional capabilities to deal with relief operations has long been a concern in Turkana. In 1985 it was argued that the TRP should become a permanent presence precisely to address this issue (ODI, 1985). It had developed personnel, logistical and infrastructural resources to cope with relief and these should not be dismantled. Likewise, it was argued that FFW, appropriate to both relief and development, should be maintained to keep the organization 'ticking over'. In practice this has not been easy to achieve.

Running the FFW programme on a long-term basis to maintain institutional preparedness during the 1980s ran into serious problems. FFW projects were open-ended and created 'permanent' FFW workers; they supported inappropriate activities; their management and accountability were sometimes weak; and women, who were the main participants, were barely, if at all, represented in their planning, management and evaluation. Suggestions have been made to improve any future FFW (or cash-for-work) programmes; for example, having detailed shelf plans and appraisals of any projects in advance of an emergency, to be of specified duration and targeted on stressed areas and communities (EC *et al.*, 1992). But the feasibility of an ongoing programme is dependent upon the availability of international aid — by no means guaranteed. Meanwhile, NGOs in the area have questioned the appropriateness of FFW programmes which are based on the unproven assumption that there is surplus labour to be absorbed.

Retaining institutional capacity within the TRP has similarly run into problems. In the period between droughts, the well-resourced TRP came under pressure to 'share' its international funds with other more impoverished government departments (Bush, 1991:14). When the crisis approached, the TRP's capacity was no longer as strong as it should have been: hence, it was unable to provide transport to move food to Kakuma in 1991. Most aid flows to the TRP have now been cut off, and it played a minimal role in the relief operation of 1992–3 because of its reduced capacity. Instead, the burden of implementation of the relief operation has been shouldered by NGOs.

The 1992 draft of the District Drought Manual identified different government departments as the principal implementors for the range of relief interventions proposed. As the government becomes increasingly impoverished, however, this no longer seems a feasible option without external assistance. The widespread dependence on NGOs in the 1992–3 operation, as compared with the mid-1980s nation-wide drought when government was the principal implementor, only serves to confirm this point.

Insecurity and the EW/response process

The incidence of drought and livestock raiding are closely linked in Turkana. Raiding increases when competition for scarce resources intensifies during periods of drought, a pattern which has repeated itself for centuries. Traditional rivalries have existed between the Turkana and neighbouring tribes such as the Toposa in Sudan, the Dongiro and Merille in Ethiopia, and the Pokot within Kenya. Raiding is practised as a means of rebuilding herds, expanding grazing lands and gaining access to new water sources. But the rivalries can sometimes be turned into alliances between tribal groups, replacing conflict with reciprocal access to grazing and water resources during periods of stress. The balance of power is critical: 'when the balance of power is upset, between rival groups competing over access to land and water, raiding rather than reciprocity can become the dominant mode of inter-tribal relations' (Oba, 1992:8).

This introduces a political dimension critical in explaining the recent upsurge in the incidence of, and violence associated with, livestock raiding in Turkana as the balance of power has shifted.[7] Within Kenya, there is increasing hostility between certain ethnic groups, fuelled by power struggles at national level. In the north-west this is played out through raiding between the Pokot and Turkana. Meanwhile, over the border in Sudan and Ethiopia, civil war and political instability have increased the availability of sophisticated weaponry with devastating consequences.

The Turkana are not passive victims. But where they have been raided, whole communities have been rendered destitute in a very short period of time, made even worse when there is large-scale loss of human life as well, which seems to be increasingly the case. One of the worst incidents in recent years was a raid on the Turkana at Kokuro in mid-December 1992 by the Dongiro from Ethiopia; approximately one hundred people were killed.

The cause of famine can thus be man-made as well as natural. The worst scenario is when the two coincide. The EW/response system in Turkana has been designed principally to prevent slow-onset drought-induced emergencies. In contrast, the effect of raiding is immediate and can be dramatic. The crisis among the displaced in Kakuma in 1991 illustrates this well. Similarly, the raid at Kokuro during the 1992 drought displaced what was left of the community; they congregated around Khaleng, in need of immediate assistance.

Livestock raiding poses a particular challenge for EW. The EWS cannot predict when it is likely to happen, but it can try to detect its incidence and impact very rapidly in order to launch an appropriate response. In Kakuma in 1991 this was done with moderate success. The first written EW report was prepared in March, on a crisis which had been developing only since

---

7   This is not the first time that raiding patterns have been affected by external political forces. It also happened at various times under the colonial administration, for example when the British tried to establish their administration in Turkana to counteract Ethiopian expansionism, and when they disarmed the Turkana people as a means of breaking their resistance thus leaving them exposed and vulnerable to raids from neighbouring tribes (Oba, 1992).

about February. The relief response did not take long to launch. The timing is impressive compared with how most centralized EWS covering larger areas in Africa would have reacted. Where raiding has occurred on a smaller scale, but with an equally devastating impact for the victims, it is much more difficult for the EWS to detect.

The TDCPU can only be reactive to the effects of raiding, as it was during the Kakuma crisis, recommending what should be done to help those who have already lost their animals. There is then a need for readily accessible resources because of the rapid onset of the crisis. The resources were available in 1991 from the FFW programme, and in 1992–3 from the ongoing relief operation. But this may not continue to be the case. Pleas have sometimes been made in TDCPU bulletins for security to be enforced in areas which have been particularly vulnerable to raiding and where grazing resources are plentiful. However, these sensitive matters are discussed in closed political committees, of which the TDCPU is not a member. Its role is confined to sharing the knowledge acquired through its monitoring network about where the threat of raiding is most negatively affecting the pastoralist economy, in the hope that this may have some impact on political decisions.

Conclusions

The performance of Turkana's EW/response system in 1990 and 1991 contrasts sharply with 1992. The first two years show the potential of a decentralized and innovative district-level system, which responded to localized pockets of food insecurity rapidly and effectively, at least in 1990 intervening early to protect livelihoods before lives were threatened. The 1992 experience, when the relief operation was launched a few months too late, shows that a well-designed system alone is not enough. The political context can be the definitive influence over whether or not a timely response is launched. In 1990 and 1991, for both the ELP and the Kakuma operation, a combination of factors worked in favour of EW information being translated rapidly into preventive action. In 1992 the reverse was the case.

The information system run by the TDCPU is an impressive example of an EWS set up to monitor pastoralists. Its key features are, first, its design to cope with a mobile nomadic population; second, the strong data base used to monitor trends and deviations from a 'baseline'; and third, the wide range of indicators used to facilitate monitoring of the sequential process of food crisis and famine. This model has since been extended to three, and eventually to six, other ASAL districts of Kenya. There has been a deliberate effort to link information to decision-making through the forum of the DMC, which involves a range of actors including both government and aid agencies. The information gatherers and analysts have been given a broader mandate than just EW. And the use of well-defined warning stages is designed to convey clear messages about the severity of the situation and the kinds of interventions required.

In 1990 and 1991, all these aspects worked to full advantage. The TDCPU proved to be a reliable and sensitive source of EW, drawing

197

attention to a deterioration in environmental indicators alone, supported by forecasts of how this could eventually threaten the pastoralist economy. It played an active role in alerting and mobilizing the decision-makers, for example by calling special meetings of the DMC, and in co-ordinating the response. At least in the case of the ELP, an alternative intervention to conventional free food distribution was implemented, in an attempt to support livelihoods *before* lives were threatened. Some additional and crucial ingredients included the political will to respond with the support of the District Commissioner, and good relations between donor agency representatives based at district level and district government officials, backed up by the availability of international aid earmarked for Turkana (although this had started to dwindle compared with the 1980s). The main problems encountered were logistical at the implementation stage, including delays in mobilizing resources in Nairobi which had been allocated to Turkana, and unclear division of responsibility. Bureaucratic inertia had not yet started to work in favour of pre-planned actions, as the designers of the system had intended. Overall, however, delays encountered between EW and implementation were only one month in the case of the Kakuma operation, and three months in the case of the ELP, compared with delays of up to a year in other countries in the Sahel and Horn of Africa dependent on the international relief system.

In 1992, the same set of factors did not conspire to ensure the timely translation of information into action. The EWS had successfully monitored the decline in food security with warnings about the likely impact, but it was less forceful and assertive in trying to mobilize a response. It did not use its mandate to the full, and was most preoccupied with its EW function. Also, it was not properly linked into a national EW system for alerting government officials and donor representatives in Nairobi. Most important of all, the political context was not conducive to a timely response. The government was trying to play down the scale of the drought-induced national food crisis, and was more concerned with preparations for the forthcoming multi-party elections. Although a system had been set up in Turkana for linking EW to decision-making through the DMC, the 1992 experience exposed its limitations. The DMC was dependent upon the most senior government officer, the District Commissioner, without whose support the committee was powerless, and no decisions were taken. Meanwhile, international donors were taking a hard line on Kenya's eligibility for development aid, until it became a multi-party state and improved its human-rights record. The common pattern emerged, of a deterioration in food-security conditions until crisis point was reached, at which stage the TDCPU's data were validated by international assessments, and eventually a large-scale relief operation was launched. Turkana slid rapidly towards famine, typical in a pastoralist economy, during a couple of months in mid-1992. Full-scale famine was averted by the launching of the relief operation, but it had started a few months too late to prevent acute food insecurity and human suffering.

Ironically, the system in Turkana had worked best for small-scale localized problems of food insecurity, which are usually overlooked by most national and international EWS geared to full-blown, unmistakable emergencies. It worked least successfully for a district-wide crisis in 1992, although no worse than elsewhere. The potential danger of an EWS being set up as an isolated 'centre of excellence' was exposed during the 1992 food crisis in Kenya. Having reliable and objective data about the number of people in need of assistance worked curiously against the district's interests. Elsewhere, the exercise was politicized and exaggerated, based on little or no objective data. As a result, Turkana's needs were initially overlooked as being less serious than those in other districts, which only served to delay the Turkana relief operation even more.

When an EW/relief system has *failed* to function effectively, the burden is borne by the food-insecure who have to fall back on their own resources, and their own coping strategies. This is what happened before the relief operation was launched in 1992. Many of these coping strategies may have long-term costs, for example, impoverishment if assets and productive resources are run down, and human costs if the effect is prolonged malnutrition. Ironically, when the relief system *succeeds* in delivering, it is often claimed to have created negative effects of 'dependency' on relief, undermining and eroding local people's ability to cope.[8] These claims were made in Turkana in 1991, when the intervention in Kakuma was evaluated (Lokong and Etheri, 1991). But no evidence was presented to support the claims. Studies elsewhere have shown that the effects of dependency are often over-stated (e.g. FSG *et al.*, 1990 on Botswana; Buchanan-Smith, 1989 on Sudan). Relief assistance is usually too erratic and unreliable to displace traditional coping strategies which are, in turn, more resilient and harder to destroy than is often assumed. At best, it adds a further dimension to the existing portfolio of strategies. Relief is based on the concept of welfare and public responsibility to alleviate stress and poverty. In Turkana, the aim is principally to counteract the negative effects of the drought cycle (and the negative and often associated effects of cattle raiding and animal disease). It is important not to throw out this objective and the rationale for some kind of welfare system, by exaggerating the dependency it hypothetically causes. Rather, the focus should be on how to scale down and eventually phase out interventions when the need has passed in order to avoid disincentive effects. The TDCPU showed itself able to signal the right moment in the Kakuma operation.

Insecurity, in the form of livestock raiding, is increasingly serious in Turkana as a cause of population displacement, impoverishment and destitution. The rising incidence and violence of the raids are related to wider political forces and interests. Although the EW/response system was not specifically geared to the impact of livestock raiding, it has proved its

---

[8] For example, the drought relief programme of the 1980s in Botswana has been hailed as a success, effectively delivering relief to a drought-stricken population. However, local government officials were extremely concerned about the dependency effects: local people becoming dependent upon, and always expecting, government assistance. An evaluation of the programme concluded that this was over-exaggerated, and the demand for income support fell away as the rural economy recovered (FSG *et al.*, 1990).

ability to trigger a rapid response, in the case of Kakuma in 1991. The challenge to react promptly to this kind of rapid-onset disaster is much greater than for a prolonged drought. If the ferocity of livestock raiding continues on the same scale as in recent years, it poses a dilemma for the TDCPU. There is little it can do to be pro-active, either in predicting the incidence and effects of raiding, or in influencing decision-making about security issues. This is a political domain, in which the 'technical' EWS plays no part. Yet, the TDCPU may be under increasing pressure to find and mobilize the resources necessary to assist families rendered destitute as a result of the raids.

The Turkana system, of both EW and relief, has so far been heavily dependent on international donor funding. There is little evidence that the EWS would continue to function effectively if financial responsibility were handed over to the Government of Kenya, which is facing growing budget constraints. There is therefore a strong case for continued donor support to maintain some of the key elements of the EWS and to support the district drought-contingency fund. This is a small price to pay to ensure that reliable information is available for relief planning, and to avoid the last-minute, expensive response to a full-scale emergency.

Based on the evidence presented in this case-study, the EW/response system in Turkana could be strengthened in the following ways:

- The lessons learned during the first half of 1992, when the EWS failed to trigger a response, need to be internalized, in particular regarding the pro-active role that the EWS should take.
- Donor funding should continue to support the EWS, at least to ensure that the key features of the system, such as the mobility of the monitors and co-ordinators, are maintained.
- A district (or possibly regional) drought-contingency fund should be set up to ensure that response decisions can be implemented rapidly, especially for small-scale localized problems. This is currently the weakest link in the chain. The decentralized decision-making system must be complemented by decentralized access to resources if it is to have any power. This contingency fund probably has to be supported by the donor community because of the government's lack of funds.
- Completing the contingency planning exercise, and integrating the drought-contingency action plan into district-level planning, are both important tasks to strengthen drought management and EW/response in the future, and to fulfil the original goals and objectives of the system.
- Finally, the Turkana EW/response system must be integrated into a wider national strategy for responding to major emergencies like 1992–3, when needs exceed district-level resources. The approach to developing EW/response capabilities in Kenya, building from the district level upwards, is the right one.

Ultimately it is the political environment which is likely to make the difference between a well-designed system performing effectively, or not. As this case-study demonstrates, the political environment can vary greatly from one year to the next.

200

A number of lessons can be drawn for other regions and countries in Africa from this important case-study. First, the EWS provides a model for an EW and monitoring system for a pastoralist economy, where the monitors must be able to cope with a mobile population, and a good understanding of the economy and of the processes leading to famine is critical.

Second, it introduces the concept of predetermined warning stages as a simple but effective tool for communicating with decision-makers, *but*, for maximum impact, this needs to be backed up by clear and detailed recommendations for action.

Third, it shows the potential advantage of a decentralized system, where the decision-makers are close to, and familiar with, the situation to which they are responding, which is likely to instil a greater sense of urgency than for a distant, national (or international) decision-maker. But if the political environment is not conducive to timely response, a decentralized system may perform no better than a centralized one.

Fourth, the decision to respond is likely to be turned more rapidly into action if it is not dependent upon the international relief system mobilizing resources outside Africa. The international system tends to be crisis-oriented and slow to respond, especially if there are larger-scale and higher-profile emergencies elsewhere. For example, it is highly unlikely that deteriorating environmental indicators in Turkana would have been able to trigger a relief response by the main donor agencies, either in Nairobi or in Western capitals, unless there was already evidence of human stress. In other words, a local-level system seems to be better able to recognize the interaction and overlap between relief and development needs, while the international system sharply compartmentalizes relief from other forms of aid for procedural, political and logistical reasons. But it is unlikely that a local-level system will ever have sufficient resources to cope with more than a localized problem.

Fifth, this highlights the prerequisite for a decentralized sub-national system to have access to resources to respond if it is to work effectively, at least for localized problems or for reacting to the early stages of a large-scale crisis. Otherwise the benefits of rapid decision-making are lost in the lengthy procedures to mobilize resources elsewhere.

Sixth, a sub-national system must be linked into a wider response system at national level for the large-scale emergencies. Even if a district drought-contingency plan exists, it should be complemented by a national contingency plan which integrates it into an overall national strategy. And this national strategy will be most effective if donors and government are working together and co-operating closely.

There are two main reasons why attempts to replicate some key features of the Turkana system may not work in other contexts: first, where there are poor relations between government systems and Western donors; and second, where planning and government systems are highly centralized. There is still a case to be made for contingency planning at national level to try and strengthen disaster preparedness, although this would be much stronger if it was built up from district-level contingency plans, as is to be attempted across the ASAL districts of Kenya.

201

CHAPTER 9

Forging the Link

Introduction

Chapter 1 identified the characteristics of an efficient and effective EW/response system for drought-related famine as:

- an EWS which is not only capable of warning of large-scale famine, but also sensitive to changes in food-security status before famine threatens and able to detect localized pockets of acute food stress;
- response which provides assistance early in the famine spiral, before the point of destitution is reached;
- interventions which protect livelihoods before lives are threatened, implying a wider range of relief than food aid, and a more developmental approach.

This chapter identifies some of the common themes emerging from the case-studies about how EW information was used, and why the relief response was invariably too little and too late. Drawing on the examples where the EW/response system was more successful, recommendations are made for 'forging the link' between EW and response, particularly within the international relief system.

In all five case-studies, assistance during 1990–91 was provided by international donors; in each case national government had inadequate resources to respond. In only one instance did the relief response come anywhere near the ideal — in Turkana District in 1990 where the very early stages of a food crisis were picked up by the EWS, an intervention was launched aimed at protecting livelihoods *before* lives were threatened, not through free food aid but through a small-scale Emergency Livestock Purchase scheme. In every other case free food aid was the predominant response, but in Ethiopia, Sudan, Chad and Turkana District in 1992, it arrived late, was supposed to save lives not livelihoods, and was less than planned. Only in Mali was the pattern different. The relief response was once again free food aid, but it was mostly distributed before the hungry season, and actual distributions came very close to target levels, even though much did not reach intended beneficiaries.

The reasons why early non-food assistance was provided in Turkana in 1990 were to do with a well-developed and sensitive EWS, some pre-planning of relief interventions, aid resources allocated in advance for destocking, responsibility delegated to district level where EW practitioners and decision-makers were in close and regular contact, and a local political environment conducive to timely response. The fact that the same pattern was not repeated throughout Kenya, nor indeed in Turkana, two years later during the more severe drought of 1992 warns against

202

Table 9.1 Summary of time-lags between EW and response

	Ethiopia relief food distribution	Sudan (Darfur) relief food distribution	Chad relief food distribution	Mali relief food distribution	Turkana ELP 1990	Turkana relief operation 1992
Time-lag:						
From early warning to decisions being taken	approx. 3 months	approx. 4 months	1.5–5 months(a)	approx. 0.5 months(b)	1 month	approx. 6 months(c)
From decisions to delivery of relief	2 months for first delivery 8–9 months for most of the deliveries(d)	5 months for first delivery >9 months for most of the deliveries(e)	3.5–7 months	1 month for first delivery 4 months to complete deliveries	2 months	2 months(f)
Scale of operation:						
Relief disbursed	>1 million tonnes (estimated requirements); 700000t delivered by November 1991	274000t (estimated requirements); 50000t delivered by beginning of December 1991	12–14000t of cereals	12000t	$21500(g)	During first 8 months of the operation >12000t relief food

Notes:

(a) Time-lag varies from one donor to another.
(b) From SAP's quantified recommendations for relief distribution (in March 1991) to decisions being taken about the programmed food-aid response; information was available earlier about the harvest prospects, but was not translated into relief needs by SAP.
(c) From the first general recommendation made by the EWS that interventions would be 'unavoidable' if the rainy season failed in 1992 (more detailed recommendations were not made) until the DFRC was formed in September.

(d) Some of the relief delivered early in 1991 was food-aid pledges carried over from the previous year.
(e) It should be noted that in the Darfur case, 11 months after recommendations had been translated into decisions to provide relief, only one-third of total requirements had been delivered.
(f) Between the forming of the DFRC in recognition of the need for a large-scale relief operation, and the first major distribution by NGOs.
(g) Converted at 1990 average exchange rate of $1 = KSh22.92.

complacency that if the system works in one year it can be relied upon in subsequent years. Instead, it highlights how rapidly the situation can change, especially the political context and willingness to respond.

In Mali, the response was more timely and followed closely the recommendations of the EWS because of the pre-positioned *Stock National de Securité*, which can be drawn upon in a small-scale crisis like 1990–91. Most decisions about the relief response in an average year can be taken locally, by government officials and donor representatives in Bamako, avoiding the inevitable delays if food aid has to be imported. More importantly, the EW/response system is linked to a wider agenda of cereals market liberalization, part of the structural-adjustment process. There is a strong commitment to donor/government co-ordination over food distribution which has been forged around a wider economic and political agenda. The by-product, at least in 1991, was that broader policy concerns made it expedient that recommendations made by the EWS were heeded and implemented.

Table 9.1 shows the differing response times for each case-study. Those countries dependent upon relief being mobilized in Europe or the US encountered the most severe delays. The worst case was Chad, where a year elapsed between recommended action by the EWS and most of the relief food arriving in-country.

EWS are necessary

In the mid-1980s, it was fashionable to blame the failure to prevent famine in the Sahel and Horn of Africa on inadequate EW. The case-studies show that by the 1990s this is no longer a convincing scapegoat. Indeed, more progress has been made in the EW domain than in almost any other part of famine prevention, not least because of the large amounts of aid invested in EWS. The Sudan case-study, however, exposes the fragility of an EWS which is heavily dependent on donor funding. International aid flows are never guaranteed, and can be cut off abruptly for political reasons, thus stunting the development of an EWS.

None of the EWS failed to sound the alarm; it was the response system which failed to take heed sufficiently early and therefore to provide timely assistance. Even in Sudan the under-resourced EWS provided clear signals early on that large amounts of relief were needed, although it was unable to carry out more refined monitoring later in the year.

EWS are a necessary but insufficient pre-condition for preventing famine. There is a danger that if an EWS fails to trigger a response, it will be regarded as redundant. But the case-studies provide sufficient evidence of the dangers of relying on alternatives to a formal information system. One-off assessments take a small, subjective snapshot of conditions on the ground, which may not be representative, and are often directed at areas where there has been most noise about the crisis, but not necessarily where it is most severe. They are likely to be misleading if team members are not already familiar with the area, and if there is no systematic monitoring system in place against which the findings can be calibrated. The case-studies also show that reliance on a free press to give early warning of famine is risky. Food crises are only newsworthy when they are visually shocking. And there is no guarantee that remote, less politically important areas and population groups will be covered. In other words, although a formal EWS may not be perfect, it is likely to be less distorting than either of these two alternatives.

There is a striking imbalance between the capabilities of EWS and the demands made upon them. Having developed multi-indicator models, most EWS are now well equipped to identify when livelihoods are under threat from drought at an early stage. But in the majority of cases they still use large-scale famine as the reference point, because this is what the international relief system demands — estimates of food aid needs in response to evidence of a crisis.

Most EWS are organizationally separate from decision-making structures, in order to preserve the objectivity of their information, and sometimes to protect the decision-makers' domain. This has been most extreme in the case of USAID's FEWS, which was not even supposed to make recommendations for action. But this strategy incurs many costs. In only one of the case-studies — Turkana's EWS during 1990–91 — were EW practitioners engaged in response planning and co-ordination. This demonstrated the benefits of using the experience of those who have collected the information, understand it best, are in the strongest position to identify an appropriate response — especially where they have had direct contact with local people — and have a vested interest in making sure that their product is used to justify continuous information-gathering to people who may be inconvenienced by regular intrusive questioning.

Common patterns in how EW information is used

We now summarize some of the complex reasons why EW information is not used to its full potential by the international relief system (especially by donor agencies), and why the relief response persists in delivering too little and too late.

Institutional constraints

Ownership of information: Who 'owns' information is critical to how it is used. An EWS that is entirely 'owned' — conceived, staffed and funded — by a national government is less likely to hold sway with international donors than one in which they too have a vested interest. Donors do not trust national EWS and rely heavily on assessments carried out by UN agencies, which possess the critical requirement of the international stamp of credibility; hence the emphasis placed on FAO's harvest assessment and WFP's needs assessment. The irony is that the data in these assessments are usually only as good as those of the national EWS on which they depend for information. Whereas international EWS are given the benefit of the doubt, national EWS are not.

The quest for certainty and quantitative evidence: In 'risk-averse' donor bureaucracies, there are institutional pressures to delay response until hard evidence of a crisis exists and relief needs can be quantified with some certainty. This invariably leads to a late response, rather than heeding the first warnings of an imminent crisis. Hence, the results of the harvest assessment, usually carried out by FAO, carry disproportionate weight compared with earlier warnings from national EWS — which are at best acknowledged but not acted upon, and at worst ignored. The food balance sheet based on the harvest assessment meets the donors' information requirements by providing apparently reliable quantitative data late in the season, and is the trigger for relief pledging. The bottom line — on the food deficit and food aid needs — appears to be simple and straightforward. Thus, it is believed to be non-controversial, although it is increasingly recognized by some to be a very approximate indicator.

Evidence of a crisis already under way is usually necessary for the response process to be treated with any urgency. Donor decision-making is driven by downstream rather than upstream events. Evidence of human stress is most influential, usually expressed as high rates of malnutrition and increased mortality, although these are signs of the outcome of *failure* to respond in time. This can set a vicious circle in motion. If donors only respond to crises, those trying to trigger donor response bid up the severity of the situation to initiate action. This can backfire if the exaggerated prophecies do not materialize; donors feel that they have been misled, and may be less willing to respond next time round. In this scenario it is easy to miss what is really happening as a result of the failure to provide adequate and timely relief: a continuous undermining of people's ability to feed themselves, and increasing vulnerability to the next drought.

Inappropriate bureaucratic procedures: Bureaucratic procedures in donor agency headquarters are not yet geared to the needs of recipient governments or people. The current schedule of decision-making and delivery times for most donor agencies fundamentally undermines the purpose of *early* warning: most food relief is arriving too late, and does not match local people's priorities of, first and foremost, protecting livelihoods.

In-built bureaucratic rigidities reinforce the tendency to delay relief decisions until clear evidence of a food crisis exists. It is accepted practice within most donor agencies that the main pledging of relief aid for countries in the Sahel and Horn of Africa takes place early in the calendar year, in January/February. This presupposes that the time-lag between decisions being taken and food reaching intended beneficiaries before the start of the hungry season (June/July) is less than six months. Evidence from the case-studies shows the time-lag to be much longer. There is an implicit assumption when donor headquarters plan and schedule that once food arrives in-country, the job is complete. In fact, distribution to rural areas can take a further three months. For some donor agencies, the phasing of the financial year is sometimes more influential in the timing of decisions than the seasonality of food shortages in Africa.

Relief and development aid are clearly compartmentalized within most donor agencies. This partly explains why the objective of relief is sharply demarcated as saving lives when there is evidence of famine. Donor agencies are not yet geared to earlier, more developmental interventions aimed at protecting insecure livelihoods. And some are unwilling to embark on this policy shift on the grounds that relief of emergencies *should* be distinct from development assistance. The recent interest in linking relief and development offers some opportunities to break down the barriers, although there are numerous obstacles to doing so, not least the political conditionality applied to aid which means that some of the most food-insecure countries, such as Sudan (and Ethiopia under the Mengistu regime), are simply ineligible for development aid.

Centralized EW/response systems: The inappropriate timing of procedures to release relief aid is exacerbated by the centralized nature of most EW and response systems. Decisions about relief and mobilization of resources are usually made thousands of miles from where assistance is needed, by people who are far removed from what is happening on the ground. EW information has to be aggregated to fit with centralized decision-making, thereby losing whatever understanding of local food economies, or of local people's coping strategies, the EWS may have detected. It is not surprising that busy decision-makers in Northern capitals are geared to getting the food to an African port without taking adequate account of how long it takes to reach beneficiaries inland.

Lack of accountability: The people involved in running EW/response systems are not those who will suffer if they fail to prevent famine, or to tackle cases of acute food insecurity. Lack of accountability if warnings are not heeded in time is a major constraint to the effective workings of an EW and response system. The real victims of late response, whose interests the system is supposed to serve, are far removed from the process of decision-making, and only loosely connected to the process by data extracted from them by the EWS. The international donor community is least accountable to the people it is supposed to protect from famine, exacerbated by physical distance between decision-makers and beneficiaries. The accountability of Western donors is limited to Western public opinion, which may act on behalf of Southern famine victims, but this is a weak and tenuous link. National governments have an indirect interest in preventing famine, but as part of a wider political, social and economic agenda, which may not coincide with the needs of famine-prone populations, especially those in remote and politically marginal parts of the country.

Logistical constraints

Waiting for EW information which proves that there is a crisis before taking action would matter less if it did not take so long to mobilize, ship and distribute internally relief aid to Africa. Considerable efforts have been made to speed up response times within most of the principal donor agencies since the mid-1980s. But it is rarely less than four months from the moment a decision is made to that relief arriving in Africa. As growing demands are being made upon donors' emergency budgets, extra delays may be encountered in mobilizing additional resources. High profile in the international media is the best way of cutting down the response time, as illustrated by the EU Special Programme for Africa in 1991. But this is an unreliable force to depend upon. The quickest response time for respective donor agencies is approximately six to nine months for WFP, four months for ODA, and six months or more for the EU. In most cases it takes much longer. If the food has to reach beneficiaries far inland, where infra-structure is poor and the transport sector undeveloped, an extra three months must often be added to delivery schedules.

Political constraints

It is a fallacy to believe that EW information is entirely objective and has no political value. The political context in which early warnings of famine are issued and the pursuit of interests by competing and unequal groups are crucial to how information is used, and to how it is interpreted. Relations between donor governments and recipient African governments are perhaps the single most important determinant of whether an adequate relief response is launched in time. Although humanitarian aid is supposed to be exempt from political conditionality, political differences can ser-iously delay a relief operation if it becomes a pawn in political controversy and negotiation. In such circumstances, EW information counts for little.

Resource-poor recipient governments, for example, keen to maximize food-aid receipts are likely to make the most generous interpretation of needs assessments, in one of the case-studies equating the national food deficit with total food aid needs. Donor governments, on the other hand, usually seek to minimize relief food allocations because of pressure to share out scarce resources. Their interpretation of EW data is likely to be much more conservative. Ultimately, however, it is the donors' interpreta-tion which prevails; they control the resources.

Forging the link

There are still improvements to be made in famine prediction, but this book shows clearly that developing more comprehensive information sys-tems cannot improve famine prevention until the response side of the equation is tackled. Better information can oil the wheels of the decision-making and response process but is no guarantee that they will start to turn. There are no easy answers; fundamental improvements on the re-sponse side will inevitably challenge a wide range of political, financial and institutional relationships between donor and recipient states. The follow-ing recommendations can nevertheless be made.

Reaching consensus on the objectives of relief: protecting liveli-hoods and saving lives

Mirroring local people's priorities during a food crisis, we have argued strongly in favour of relief operations which attempt to save livelihoods as well as lives. Increasingly, NGOs working in Africa are adopting this ap-proach, especially those engaged in both development and relief activities, as the limitations of a single-tracked 'saving lives' approach become evi-dent in subsequent rehabilitation work. Many donor agencies, however, have not yet made this transition. Indeed, there are strong institutional reasons why relief continues to carry the more narrowly defined objective. But there is an urgent need to re-programme donor bureaucracies — and the Western media that watch over them — to focus on saving livelihoods.

This issue must be placed at the centre of the current debate about linking relief and development.

One way of approaching this link is to develop alternative uses of emergency food aid, as well as non-food responses. Such alternative response options require far more attention, especially field-testing and costing, than is currently the case. Relief should be used more flexibly, as far as possible incorporating the longer-term objective of 'drought-proofing' the rural economy.

EWS as jointly funded ventures

Information provided by national and sub-national EWS is most likely to be used by all parties, and to be sustainable, if these systems are jointly funded by donors and government, giving both a stake in the system. In these circumstances, it is more likely that the political influences an EWS is subject to can be negotiated over, and the problem of a purely national EWS being bypassed by the international community insisting on its own assessments is less likely to arise. This may be incompatible with the habitual approach to aid-funded projects which have a limited lifespan, at the end of which national (or local) government is expected to assume full funding and other responsibilities for the EWS. But most impoverished African governments cannot maintain the system at its former capacity. The costs of a good information system are hard to justify in a country struggling to provide basic services. Often the most food-insecure are also the most marginalized groups in the population, and they may not rank high on the government's list of priorities. If it is likely that the international donor community will be called upon to provide relief in the event of a food crisis, then the cost of maintaining an EWS must be weighed against the benefits of a relief operation planned on the basis of sound and timely information. The benefits include the cost-effectiveness of targeting according to need, rather than blanket distributions. They also include savings if the relief response is launched in time, enabling the cheapest means of ground transport to be used during the dry season, compared with the costs of response at the height of an emergency when expensive airlifts are needed. As the cost of running an EWS is small compared with the costs of running a large relief operation, it is hypothesized that the calculation is likely to be positive.

There are thus both economic and institutional arguments for jointly funded national EWS. Realistically, this is more feasible where donor/government relations are good. Where they are not, co-operation over information is much less likely to succeed.

Responding to early indicators: a phased response

Decision-making relies too heavily on harvest assessments carried out at the end of the growing season, which results in late response by the international community if there are no food-security reserves in-country. It is time for information made available earlier to play a more prominent role, and thus to make better use of the capacity of existing EWS. This means taking due account of *predictive* indicators.

Although the quest for 'certainty' on which to base decisions within donor agencies cannot be ignored, there is scope for starting the response process earlier, if relief resources have to be mobilized in the North for the African continent. For countries in the Sahel and Horn of Africa, a preliminary estimate in September could provide a figure for the minimum amount of relief required for the following 12 months, to set the wheels of response in motion if the first round of pledges is made at this stage. When the final assessment of relief needs is carried out at the end of the calendar year, additional resources could be fed into a system which is already up and running. This requires some re-programming of existing donor bureaucracies, above all to take into account the time-lags involved in mobilizing, shipping and transporting relief in-country, to the final beneficiaries. This could make a very substantial difference in the timeliness of the relief response as a much greater proportion would arrive before the hungry season.

In situations and countries of endemic food crisis, the response process need not start from scratch every time. A certain minimum requirement of emergency aid should be recognized and pledged yearly to avoid delay.

Decentralizing EW/response systems

The limitations of a highly centralized EW/response system have been shown. There are many potential advantages to a more decentralized system, although the case is not clear-cut (illustrated by the Turkana system). A decentralized EWS can take better account of local variations in the food economy, can be more sensitive to local strategies and vulnerability to food stress, and can recommend more appropriate interventions. The management of EW information is usually less cumbersome if decentralized. The disadvantages include problems of standardization of data where resources have to be allocated at national level, and inadequate skilled personnel to run the EWS. If decision-making is also decentralized, decision-makers are closer to what is happening, interpretation of information is usually less distorted, and they have a greater sense of urgency to respond to a problem close at hand. Against this, there is once again the problem of inadequate personnel capacity, and distortion by powerful local elites. There is little sense in decentralizing EW and decision-making if control over resources and the capacity to respond are not also decentralized. This would speed up the response process and the scope for developing more flexible and appropriate response options. But a decentralized response system must be linked into a wider national strategy which can mobilize resources for large-scale food crises. Constraints to a decentralized response system include central government's reluctance to relinquish control over resources, and fear of misuse. On balance, despite these problems, a decentralized approach to EW and response is more likely to be effective and efficient.

Some of the same arguments apply to decision-making within donor agencies, notably decentralizing power from donor agency headquarters to donor country representatives. This should simplify many issues of management, bureaucratic procedures, and improve interpretation of EW indicators. The response process can be speeded up and flexibility and room for manœuvre increased. But this would only work if accompanied by a certain decentralization of resources. This, of course, would reduce the flexibility and control of donor headquarters.

Pre-positioning of relief resources
Where relief resources were pre-positioned, the time-lag between decisions being made and relief being delivered to beneficiaries was much shorter than where relief had to be imported from overseas: in Mali where the SNS supplied the relief operation, and in Turkana where funding for restocking had been committed in advance. Indeed, in Chad, where the longest response time was recorded, fortuitously there was some grain in the reserve stock which could supply the relief operation during 1991 when the imported relief arrived too late.

Pre-positioning resources is one of the strongest options for cutting down the response time for mobilizing and delivering international relief. It carries the added advantage of increasing the autonomy of decision-making at national level, which should speed up the process of translating recommendations into decisions. There is currently substantial support from both government and donors for an Emergency Food Security Reserve in Ethiopia, specifically to cover the bridging period while relief is being imported, and thus acts as a form of loan. It should not be a large buffer stock, incurring high storage and management costs, of which there have been many unsuccessful examples in Africa. Instead, it should be a small, easy-to-manage strategic reserve, supported by donors with a long-term commitment as, in most countries, they will be required to replenish it. Such a reserve is unlikely to be adequate for any large-scale emergencies, but it will cover the critical bridging period while relief is mobilized overseas, thus speeding up the response time. The feasibility of this option is likely to depend upon the state of donor/government relations. If they are strained, it is unlikely to be politically acceptable, although there are other options: donors might set up their own food-aid pool, entirely under their control, or draw on a regional reserve.

It is tempting to argue that good political relations between government and donors are the essential prerequisite for effective EW and response. But this does little to address the current climate of political instability in much of the Horn of Africa and the Sahel and associated tensions between governments and donors. The immediate need is to find pragmatic solutions to the problem of delayed emergency responses — hence the policy options outlined here. We have considered early warning of, and response to, drought-induced famine, although war is increasingly associated with famine. Finding ways of reconciling the political interests vested in EW and response is the central challenge in preventing future famines, which better information alone can do little to tackle. Nevertheless, changing perceptions of what constitutes *early* warning and of the objectives of relief, shared responsibility for information provision, synchronizing the seasonality of response with that of need, pre-positioning resources, and decentralizing the whole process to move it closer to where the action is, will all help to strengthen the context within which decisions to respond are made, to break the cycle of relief arriving always *too little and too late*.

References

General references

ACC/SCN, 1992, *Second Report on the World Nutrition Situation*, Volume 1, Global and Regional Results, UN, October.

Borton, J.N., 1993, 'Recent Trends in the International Relief System', *Disasters*, 17 (3):187–201.

Borton, J.N., Stephenson, R.S., and Morris, C., 1988, 'ODA Emergency Aid to Africa, 1983–86', Overseas Development Administration Evaluation Report EV 425, August (mimeo).

Buchanan-Smith, M., 1990, 'Food Security Planning in the Wake of an Emergency Relief Operation: The Case of Darfur, Western Sudan', *IDS Discussion Paper* No. 278, Brighton: IDS.

Buchanan-Smith, M., and Maxwell, S., 1994, 'Linking Relief and Development: An Introduction and Overview', *IDS Bulletin*, 25 (4):2–16, Brighton: IDS.

Buchanan-Smith, M., and Tlogelang, G.L., 1994, 'Linking Relief and Development: A Case Study of Botswana', *IDS Bulletin*, 25 (4):55–64, Brighton: IDS.

Clay, E.J., and Schaffer, B.B., 1984, 'Introduction – Room for Manœuvre: The Premise of Public Policy' in E.J. Clay and B.B. Schaffer (eds) *Room for Manœuvre: an Exploration of Public Policy in Agriculture and Rural Development*. London: Heinemann.

Corbett, J.E.M., 1988, 'Famine and Household Coping Strategies', *World Development*, 16 (9).

Curtis, D., Hubbard, M., and Shepherd, A. (eds), 1988, *Preventing Famine: Policies and Prospects for Africa*. London: Routledge.

Cutler, P., 1985, 'The Use of Economic and Social Information in Famine Prediction and Response'. Report for the ODA, FERU/LSHTM, London, (mimeo).

Cutler, P., 1993, 'Responses to Famine: Why They are Allowed to Happen', in J.O. Field (ed.) *op. cit.*

Davies, S., 1993, 'Are Coping Strategies a Cop Out?', *IDS Bulletin*, 24 (4):60–72, Brighton: IDS.

Davies, S., 1994, 'Introduction: information, knowledge and power', *IDS Bulletin*, 25 (2):1–13, Brighton: IDS.

Davies, S., 1995 (forthcoming), *Adaptable Livelihoods: Coping with Food Insecurity in the Malian Sahel*. Basingstoke: Macmillan Press Limited.

Davies, S., Buchanan-Smith, M., and Lambert, R., 1991, 'Early Warning in the Sahel and Horn of Africa: The State of the Art: A Review of the Literature', Volume 1 of 3, *Research Report* No. 20, Brighton: IDS.

De Waal, A., 1989, *Famine that Kills: Darfur, Sudan, 1984–1985*. Oxford: Clarendon Press.

De Waal, A., 1990, 'A Re-assessment of Entitlement Theory in the Light of the Recent Famines in Africa', *Development and Change*, 21 (3), London: SAGE.

De Waal, A., 1993, 'War and Famine In Africa', *IDS Bulletin*, 24 (4):33–40, Brighton: IDS.

Devereux, S., 1993, 'Goats Before Ploughs: Dilemmas of Household Response Sequencing During Food Shortages,' *IDS Bulletin*, 24 (4):52–9, Brighton: IDS.

Downing, T.E., Gitu, K.W., and Crispin, M.K. (eds), 1989, *Coping with Drought in Kenya*. Boulder and London: Lynne Rienner.

Drèze, J., and Sen, A., 1989, *Hunger and Public Action*. Oxford: Clarendon Press.

Duffield, M., 1991, 'War and Famine in Africa', *Oxfam Research Paper* No. 5, Oxford: Oxfam Publications.

Dyson, T., 1993, 'Demographic Responses to Famines in South Asia', *IDS Bulletin*, 24 (4):17–24, Brighton: IDS.

Elbadawi, I., Ghura, D., and Uwujaren, G., 1992, 'Why Structural Adjustment has not Succeeded in Sub-Saharan Africa', *WPS 1000*, Washington, DC: World Bank.

FAO, 1986, 'Food and Agricultural Statistics in the Context of a National Information System', *FAO Statistical Development Series* No. 1, Rome: FAO.

Field, J.O. (ed.), 1993a, *The Challenge of Famine. Recent Experiences, Lessons Learned*. Hartford, CT: Kumarian Press.

Field, J.O., 1993b, 'Beyond Relief: Toward Improved Management of Famine', in J.O. Field (ed.) *op. cit.*

Gill, P., 1986, *A Year in the Death of Africa: Politics, Bureaucracy and the Famine*. London: Paladin, Grafton Books.

Glantz, M.H. (ed.), 1987, *Drought and Hunger in Africa: Denying Famine a Future*. Cambridge: Cambridge University Press.

Holt, J., and Lawrence, M., 1993, *Making Ends Meet. A Survey of the Food Economy of the Ethiopian North-East Highlands*. London: SCF (UK).

House of Commons Foreign Affairs Committee, 1992, *Recent Developments in the Horn of Africa*, Second Special Report, London: HMSO.

Hubbard, M., 1989, 'Why and How the Famine Prevention Capability of Rural Local Government in Western Sudan should be Strengthened: Learning from the Kordofan Experience', Birmingham: University of Birmingham, Development Administration Group, (mimeo).

Lambert, R., Gershon, M., Buchanan-Smith, M., and Davies, S., 1991, 'Famine Early Warning and Food Information Systems in the Sahel and Horn of Africa: An Annotated Bibliography, Volume 3', *Development Bibliographies Series* No. 7, Brighton: IDS.

Machlup, F., 1979, 'Uses, Values and Benefits of Knowledge', in D.W. King *et al.* (eds) *Key Papers in the Economics of Information*. New York: American Society for Information and Science, Knowledge Industry Publications.

March, J.G., and Olsen, J.P., 1989, *Rediscovering Institutions: The Organisational Basis of Politics*. New York and London: Free Press.

Mosley, P., Harrigan, J., and Toye, J., 1991, *Aid and Power. The World Bank and Policy-based Lending. Volume 1. Analysis and Policy Proposals*. London and New York: Routledge.

ODI, 1992, 'Aid and Political Reform', *ODI Briefing Paper*, London: ODI, January.

OECD, 1994, *Development Co-operation. Development Assistance Committee, 1993 Report*, Paris: OECD.

Robinson, M., 1994, 'Governance, Democracy and Conditionality: NGOs and the New Policy Agenda', in A. Clayton (ed.), *Governance, Democracy and Conditionality: What Role for NGOs?*, Intrac NGO Management and Policy Series No. 2, Oxford: Intrac Publications.

Roskens, R., 1991, 'Meeting the Development Test in Africa', Washington, DC: USAID Office of External Affairs, May.

SADC, 1993, 'Drought Management Workshops in Southern Africa: Final Report', Harare: Southern Africa Development Community, Food Security Technical and Administrative Unit.

Sen, A., 1981, *Poverty and Famines: An Essay on Entitlement and Deprivation*. Oxford: Clarendon Press.

Shaw, J., and Clay, E., 1993, *World Food Aid*. London: WFP in association with James Currey and Portsmouth, NH: Heinemann.

Swift, J., 1989, 'Why Are Rural People Vulnerable to Famine?, *IDS Bulletin*, 20 (2):8–15, Brighton: IDS.

Tabor, S., 1983, 'Drought Relief and Information Management: Coping Intelligently with Disaster', Botswana: Gaborone (mimeo).

Uvin, P., 1994, *The International Organization of Hunger*. London: Kegan Paul International.

Von Braun, J., Tesfaye, T., and Webb, P., 1993, 'Famine as the Outcome of Political, Production and Market Failures', *IDS Bulletin*, 24 (4):73–9, Brighton: IDS.

WFP, 1992, 'Disaster Mitigation and Rehabilitation in Africa', Rome: WFP.

WFP, 1994, 'WFP Resource Situation', Thirty-seventh Session, CFA, Rome, 19–27 May.

Case-study references

Ethiopia

Belshaw, D., 1990, 'Food Strategy Formulation and Development Planning in Ethiopia', *IDS Bulletin*, 21 (3):31–43, Brighton: IDS.

Buchanan-Smith, M., Davies, S., and Lambert, R., 1991, 'A Guide to Famine Early Warning and Food Information Systems in the Sahel and Horn of Africa', Volume 2 of 3, *Research Report* No. 21, Brighton: IDS.

Clark, L., 1986, 'Early Warning Case Study: the 1984–85 Influx of Tigrayans into Eastern Sudan', *Working Paper* No. 2, Oxford: Refugee Policy Group (mimeo).

CRDA, 1990–91, monthly, 'Summary telefax' to CRDA donor partners, Addis Ababa, (mimeo).

CSA, 1990a, 'Report on 1990/91 Crops, Weather and Food Situation', CSA Statistical Bulletin No. 82, Addis Ababa, November.

CSA, 1990b, 'Crop Production Forecast 1990/91. Results of Area and Production of Major Crops', CSA Statistical Bulletin No. 84, Addis Ababa, December.

Curtis, D., Hubbard, M., and Shepherd, A. (eds), 1988, *Preventing Famine: Policies and Prospects for Africa*. London: Routledge.

Dagnew, E.T., 1993, 'The Impact of Food Shortages on Rural Households of Different Income Groups and their Crisis Coping Strategies: A Case Study of Wollaita District in Ethiopia', Ph.D. thesis, Sussex University, (mimeo).

EWPS, 1990a, '1990 Belg (small) Crop Season Synoptic Report', Addis Ababa: RRC, August.

EWPS, 1990b, 'Food Supply Prospect in 1991 (Crop growers and nomads)', Addis Ababa: RRC, October.

EWPS, 1991a, 'Famine Threat in the Ogaden', Addis Ababa: RRC, January.

EWPS, 1991b, 'Food Supply of the Crop Dependent Population in 1991', Addis Ababa: RRC, February.

EWPS, 1992, 'Relief Plan of Operation for 1992', Addis Ababa: RRC, March.

FAO, 1990, 'Special Report, FAO Crop Assessment Mission to Ethiopia', Rome (mimeo).

FAO, 1991a, 'FAO Crop Assessment Mission Report, Ethiopia, October-December 1990', Rome: GIEWS, January (mimeo).

FAO, 1991b, 'Assistance on the Implementation of the National Disaster Prevention and Preparedness Strategy', Study Project 4, Early Warning and Information Systems, Rome: FAO (mimeo).

FEWS, 1990, 'Pre-Harvest Assessment of Cereal Production', Washington, DC: USAID, Tulane/Pragma Group, October (mimeo).

FEWS, 1991, 'Harvest Assessment of Cereal Production', Washington, DC: USAID, Tulane/Pragma Group, January (mimeo).

FEWS, 1993, 'Pre-harvest Assessment', Washington, DC: USAID, Tulane/Pragma Group.

Goyder, H., and Goyder, C., 1988, 'Case Studies of Famine: Ethiopia' in D. Curtis, M. Hubbard, A. Shepherd (eds), *Preventing Famine: Policies and Prospects for Africa*. London: Routledge.

Holt, J., and Lawrence, M., 1993, *Making Ends Meet. A Survey of the Food Economy of the Ethiopian North-East Highlands*. London: SCF (UK).

Kumar, B.G., 1990, 'Ethiopian Famines 1973–1985: A Case Study' in J. Drèze and A. Sen (eds) *The Political Economy of Hunger, Volume II: Famine Prevention*. Oxford: Clarendon Press.

Lawrence, M., Tayech, Y., and O'Dea, J.K., 1994, 'Nutritional Status and Early Warning of Mortality in Southern Ethiopia, 1988–1991', *European Journal of Clinical Nutrition*, 48:38–45.

Maxwell, S., 1993, 'State Action for Food Security: Horses for Courses in Sub-Saharan Africa', Brighton: IDS (mimeo).

ODNRI, 1987, 'The Size, Location, Infrastructure and Management of a Food Security Reserve to Assist Famine Relief in Ethiopia', 10 July to August 1987, London: ODA (mimeo).

People's Democratic Republic of Ethiopia, 1990, 'Guidelines on Nutritional Status Data and Food Relief', Addis Ababa: EWPS.

RDI, 1985, 'Strengthening Disaster Preparedness in Six African Countries', Study prepared for the Ford Foundation, London: RDI (mimeo).

RRC, 1991, 'Review of Current Relief Activities and Assistance Requirements for the Period May–Dec., 1991', Addis Ababa: RRC, June.

SCF (UK), 1991, 'Strong Evidence of Famine in Ethiopia', Addis Ababa, April (mimeo).

Sen, A., 1981, *Poverty and Famines. An Essay on Entitlement and Deprivation*. Oxford: Clarendon Press.

UN, 1991, 'Consolidated Interim Appeal for Emergency Operations in the Horn of Africa Area (Ethiopia, Sudan, Somalia, Djibouti, Kenya)', New York: UN, 19 July (mimeo).

University of Leeds, 1988, 'Eritrea Food and Agricultural Production Assessment Study, Final Report', An Independent Evaluation of the Food Situation in Eritrea, submitted to the Emergency Relief Desk, Leeds: University of Leeds (mimeo).

Walker, P., 1989, *Famine Early Warning Systems: Victims and Destitution*. London: Earthscan Publications.

Webb, P., von Braun, J., and Yohannes, Y., 1991, 'Famine in Ethiopia: Policy Implications of Coping Failure at National and Household Levels', Washington, DC: IFPRI, draft.

Webb, P., and von Braun, J., 1994, *Famine and Food Security in Ethiopia: Lessons for Africa*. Chichester: Wiley.

WFP, 1990, 'WFP/NGO Food Aid Assessment Mission Ethiopia 1990. Briefing Note', Rome (mimeo).

World Bank, 1988, 'The Challenge of Hunger in Africa: A Call to Action', Washington, DC, September (mimeo).

World Bank, 1992, *World Development Report*. Oxford and New York: Oxford University Press.

215

Sudan

APU, 1988–90, various, 'Darfur Region Food and Agriculture Bulletin', El Fasher, Darfur (mimeo).

APU, 1988, 'Results of North Darfur Pre-Harvest Survey, October 1988', El Fasher, Darfur, November (mimeo).

APU, 1990, 'Results of North Darfur Pre-Harvest Survey, October 1989', El Fasher, Darfur, January (mimeo).

APU, RRC, SCF, WFP, Oxfam and SRC, 1990, 'Rapid Assessment Report on Food Security Situation, Darfur Region, September 1990', El Fasher, Darfur, October (mimeo).

Buchanan-Smith, M., 1989, 'Evaluation of the Western Relief Operation 1987/88', EC and Khartoum: Ministry of Finance and Economic Planning (mimeo).

Buchanan-Smith, M., 1990, 'Food Security Planning in the Wake of an Emergency Relief Operation: The Case Of Darfur, Western Sudan', *IDS Discussion Paper* No. 278, Brighton: IDS.

Buchanan-Smith, M., and Mohammed, M.I., 1991, 'Regional Policy and Food Insecurity: The Case of Darfur, Western Sudan', in *Conference Papers* of Second International Sudan Studies Conference, Durham, 8–11 April, Durham: Sudan Studies Society of UK.

Clift-Hill, A., 1987, 'Darfur Rainfall Records', London: ODA (mimeo).

De Waal, A., 1989, *Famine that Kills: Darfur, Sudan, 1984–1985*. Oxford: Clarendon Press.

Eldredge, E., and Rydjeski, D., 1988, 'Food Crises, Crisis Response and Emergency Preparedness: The Sudan Case', *Disasters*, 12 (1):1–4.

EWSU, 1990/91, various, 'Early Warning System Bulletin', Khartoum: RRC.

EWSU, 1991, 'Grain Production and Consumption in the Sudan for the Year 1991', prepared by Early Warning and Food Information System staff, Addis Ababa: RRC, January.

FAO, 1990a, 'Foodcrops and Shortages', Special Report, Rome: GIEWS, April (mimeo).

FAO, 1990b, 'Joint FAO/GOS Release on the Food Grain Plantings and Crop Conditions in the Sudan – 1990/1991', Khartoum, October (mimeo).

FAO, 1990c, 'FAO Crop Assessment Mission Report, Sudan (November 1990)', Rome: FAO, December (mimeo).

FAO, 1991a, 'FAO Wheat Crop Assessment Mission to Sudan', Special Report, Rome: GIEWS, 18 April (mimeo).

FAO, 1991b, 'Special Alert No. 222', Rome: GIEWS, 14 June (mimeo).

FEWS, 1990a, 'Vulnerability Assessment', Washington, DC: USAID, Tulane/Pragma Group, June (mimeo).

FEWS, 1990b, 'Pre-Harvest Assessment of Cereal Production', Washington, DC: USAID, Tulane/Pragma Group, October (mimeo).

Graham, R., 1990, 'Food Security Analysis Summary', Oxfam (Sudan), October (mimeo).

ILO, 1987, 'Employment and Economic Reform: Towards a Strategy for the Sudan', Geneva: ILO/Jobs and Skills Programme for Africa (mimeo).

Kelly, M., and Buchanan-Smith, M., 1994, 'Northern Sudan in 1991: Food Crisis and the International Relief Response', *Disasters*, 18 (1):16–34.

Maxwell, S., 1989, 'Food Insecurity in North Sudan', *IDS Discussion Paper* No. 262, Brighton: IDS.

Maxwell, S. (ed.), 1991, *To Cure All Hunger: Food Policy and Food Security in Sudan*. London: Intermediate Technology Publications.

Oxfam, 1991, 'Situation Report: Nutrition Programme, Oxfam Darfur, January–April 1991', Darfur, April (mimeo).

SCF (UK), 1992, various, 'SCF (UK) Food & Information System Bulletin, Darfur State, Sudan' (mimeo).

SEPHA, 1991–2, two-weekly reports, various, Khartoum (mimeo).

Sharp, K., 1990, 'North Darfur Food Security Situation, October 1990', APU, El Fasher, Darfur, October (mimeo).

Shepherd, A., 'Case Studies of Famine: Sudan', in D. Curtis, M. Hubbard, A. Shepherd (eds), *Preventing Famine: Policies and Prospects for Africa*. London: Routledge.

Swift, J., and Gray, J., 1989, 'Report on Darfur Region Food Security Policy and Planning', Darfur Regional Government, Republic of Sudan (under assignment from ODA) (mimeo).

Teklu, T., von Braun, J., and Zaki, E., 1991, 'Drought and Famine Relationships in Sudan: Policy Implications', *Research Report* No. 88, Washington, DC: IFPRI.

WFP, 1990, 'Emergency Food Aid Assessment Mission Sudan: Summary of Conclusions and Recommendations, 27 November–19 December', Khartoum, December (mimeo).

Chad

Arditi, C., and Bouquin, P., 1990, 'Evaluation de l'Office National des Céréales, Version Préliminaire', Brussels: Commission of the European Communities (mimeo).

Brown, V.W., Patterson Brown, E., Eckerson, D., Gilmore, J., and Swartzendruber, H.D., 1987, 'An Evaluation of the African Emergency Food Assistance Program in Chad, 1984–1985', AID Evaluation Special Study, No. 48, Washington, DC: USAID (mimeo).

CARE, 1991, 'Projet de Distribution de 5,000 Tonnes Métriques Prélevées sur le Stock de Sécurité. Rapport Final', August (mimeo).

Direction de la Sécurité Alimentaire, 1990, 'Requête pour une Aide Alimentaire à la République du Tchad, 1990–1991', République du Tchad.

Direction des Ressources en Eau et de la Météorologie, 1990, 'Bulletin Agro-Hydro-Météorologique', par decade.

FAO, 1990, 'Evaluation du Niveau Actuel de Sécurité Alimentaire, Problèmes à Résoudre', Assistance pour l'Elaboration d'un Programme National de Sécurité Alimentaire, Première Phase, Rome: FAO (mimeo).

FEWS, 1990a, 'Vulnerability Assessment', Washington, DC: USAID, Tulane/Pragma Group (mimeo).

FEWS, 1990b, 'Pre-Harvest Assessment of Cereal Production', Washington, DC: USAID, Tulane/Pragma Group (mimeo).

FEWS, 1991, 'Harvest Assessment of Cereal Production', Washington, DC: USAID, Tulane/Pragma Group (mimeo).

Lalau-Keraly, A., and Magos, L., 'Evaluation du Système d'Alerte Précoce (SAP), financé par la Communauté Européenne au Tchad. Rapport Final', Centre Européen de Formation des Statisticiens Economistes des Pays en Voie de Développement, Malakoff (mimeo).

Lea, J.D., and Reed, C., 1991, 'Chad Food Security Programme Case Study, Draft', Kansas State University, USAID (mimeo).

SAP, monthly, various, 'Bulletin Mensuel', N'djamena: MSAPS.

SAP, 1990a, 'Le Système d'Alerte Précoce au Tchad', AEDES/SAP/Tchad.

SAP, 1990b, 'Crises Alimentaires en Zone Sahélienne, Prévisions pour 1991', N'djamena: MSAPS.

SAP, 1990c, 'Crises Nutritionelles en Zone Sahélienne. Prévisions pour 1990/91', N'djamena: MSAPS.

SAP, 1990d, 'Proposition d'un Mode de Calcul pour l'Evaluation Quantitative de l'Assistance Alimentaire Nécessaire au Tchad pour la Saison 1990/91' N'djamena: MSAPS.

SAP, n.d.,'Limite de la Méthode de l'Analyse: la Non-Intégration des Populations Nomades' N'djamena: MSAPS.

USAID, 1991, 'Project Implementation Report, Famine Early Warning System, 698–0466, 1 April–30 September 1991', N'djamena (mimeo).

Valère-Gille, F., 1990, 'Rapport de Mission sur la Création d'un Stock de Sécurité Alimentaire au Tchad', Rome: WFP (mimeo).

World Bank, 1991, *World Development Report 1991*. Oxford and New York: Oxford University Press.

Mali

Acord Mali, 1991, 'Mise à Jour de la Situation au Nord du Mali', Bamako and London, July (mimeo).

Buchanan-Smith, M., Davies, S., and Lambert, R., 1991, 'Guide to Famine Early Warning and Food Information Systems in the Sahel and Horn of Africa', Volume 2 of 3, *Research Report* No. 21, Brighton: IDS.

CCE, 1992, 'Action de Substitution aux Livraisons d'Aide Alimentaire au Mali', Draft Report by J.P. Dumas, Société Française de Conseil en Développement, Boulogne, for the EU Delegation, Bamako, March.

Cekan, J., 1991, 'The Système d'Alerte Précoce (SAP): Mali's Famine Early Warning System: An Overview and Assessment', Medford, MA: Fletcher School of Law and Diplomacy, July (mimeo).

CILSS, 1990, *Situation Alimentaire Exercice 1989/90 et Perspectives 1990/91*, Suivi de la Situation Alimentaire dans les Pays du CILSS, Project Diagnostique Permanent II, PR/DIAPER/12/ 90/ECA/D88/90, Ouagadougou, December.

Davies, S., 1995 (forthcoming), *Adaptable Livelihoods: Coping with Food Insecurity in the Malian Sahel*. Basingstoke: Macmillan Press Limited.

De Waal, A., 1989, *Famine that Kills: Darfur, Sudan, 1984–85*. Oxford: Clarendon Press.

Egg, J., and Teme, B., 1990, 'Rapport de Mission d'Evaluation du "Project Système d'Alerte Précoce" (SAP) au Mali', PRMC, Montepellier: INRA-ESR and Bamako: IER, November (mimeo).

FAO, 1990, 'Back to Office Report: Assessment of the 1990–91 Cropping Season, jointly with CILSS and National Authorities: Mali', by P. Behal and R. Gommes, Rome (mimeo).

FEWS, 1990, 'Vulnerability Assessment'. Washington, DC: Tulane/Pragma Group USAID, (mimeo).

FEWS, 1991a, 'Harvest Assessment of Cereal Production'. Washington, DC: USAID, Tulane/Pragma Group (mimeo).

FEWS, 1991b, 'Vulnerability Assessment'. Washington, DC: Tulane/Pragma Group for USAID, (mimeo).

Lalau-Keraly, A., and Winter, G., 1988, 'Evaluation du Projet Système d'Alerte Précoce (SAP) au Mali', Bamako: OSCE, November (mimeo).

Pirzio-Biroli, D., 1988, 'Mali Cereals Policy and Food Sector Work: Institutional Structure and Efficiency of Emergency Food Aid and Early Warning Systems', Mission to Mali Report (mimeo).

République du Mali, 1982, 'La Stratégie Alimentaire du Mali', Bamako: Ministère de l'Agriculture.

République du Mali, 1991a, 'Rapport de Mission: Suivi des Opérations de Transport et de Distributions Alimentaires Gratuites dans la Région de Mopti (1991)', Bamako: CADB, MATDB, July.

République du Mali, 1991b, *Enquête Budget Consommation (1988–1989): Résultats*. Bamako: PADEM/World Bank and Planning Ministry (DNSI), March.

République du Mali, 1991c, 'Rapport d'Execution du Plan de Ravitaillement 1991', Bamako: OPAM.

République du Mali, 1991d, *Enquête Agricole de Conjoncture: Campagne 1990– 1991, Résultats Définitifs*. Bamako: PADEM/CILSS–DIAPER et Ministères du Plan (DNSI) et de l'Agriculture (DNA), July.

SADS, n.d., 'Survey of Readers' Reactions to the SADS Bulletin', Mopti: SADS (mimeo).

WFP, 1986, 'Evaluation of WFP Emergency Response in West Africa 1983–1985: Country Report: Mali', Rome: WFP, October (mimeo).

Turkana District, Kenya

Buchanan-Smith, M., 1989, 'Evaluation of the Western Relief Operation 1987/88', Khartoum: EC and Ministry of Finance and Economic Planning (mimeo).

Buchanan-Smith, M., 1993, 'A Review of Oxfam's Approach to Relief Food Distribution in Samburu and Turkana Districts of Kenya, 1992/93: "The Entitlement System"', Oxford and Brighton: Oxfam and IDS, (mimeo).

Bush, J., 1991, 'Case Study of WFP Project 2669/Ext.1, Integrated Livestock Development and Soil Conservation in Turkana District, Kenya'. Paper prepared for WFP/IGADD Seminar on Soil Conservation, Forestry and Drought Control Projects, WFP Turkana Sub-office, March (mimeo).

Bush, J., 1992, 'Destocking, Restocking and Tree Planting: A Review of Select Activities in WFP Project 2669/Ext.1 – Turkana District', Final Report to WFP, WFP Turkana Sub-office, January (mimeo).

Cohen, J.M., and Lewis, D.B., 1987, 'Role of Government in Combating Food Shortages: Lessons from Kenya 1984–85' in M.H. Glantz (ed.), *Drought and Hunger in Africa: Denying Famine a Future*. Cambridge: Cambridge University Press.

Cullis, A., and Pacey, A., 1992, *A Development Dialogue: Rainwater Harvesting in Turkana*. London: Intermediate Technology Publications.

EC, WFP and Royal Netherlands Embassy, 1992, 'Drought Preparedness Intervention and Recovery in Arid and Semi-Arid Lands of Kenya', Formulation Mission Report, Nairobi: Ministry of Reclamation and Development of Arid and Semi-Arid Areas and Wastelands (mimeo).

Engomo, D.K., 1992, 'Putting Decision-making Back into the Hands of the People', *Appropriate Technology*, 19 (3), December, London: Intermediate Technology.

FSG, DAG and IDS, 1990, 'More Rural Development With Less Rain, Drought and the Rural Economy in Botswana: An Evaluation of the Drought Programme, 1982–1990', Study Report prepared for Ministry of Finance and Development Planning, Government of the Republic of Botswana (mimeo).

Government of Kenya and WFP, 1990, 'Plan of Operations Agreed Upon Between the Government of Kenya and the World Food Programme Concerning Assistance for Integrated Livestock Development Including Soil Conservation in Turkana District, WFP Project 2669/Ext.1', Nairobi: Government of Kenya (mimeo).

Lokong, M.O., and Etheri, A.J., 1991, 'Interim Report on Food Emergency in Kakuma and Lokichoggio Divisions', Drought Stress Evaluation Team, Ministry of Regional Development, Lodwar: TRP, June (mimeo).

McCabe, J.T., 1990, 'Turkana Pastoralism: A Case Against the Tragedy of the Commons', *Human Ecology*, 18 (1):81–103.

Oba, G., 1992, 'Ecological Factors in Land Use Conflicts, Land Administration and Food Insecurity in Turkana, Kenya', *Pastoral Development Network Paper* No. 33a, London: ODI.

ODI, 1985, 'Turkana District: Development Strategy and Programme 1985/86 to 1987/88', London: ODI, July (mimeo).

Prigan, M., and Chirchir, J., 1991, 'Famine Stress Report for Kakuma/ Lokichoggio Divisions', Report to Project Manager, Lodwar, TRP, March (mimeo).

RDI, 1985, 'Strengthening Disaster Preparedness in Six African Countries', study prepared for Ford Foundation, London: RDI (mimeo).

Swift, J., 1985, 'Planning Against Drought and Famine in Turkana, Northern Kenya', Nairobi: Oxfam and TRP (mimeo).

TDCPU, quarterly, 1990–92, 'Early Warning System Bulletin, Turkana District', Lodwar.

TDCPU, 1991, 'Analysis Report Survey Among Displaced Population Kakuma Division', report prepared for DMC members, Lodwar, May.

TDCPU, 1992a, 'Turkana District Drought Manual', draft, Lodwar, June.

TDCPU, 1992b, 'Post Evaluation Mission Report', Lodwar, May.

TDCPU, 1993, 'Planning for Drought in Turkana', *Appropriate Technology*, 20 (2), September, London: Intermediate Technology Publications.

Wekesa, F., and Bush, J., n.d., 'Impacts of Emergency Livestock Purchasing, Presentation of Survey Findings', Lodwar (mimeo).

INDEX

ACC/SCN, 7
access, to food, 3–5 *passim*, 17
to markets, 87
accountability, 25, 27, 30, 32, 33, 42, 162,
172, 207
Acord Mali, 160
actions de substitution, 162
adaptation capacity, 144
advisers, expatriate, 88, 89, 89n4, 131, 138
AEDES, 116
agriculture, 7, 57, 60, 61, 81, 86–7, 93, 113–16
passim, 169, 186
aid, 5–6, 9, 27–36, 61, 83, 87–8, 109, 110, 169,
170, 180, 192, 195, 198, 200, 204 *see also*
donors; relief
budgets, 9, 26, 28, 33–4, 44, 53, 54
conditionality, 23, 27, 28, 34–6, 35n8;
political 34, 53, 54, 88, 94, 101, 108, 193,
198, 207, 208
development, 5, 9, 33, 35, 53, 55, 60, 74,
82, 104, 109, 121, 206–7
food, 6, 14, 16–19, 32–3, 35, 36, 43–4, 56,
65–74, 92–5, 110, 115–17, 122–4, 134–9,
142–3, 147n9, 150–64, 184–5, 202, 208;
Convention, 32
humanitarian, 27–30, 35, 43, 44, 46, 48, 49,
53, 82, 88, 94, 208
politics of, 33–5, 55–6, 100–3, 109, 192–3
see also under individual countries
suspension, 34, 35, 49, 84, 88–9, 170, 173,
180, 193
airlifts, 66, 71, 79–80, 95, 104, 105, 209
Amin, Mohammed, 42
Anatomy of a Famine, 102, 103
Arditi, C., 115
assessments, of need, 17, 18, 62, 71–4, 92,
135, 149, 210
APU, 92, 93, 103
FAO harvest, 36, 38, 46, 51, 52, 56, 63, 65,
66, 71, 72, 75, 81, 82, 89, 92–4, 99, 102,
103, 117, 120, 126–7, 129, 132, 136, 137,
141, 146–51 *passim*, 155, 190, 205, 206,
209
one-off, 96, 100, 104, 121, 131, 136, 204
WFP, 36, 38, 46, 51, 52, 56, 63, 65, 71, 75,
81, 82, 90, 92, 93, 98, 99, 103, 115, 205
assets, 3, 7

depletion of, 3, 74, 91, 99, 106, 109, 111,
119, 125, 199
destruction of, 4, 106, 115, 135, 144
preservation of, 5, 98
auctions, livestock, 177, 179, 180
availability, food, 3, 17, 60, 115, 144

balance-sheet, food, 16, 17, 66, 71, 72, 81, 92,
113, 116, 126–7, 131, 136, 142, 149, 155,
206
Bangladesh, 26
Banikane (Mali), 158
al-Bashir, President, 84, 93, 101
Batha *préfecture* (Chad), 128
Belgium, 35
Belshaw, D., 57, 58
Biltine *préfecture* (Chad), 121, 135
blood, 169, 173
Borana (Ethiopia), 63
Borkou–Ennedi–Tibesti (Chad), 133, 138
Borton, J. N., 9, 10, 28, 28n3, 39, 51
Bosnia, 33, 43n15
Botswana, 21n5, 199, 199n8
Bouquin, P., 115
Britain, 33, 35, 39, 40, 42, 90, 102 *see also*
ODA
British Council, 35
House of Commons Foreign Affairs
Committee, 28
Brown, V. W., 116, 135
Buchanan-Smith, M., 21n5, 63, 87, 91, 95, 97,
98, 184, 199
Buerke, Michael, 42
bureaucracy, 5, 16, 19, 21–3, 36, 44, 46–8, 52,
56, 121, 132, 133, 147, 198, 206, 208, 210
Bush, J., 169, 179, 180, 195

camels, 167
Cameroon, 124
camps, destitute/displaced, 98, 106–7, 172,
184
Canada, 147n9
CIDA, 63, 147n9
CARE, 63, 76, 93, 104, 122, 124, 127, 150,
154
cash-for-work, 61, 195
Catholic Relief Services, 182

cattle, 167, 181
censuses, population, 126, 141, 159
centralization, 11, 62, 73, 81, 89, 119, 125, 138, 207
cereals, 9, 57, 66, 86, 92, 113, 119, 123, 141–2, 146, 161, 204 *see also* markets
certainty, quest for, 11, 22, 25, 27, 28, 36, 46, 52, 65, 205–6, 210
Chad, 1, 7, 11, 34, 35, 38, 44, 46, 47, 111–38, 189, 211
  AGRHYMET, 117, 119
  CASAAU, 117, 119–22 *passim*, 128, 131–4 *passim*
  CNNTA, 116, 121, 128
  economy, 113
  food policy, 114–16
  food security, 113–14
  government-donor relations, 132, 133, 136
  ONC, 115, 123, 134
  Opération Viande, 124, 136
  politics, 113, 120, 122, 132, 133, 135, 136
  response system, 117, 119–24, 135, 148
  SAP, 111, 116–17, 119–21, 124–9, 131–3, 135–8 *passim*, 202, 203
  Sudanian zone, 113, 114, 117, 123, 124, 126, 127, 134, 138
Chad, Lake, 113, 127
chiefs, 158, 182
children, 98, 150, 174, 181, 183
  under-fives, 7, 18, 68, 70, 98, 174
Chirchir, J., 186
Christian Relief and Development Association, 63, 70
CILSS, 46, 117, 132, 147
  DIAPER, 126, 145
Clark, L., 78
Clay, E. J., 22, 32, 46
Clift-Hill, A., 87
Cohen, J. M., 21, 178
Commonwealth of Independent States, 33
conflict, 2, 4, 5, 7–10 *passim*, 32, 33, 57, 63, 79, 82, 88, 113, 139, 144, 148, 150, 159–60 *see also* raiding
  tribal, 106, 107, 135, 159, 196
consumption, 3–5 *passim*, 71–2, 86, 92, 98, 126–7, 141, 144, 149, 154, 155, 173–4
Coopération Française, 121, 154
co-ordination, 22, 83, 90, 161, 178, 184, 190, 205
  Destocking–Committee, 180, 181
  Logistics–Plan, 94
  Technical–Committee, 90
coping strategies, 3–4, 8, 9, 16, 58, 62, 74, 81, 87, 98, 125, 131, 144, 150, 156, 165, 170, 174, 199
Corbett, J.E.M., 3
cost recovery, 179, 181
counterpart funds, 142, 143, 146, 147n9, 191

Cullis, A., 172, 173
Cutler, P., 22, 39, 46

Dagnew, E.T., 74
Darfur, 84, 86–8, 91–3, 95–100, 103–10 *passim*
  Agricultural Planning Unit, 88, 89, 91–3, 101, 103, 104, 106
  Regional Emergency Food Security Committee, 91–3 *passim*
Dar Zaghawa (Sudan), 96
data collection, 1, 4, 12–14, 25, 62, 89, 99, 100, 107, 125, 126, 146, 162, 175, 178, 182, 188, 205
Davies, S., 3, 4, 9, 16, 141n1
deaths, 5, 6, 84, 87, 96, 98, 103, 109, 125, 182, 184
  'mega', 103, 104, 109
debt, 8, 16, 86
Deby, President Idriss, 113
decentralization, 10, 11, 56, 61, 73, 81, 99, 138, 162, 164, 165, 169, 177, 178, 185, 190, 194, 197, 200, 201, 210–11
decision-making, 1, 2n2, 8, 11, 15, 16, 18, 21–2, 24, 26, 27, 44–8, 52, 66, 74–7, 83, 84, 90–1, 104, 108, 117–19, 121, 130, 133, 162, 189–93, 200, 201, 205–7, 210, 211
  timeliness of, 24, 46–7, 83, 108, 120–1, 162
deficits, budget, 8, 86
  food, 57, 80, 86, 92, 93, 99, 107, 113, 120, 126–7, 132, 141, 142, 149, 154, 155, 206, 208
degradation, environmental, 58, 169
delivery, 6, 50, 56, 70, 78, 82, 84, 95, 105, 134, 202, 206, 210
democratization, 10, 163
destitution, 3, 5, 11, 52, 104, 172, 199
destocking, 177, 179, 194, 202
  Co-ordination Committee, 180, 181
de Waal, A., 3, 4, 87, 98, 143
Dinangourou (Mali), 157
Dire Dawa (Ethiopia), 68
'disaster tourism', 100, 109, 110
disease, 3, 5, 61, 172
  livestock, 170, 178, 199
displacement, population, 8, 17, 55, 69, 79, 84, 91, 97, 98, 106–7, 113, 115, 126, 137, 157–9 *passim*, 175, 181, 182, 199
distribution, 17, 47, 60, 65, 70, 77, 90, 95, 107, 119, 121, 123, 124, 127–9 *passim*, 131, 136, 139, 142, 144, 152–9 *passim*, 163, 164, 183, 206, 209
donors, 1–3 *passim*, 5, 8–10, 15, 19, 21–56 *passim*, 65, 68, 74, 75, 81–3, 90, 91, 94, 97–108 *passim*, 119, 121, 126, 128, 129, 131–6 *passim*, 143, 143n6, 149, 163, 198, 200–2, 205–10 *passim*

co-ordination, 50–1, 102, 147, 163
pledging, 49, 52, 56, 66, 68–70, 75–7
  passim, 83, 93, 95, 105, 115, 206
relations with governments, 2, 4, 9, 11, 23,
  53 *see under individual countries*
relations with NGOs, 10, 39, 49–50, 52,
  76, 104, 105, 124, 163, 185
relations with WFP, 95, 102, 108
Drèze, J., 8, 12
drought, 1, 2, 7–9 *passim*, 35, 36, 55, 57, 60,
  61, 66–8 *passim*, 74, 76, 80, 84, 86, 87, 91,
  111, 113–15 *passim*, 119, 120, 141, 148,
  165, 167, 170–3 *passim*, 177, 183, 196–7,
  199 *see also* TDCPU
  contingency fund, 194–5, 200
  management, 165, 169, 175–8, 195, 200
  'proofing', 209
Duffield, M., 7, 79
Dyson, T., 3

Egg, J., 147
Egypt, 32
Elbadawi, I., 7
Eldredge, E., 99
elites, 23, 210
emergency, declaration of, 46, 94, 101, 143,
  172, 183, 192
employment, 9, 57, 93n7, 144, 177
  generation scheme (Ethiopia), 61
Engomo, D. K., 188
entitlement, to food, 3, 4, 60, 87, 144
Eritrea, 57, 63, 66, 67, 71, 78
  ERA, 63, 78
'escape hatches', 22, 46
Etheri, A. J., 182, 199
Ethiopia, 1, 9, 11, 27n2, 35, 38, 39n10, 40n11,
  41–5 *passim*, 41n12, 47, 50, 55–83, 137,
  196, 202, 203, 207, 211 *see also* Tigray
  Directives for Disaster Prevention etc.,
  60, 83
  economy, 57, 59
  Emergency Code, 60; – Food Security
    Reserve, 74, 78
  food aid to, 55, 56, 59, 60, 63, 65–8 *passim*,
    71
  food insecurity, 55, 57–8, 60, 65, 78–9, 81–
    3
  food policy, 60, 61; National Food and
    Nutrition Strategy, 60
  EWPS, 61–8, 71, 73, 75, 78, 79, 81–3
    passim
  government–donor relations, 55–6, 63, 65,
    76, 80
  NDPPS, 60, 81
  politics, 55–6, 76, 79
  Relief and Rehabilitation Commission,
    21, 58, 65–76 *passim*, 79, 82
  response system, 65–6, 69–71, 79, 80, 83

security situation, 55, 66, 68, 69
Southern Line operation, 65, 71, 79
ethnic factors, 106, 135, 196
Europe, Eastern, 27, 33, 135
European Union, 26, 28, 32, 34, 37–9, 42–5,
  47–51 *passim*, 53, 88, 90, 93, 95, 100, 106,
  116, 120, 122, 123, 128, 131, 133, 134,
  147n9, 169, 172, 207
  Commission, 26, 30–2 *passim*, 39, 40, 44,
    48, 148, 161, 162, 165, 181, 195
  ECHO, 30, 39, 47, 53
  Food Aid Committee, 121, 123; Division,
    39
  Parliament, 30, 39, 43–4, 102–3
  Special Programme for Africa, 39, 44, 46–
    8 *passim*, 50, 52, 94, 132, 207
evaluations, 2, 12, 19, 24, 71–4, 97–100,
  124–8, 147–8, 151, 156–8 *passim*, 161, 163,
  164, 172, 180, 182, 185–9
EWS, 1, 2, 4–5, 11–25, 36–8 *passim*, 40, 202,
  204–6, 209 *see also under individual*
  countries
  donor funding, 2, 61, 109, 128, 137–8, 147,
    200, 204
  local-level, 4, 5, 8, 81, 83, 110, 165, 175,
    178, 210 *see also* Turkana
  sustainability, 147, 187–9
exchange rate, 27n2, 35n9, 94
expenditure, cuts in, 10, 33

famine, 4, 5, 55–8 *passim*, 73, 74, 78, 81, 84,
  87, 88, 97–8, 102, 104, 115, 119, 126, 164,
  167, 169, 172, 173, 205
  causality of, 3, 7, 60
FAO, 18, 36, 43, 48, 51, 57, 72, 77, 89, 124,
  134 *see also* assessment, harvest
el Fasher, 95, 98, 100, 106
FEWS, 38, 40, 41n12, 52, 57, 63, 66, 68, 71,
  90, 91, 100, 113, 117, 119, 120, 124–6, 133,
  145, 146, 149, 150, 155–6, 205
Field, J. O., 36, 46
fish/fishing, 113, 114, 141, 149, 169, 186
food-for-work, 18, 61, 163, 167, 172, 173,
  177, 181–2, 187, 192–5 *passim*
forecasts, production, 4, 38, 61, 66, 79, 92 *see*
  also assessments
foreign exchange, 57
France, 35, 121, 123, 147n9
fraud, 172–3
FSG, 199

G-7, 51
game, 169
Gao (Mali), 159, 160
gaps, food, 9, 93, 101, 103
  information, 95–6, 98–100, 109
Geneina (Sudan), 95
geopolitical factors, 8, 23, 34

Germany, 121, 123, 147n9
GIEWS, 4, 36, 38, 89–92 *passim*, 96, 117, 145, 178
goats, 9, 167, 179, 181
governance criteria, 8, 88
governments, recipient, 1, 5, 8–10 *passim*, 19, 21–4 *passim*, 27, 28, 52, 208
    relations with donors, 2, 4, 9, 11, 23, 53 *see also under individual countries*
    requests for relief, 47–8, 75, 93, 94, 101, 120–1, 133, 153–4
Goyder, H. and C., 58, 75
Graham, R., 91
Gray, J., 87, 106
Guido Sah (Mali), 157
Guera *préfecture* (Chad), 125
Guinea, 154

Habré, President Hassan, 113
Harerghe (Ethiopia), 63, 68–70 *passim*, 73, 76
health, 3, 5, 99, 106, 172, 177
Holt, J., 9, 58, 74
Horn of Africa, 1–3 *passim*, 6–8, 10, 12, 25, 28, 30, 32, 47, 50, 52, 53, 77, 82, 107, 108, 137, 198, 206, 210, 211
    UN Consolidated Appeal for, 69; Special Emergency Programme for, 51
Hubbard, M., 23
human rights, 23, 34, 35, 88, 193, 198
hungry season, 6, 18, 47, 50, 52, 56, 65, 70, 82, 95, 103, 119, 144, 150, 155, 164, 202, 210
hygiene, 106, 172

IFPRI, 7, 57
Illubabor (Ethiopia), 79
ILO, 86
IMF, 34
imports, food, 57, 92, 93, 142, 154
incomes, 7, 9, 86, 93n7, 115, 120
India, 7, 7n3, 8, 60
indicators, EW, 1, 2, 4–5, 16–18, 61, 75–6, 81, 103–4, 109, 117, 125, 126, 175–6, 178–9, 185, 189–90, 197
information, EW, 1, 2, 11, 12, 15–19, 22, 26, 36–41, 71–4, 95, 97–104, 111, 117, 124–8, 146, 148–51, 159, 160, 164, 192
    politicization of, 100–4
    use of, 1, 2, 8, 11–13, 18–25, 56, 74–7, 100–5, 128–34, 137–9, 148, 155–6, 160, 161, 163, 164, 185, 188–93, 202, 205–9
information systems, 12–25, 173, 204, 208, 209
    indigenous, 4, 5, 12
infrastructure, 24, 59, 60, 78, 82, 88, 113, 144, 172, 178, 208

insecurity, 33, 82, 106–7, 135, 154, 158, 160, 170, 183, 199 *see also* conflict
    food, 2, 7, 36, 55, 57, 59–60, 63, 68, 73, 82–4 *passim*, 87, 98, 106, 109, 114, 143, 163–5 *passim*, 172, 174
instability, political, 3, 27, 55, 82, 135, 196, 211
institutions, 1, 2, 4, 5, 11, 25, 104–5, 131–2, 139, 190–2, 195
    constraints, 19–20, 22–3, 25, 44–6, 108–9, 132, 165, 205–7
    memory, 23, 105, 108
interest groups, 10, 23, 24, 163, 208
investment, 3, 35, 82, 87, 109
Iraq, 26, 101, 108, 137
irrigation, 169

Kakuma Division (Turkana), 167, 181–3 *passim*, 186, 187, 189, 191, 193–200 *passim*
Kanem *préfecture* (Chad), 121, 131
Kayes (Mali), 157
Kelly, M., 91, 97, 98
Kenya, 1, 7, 8, 11, 35, 165–202
    ASAL districts, 165, 167, 169, 177–8, 197, 201 *see also* Turkana
    District Focus Strategy, 169
    EWS, 178
    politics, 167, 178, 192, 198, 200
    response, to drought, 178
    Freedom from Hunger, 184
Khaleng (Turkana), 172
Kidal (Mali), 159, 160
Kokuro (Turkana), 196
Kordofan (Sudan), 91–3 *passim*, 95, 98, 99, 104, 107
Koro (Mali), 157
Koulikoro (Mali), 157
Kumar, B. G., 60, 78
Kurds, 26–9 *passim*, 49, 51, 53

Lalau-Keraly, A., 151
land, grazing, 170, 181, 183, 196
    tenure, 60
Lawrence, M., 9, 58, 74
Lea, J. D., 131, 134
Lewis, D. B., 21, 178
liberalization, market, 8, 60, 115, 144, 146, 163, 204
Libya, 93
livelihoods, 8, 43, 62, 87, 106, 111, 119, 125, 136, 144, 164, 169, 185, 205
    protection, 2, 5, 11, 17, 18, 24, 52–4 *passim*, 111, 185, 189, 190, 197, 198, 202, 206, 208
livestock, 7, 9, 57, 86, 93, 106, 113, 114, 127, 141, 167, 169, 170, 175, 178–81, 183, 186, 189

Emergency – Purchase scheme, 167, 173, 177–81, 186, 187, 189–92 *passim*, 194, 197, 198, 202, 203
lobbying, 22, 33n6, 39, 42, 93
local government, 10, 81, 157, 158, 162, 169, 177, 188, 191–2, 198
logistical constraints, 1, 2, 24, 26, 60, 78, 83, 108, 109, 144, 198, 207–8
Lokichoggio Division (Turkana), 181, 183
Lokitaung Division (Turkana), 172, 183
Lokong, M. O., 182, 199
Lomé IV, 88

el-Mahdi, Sadiq, 84
maize, 142, 143, 174, 182, 183
Mali, 1, 11, 17, 21, 35, 38, 48, 50, 138–64, 202–4, *passim*, 211
  CNAUR, 146, 157, 158, 162–4 *passim*
  COC, 152, 160, 162
  EWS, 21, 139, 145; SADS, 145, 146, 148, 149, 151, 161, 163–4; SAP, 139, 145–52 *passim*, 155, 156, 159–64 *passim*
  food security, 141–4, 163–4
  government-donor relations, 11, 48, 139, 161
  politics, 144, 152, 154, 159–60, 163
  PRMC, 143, 146–8 *passim*, 152, 154, 155, 158–63 *passim*
  response system, 139, 147, 148, 151–60, 162–4, 204
  SNS, 146–7, 151–2, 154, 155, 160, 161, 204, 211
malnutrition, 7, 68, 70, 72, 84, 91, 96–8 *passim*, 104, 109, 111, 122, 124, 125, 131–6 *passim*, 174, 181–5 *passim*, 189, 190, 199, 206
March, J. G., 22
marketing, 60, 78, 113, 115, 177, 180
markets, 87
  cereals, 8, 60, 143, 144, 146, 158, 161–4 *passim*, 167, 204
  labour, 8, 60
Mauritania, 154, 159
Maxwell, S., 57, 60, 86n1
meat, 167, 173, 174n, 181 *See also Opération Viande*
media, 8, 9, 12, 23, 28, 39, 41–4, 46, 49, 52–3, 56, 58–60, 66, 76, 80, 102–3, 111, 133, 137, 163, 187, 190, 193, 204, 207
Médecins sans Frontières, 116
Mengistu, President, 35, 55, 56, 60, 61, 65
migration, 3, 9, 61, 125, 126, 128, 144, 156, 170, 184
milk, 167, 173, 178
millet, 141, 146, 148, 150, 183
misappropriation, 157, 158, 184
mobility, of population, 144, 169, 184, 197, 201

Mobutu, President, 35
Mohammed, M.I., 87
monitoring, 4, 5, 21, 36, 61, 63, 73, 74, 78–9, 82, 83, 89, 95–100 *passim*, 107, 110, 111, 116, 127, 148, 158, 163–5 *passim*, 181, 185, 186, 197, 201, 204
Mopti Region (Mali), 157–9 *passim*
mortality, 3, 5, 6, 36, 74, 80, 91, 97, 98, 104, 135, 137, 206
  child, 98, 109
  livestock, 175, 178, 180, 181
Mosley, P., 34
movement, population, 4, 8, 36, 74, 120, 121, 156, 181–2
Mozambique, 137
mutual support networks, 170

NDVI, 175
Netherlands, 147n9, 169, 173, 188
NGOs, 2, 9, 10, 15, 21–4, 28–30 *passim*, 38–9, 42, 49–52, 63–5 *passim*, 70, 76–7, 90, 99, 110, 136, 153, 154, 157–61 *passim*, 174, 178, 184, 191, 195, 208 *see also individual headings*
  information systems, 39
  relations with donors, 10, 39, 49–50, 52, 76, 104, 105, 124, 163, 185
Niafunké (Mali), 158
Nigeria, 124
Nimeiri, President, 27, 101
Nordic Countries Trust Fund, 88
Norway, 170
  NORAD, 170, 180, 181, 193, 194
nutritional status, 61, 74, 173, 189
Nyala (Sudan), 106

Oba, G., 196
El Obeid (Sudan), 95
objectives, 23, 80, 132, 208–9, 211
  of EWS, 16–17, 82, 187
ODA, 26, 28, 30–2, 37–40 *passim*, 42, 44, 45, 47–50 *passim*, 53, 88, 93, 95, 102, 207
  Disaster Unit, 47
  Emergency Aid Department, 30
ODI, 34, 172, 195
ODNRI, 77
OECD, 33
Ogaden, 39n10, 66, 68, 70, 71, 74, 79
Olsen, J.P., 22
Omdurman (Sudan), 95
Omo (Ethiopia), 68, 69, 73
Ouaddai *préfecture* (Chad), 128
ownership, of information, 12, 25, 205
Oxfam, 70, 89, 92, 95–7 *passim*, 102n8, 184

Pacey, A., 172, 173
pastoralists/pastoralism, 7, 17, 61, 87, 106, 114, 127, 138, 165, 167–201

pests, 148, 148n11
Petty, Celia, 26n1
Pirzio-Biroli, D., 143
planning, 12, 21, 81, 82, 88, 103, 108, 115,
129, 133, 158, 164, 177, 188, 200, 205
contingency, 164, 165, 172, 173, 175, 178,
194, 200, 201 *see also* TDCPU
political factors, 2, 5, 7, 9, 10, 22–7 *passim*,
30, 34, 43–4, 48, 52–3, 55–6, 76, 100–3,
105–8 *passim* 132–3, 135, 159, 160, 192–3,
196–8, 200, 208, 211
pool, food, 106, 110, 211
population, 141, 144, 167, 186
growth, 7, 57, 86, 87, 144
Port Sudan, 95, 106, 110
poverty/impoverishment, 55, 57, 74, 80, 81,
84, 104, 109, 141, 169, 199
prediction, 151, 161, 164, 186
famine, 1, 2, 4, 11, 18, 80, 82, 163, 208 *see
also* assessments
pre-positioning of resources, 77, 83, 105,
106, 110, 134–5, 137, 138, 161, 211
prevention, famine, 2–12 *passim*, 18–21,
27–8, 58, 59, 63, 110, 114, 135, 144, 175,
204, 207, 208
prices, 4, 57, 86, 92, 96, 115, 119, 123–4, 144,
146, 148–50 *passim*, 154, 175, 179, 183
Prigan, M., 186
private sector, 8, 60, 78, 115, 146, 161
privatization, 115
production, food, 7, 17, 38, 57, 92, 93, 113–15
passim, 119, 141, 142, 144, 148–9
capacity, 3, 5, 17, 98
public opinion, 9, 28, 42, 103, 207

quotas, 60

raiding, livestock, 165, 167, 170, 172, 174,
181, 183, 185, 196–7, 199–200
rainfall, 15, 57, 63, 78, 87, 115, 117, 119, 142,
160, 169, 170, 175, 186
rapid-onset disaster, 181, 185, 197, 200
ration rates, 71–2
reciprocal ties, 9, 150, 156
Red Cross, International Committee, 182;
Federation, 184
Reed, C., 131, 134
RDI, 178
refugees, 8, 26, 28–9, 55, 68–9, 71, 78, 79, 82,
86, 121
regionalization, 61, 62
rehabilitation, 11, 88, 172, 173, 208
relief, 2, 4, 6, 8, 9, 11, 16, 23, 25–54, 56, 58,
60–2 *passim*, 65, 69–71, 74, 79–84 *passim*,
87, 91, 94–7, 105, 107, 108, 110, 111, 115,
122–6, 128, 136–8, 167, 170, 172, 174,
182–4, 190, 198, 201, 202, 205
dependence on, 172, 199

Planning Workshop, 91
replicability, 139, 165, 178, 186, 201,
202
representatives, in-country, 40, 51, 52, 193,
210
reserves, food security, 48, 77–8, 82, 83, 87,
106, 115, 137, 138, 161, 209, 211
responses, 2, 3, 5–6, 18, 19, 48–50, 202,
206–10 *passim see also under individual
countries*
phasing, 138, 209–10
procedures, 5, 26, 46–8, 50, 52, 206, 207
timeliness of, 21, 47, 50, 52, 58, 77, 82, 83,
95, 105, 120, 122–4, 129, 132, 207
responsibility, 21, 22, 27–8, 90, 94, 108, 110,
177, 180, 192, 194, 198, 211
restocking, 170, 177, 179
restructuring, 143, 164
returnees, 55, 68, 69, 79
rice, 142, 148, 149, 154
rinderpest, 114, 115
risk avoidance, 44, 46, 52, 205
roads, 24, 82, 144
Robinson, M., 34
Roskens, Ronald, 33
Rwanda, 7, 8, 33
Rydjeski, D., 99

SADC, 3
safety nets, 8, 9, 81, 128
Sahel, 1–4 *passim*, 6–8, 10, 12, 25, 32, 47, 50,
52, 77, 82, 107, 108, 186, 198, 206, 210, 211
Salamat *préfecture* (Chad), 114, 123, 127
satellite imagery, 16, 41, 78, 117, 175
SCF (UK), 39n10, 63, 68, 70, 74, 76, 89, 91,
92, 98
Schaffer, B. B., 22, 46
school attendance, 175
security, 55, 66, 68, 69, 71, 181, 197
food, 3, 5, 11, 16, 24, 32, 36, 61, 78–9, 163,
164
self-sufficiency, food, 7, 60, 84, 86, 101, 108,
113, 115, 129, 169
sedentarization, 169, 172, 175
Sen, A., 3, 8, 12, 60
Sharp, K., 92
Shaw, J., 32
sheep, 167, 179, 181
Shewa (Ethiopia), 63, 66, 68
shocks, 7–9 *passim*, 35, 74, 86
shortages, food, 3, 11, 21, 27, 33, 60, 66, 74,
87, 136, 139, 143, 144
fuel, 71, 95
Somalia, 7, 35, 55, 69, 79, 137, 185
socialization, 60
sorghum, 86, 121–3 *passim*, 141, 142, 147,
154, 169
Soviet Union, former, 27

starvation, 3, 5, 6, 18, 33, 96, 98, 104, 159, 183, 190
stocks, 7, 77–8, 91, 106, 123, 134–5, 137, 139, 146–7, 152, 154
  household, 16, 141, 144
stress, 17, 61, 175, 179, 189, 206
  food, 11, 138, 150, 173, 202
structural adjustment, 34, 161, 204
  programmes, 3, 7, 8
Sudan, 1, 7, 9, 11, 16, 23, 27, 27n2, 28, 35, 38–47 *passim*, 40n11, 41n12, 50, 51, 80, 84–110, 124, 137, 189, 196, 199 *see also* Darfur
  Drought Monitoring Programme, 89
  economy, 86
  EWS, 88, 89, 91, 92, 94, 98–102, 104, 107, 109, 110, 204
  food insecurity, 86–8
  government–donor relations, 11, 39, 48, 84, 86, 88–90 *passim*, 93, 95, 101, 103–8 *passim*
  government–foreign NGO relations, 50
  politics, 27, 35, 84, 87, 90, 100–3, 105–8 *passim*, 110
  Relief and Rehabilitation Commission, 21, 88, 90, 92, 105, 110
  response system, 103, 105, 107, 110
  Western Relief operation, 87, 91, 95, 105, 106
supplementary feeding programmes, 70, 181, 182, 185
surpluses, food, 6, 32, 33, 144
surveillance, nutritional, 16, 68, 71, 75–6, 89, 95–6, 116, 121–2, 128, 135, 138, 150, 183
Swift, J., 3, 87, 106
Switzerland, 121, 123

Tabor, S., 23
Tamanrasset agreement (1991), 159
targeting, 16–18 *passim*, 34, 38, 73, 89, 99, 148, 156–8 *passim*, 163, 184, 188, 209
technical assistance, 89, 116, 147, 147n9
Teme, B., 147
Thailand, 122
Tigray, 57, 60, 63, 65, 66, 78
  People's Liberation Front, 55, 63, 68
  REST, 63, 78, 79
time-lags, 4, 47, 48, 50, 52, 77, 82, 129, 137, 148, 162, 167, 179, 190, 203, 204, 206–8 *passim*, 210, 211
timing, of decision-making, 46–7, 108, 129, 130, 161, 205–6
  of response, 2, 3, 5, 6, 11, 21, 26, 46–7, 50, 52, 77, 82, 105, 121–3 *passim*, 130, 132, 134, 136, 143, 148, 184, 198, 202–4 *passim*, 206, 210
  of warning, 2, 11, 19, 25, 83, 100, 105, 125, 128, 136, 161, 181–4 *passim*, 186, 202
Tine *préfecture* (Chad), 134

Tlogelang, T., 21n5
Tombouctou, 11, 157, 160
training, 83, 158
transport, in-country, 24, 50, 60, 65, 70–1, 78, 90, 95, 105, 107–9, 156–8 *passim*, 172, 180–2 *passim*, 194, 195, 208, 209
Traoré, President Moussa, 144, 152, 154, 159, 160
triangular transactions, 32
Tuareg, 144, 159, 160
Turkana, 17, 18, 165–201, 202, 203, 210, 211
  economy, 167, 169
  Emergency Livestock Purchase scheme, 167, 173, 177–81, 186, 187, 189–92 *passim*, 197, 198, 202
  EWS, 165, 167, 174–6, 178–9, 183, 185–93, 197–202, 205
  response system, 167, 174, 177, 179, 182, 183, 189–93, 196–7, 200
  TDCPU, 165, 172–3, 175, 177, 181–93 *passim*, 197, 199, 200
  TRDP, 170, 179
  TRP, 169, 170, 172–3, 182, 193, 195

Uganda, 172, 181
UNDP, 88, 89
UNDRO, 51
UNICEF, 89, 100, 183, 185
United Nations, 4, 27, 28, 32, 34, 36, 38, 42–3, 51, 53, 65, 68, 69, 78, 79, 88, 93, 94, 102, 110, 120, 205 *see also individual headings*
  Consolidated Appeal for Horn of Africa, 69
  Department of Humanitarian Affairs, 51
  Emergency Operation Group, 90, 96
  Emergency Prevention and Preparedness Group, 63, 65, 78
  Emergency Unit, 90, 90n5, 102
  Special Emergency Programme for Horn of Africa, 51, 107
United States, 32–5 *passim*, 41, 43, 49, 88, 117, 122, 147n9 *see also* USAID
  Agricultural Development and Trade Act (1990), 32
  Brooke Amendment, 35n8, 41n12, 56n1, 63
  Bureau of Food for Peace, 47
  OFDA, 43, 47, 49
  Select Committee on Hunger, 43
University of Leeds 78
urban areas, 8, 9, 61, 144
urbanization, 86, 144
USAID, 26, 30–2 *passim*, 34, 34n7, 37, 38, 40–5 *passim*, 47, 49, 53, 76, 90, 93, 95, 96, 100, 102, 106, 120–1, 126, 133–5 *passim*, 145, 146, 148, 154, 156, 157, 161, 205
  Famine Early Warning System *see* FEWS

Food Security Operations Reports, 40, 41
  'waiver authority', 49
Uvin, P., 32

vaccinations, 180, 181
Valère-Gille, F., 134
veterinary campaigns, 177
Von Braun, J., 7, 57, 74
vulnerability, 5–7 passim, 9, 56, 60, 74, 81,
  83, 84, 86, 87, 91, 120, 125, 149, 206

Wajir District (Kenya), 193
Walker, P., 74
war, 4, 7, 9, 57, 78, 82, 84, 86, 106, 113, 115,
  211
  civil, 7, 33, 35, 55, 57, 84, 86n2, 111, 126,
    135, 196
  Cold, 7, 34, 55
  Gulf, 42, 44, 52, 77, 80, 101, 102, 108
water supplies, 5, 172, 196
Webb, P., 57, 74
Wekesa, F., 179
WFP, 19, 26, 30–2 passim, 38, 40, 43–5,
  48–51 passim, 66, 68–77 passim, 90, 94,

109, 121, 122, 124, 134, 136, 160, 163, 170,
  179, 180, 192–4 passim, 207 see also
  assessments
  CFA, 32
  Disaster Relief Service, 48
  IEFR, 32, 49
  relations with donors, 95, 102,
    108
  relations with NGOs, 185
WHO, 126
wild foods, 96, 141, 150, 169,
  170
Winter, G., 151
Wollayita (Ethiopia), 68, 73
Wollega (Ethiopia), 79
Wollo (Ethiopia), 60, 63, 65, 78, 79
women, 18, 184, 195
World Bank, 34, 57, 113
World Vision, 184

Youvarou (Mali), 157
Yugoslavia, former, 30, 185

Zaire, 35